The Moth

The Casey Anthony Story

By David Kennedy

First Printing, 2017

I dedicate this book to Christina Batchelor
Just when I thought I was done, you said that you wanted to read this story:
So this one's for you

Prologue

Thousands of people go missing in the United States each year and many are never heard from again.

According to the National Center for Missing and Exploited Children, roughly 800,000 children are reported missing each year in the United States—that's roughly 2,000 per day. Of those, there are 115 child "stranger abduction" cases each year, which means the child, was taken by an unknown person.

In January, 2006 Jennifer Kesse from Orlando Florida was one of those people.

We are dedicating the prologue of this book to her in hopes that maybe somebody can help bring this young woman home.

-The Search for Jennifer Kesse –

Jennifer, was reported missing when she failed to show up for work at Central Florida Investments, on the morning of Tuesday January 24th, 2006 in Orlando Florida after a long weekend in St. Croix with her boyfriend and other friends (they Flew both ways, there was no cruise as some people think).

Those closest to Jennifer knew something was wrong immediately. If she was going to be late for work or a meeting she would call. In fact Jennifer had good routines she and her boyfriend (who lives hours away in south Florida and Jennifer in Orlando) called each other every day while driving to work in the morning and would speak with each other every night before going to bed, having a long distance relationship, seeing each other on weekends and Holidays.

Jennifer Kesse 2006– age 24 Age Progressed Picture 2015– age 33

On Monday, the morning of January 23rd, Jennifer left her boyfriend's home in south Florida and drove directly to work in Ocoee Florida, not going home first but directly to her work as she usually did when she stayed the weekend in south Florida.

On the night of Monday January 23rd, Jennifer left work around 6 p.m., walking out of the building, where she worked with her boss and wishing each other a good evening and will meet again in the morning.

That evening, Jennifer talked to her father, mother and brother. Later she spoke with some friends and at 9:57 p.m. she spoke with her boyfriend by phone as usual and that was the last anyone has seen or heard from Jennifer.

Jennifer and her boyfriend did not talk the morning of Tuesday, January 24th. Her boyfriend called Jennifer at work and was told she had not arrived yet. When she did not show up for work, her employer immediately called her family to see if they knew where Jennifer was.

Her family tried to reach her at her condo and on her cell phone and computer but their attempts was unsuccessful. Police were notified and the journey into Jennifer's personal Hell began.

Reaction was quick, within 2 hours of not being at work - her disappearance was known and being acted on by family and police.

Upon reaching Jennifer's condominium by midafternoon, her family found it to be "normal."

Everything was clan and in place. She had obviously slept in her bed, taken a shower (wet towel and shower) and had a couple outfits on the bed she was choosing to wear. Her tracks seem to cease from when she left her condo for work usually around 7:30-7:45 a.m. each work day. By 4 p.m., family and friends of Jennifer had fliers made and being distributed within the immediate area of her condominium located at Mosaic at Millenia Condominiums next to the Mall at Meillenia, Orlando, Florida. And awareness has not stopped since.

On Thursday January 26th, 2006, police were notified that Jennifer's car was abandoned in a condominium complex 1.2 miles down the same road from where she lived in The Huntington on the Green Condominiums at the corner of Texas and Americana Ave in Orlando, Florida.

Her car was parked by a Suspect (on video) who pulled into a visitor parking space waited 32 seconds to exit her car and walked away, never looking back.

Please search google for the Jennifer Kesse case and watch the video of the suspect that they have on video.

There is a reward of up to $5,000 for the identification and/or whereabouts of Jennifer. Tips may be called into Crimeline 1-800-423-8477 or to FBI directly @ 1-866-838-1153.

There were valuables left in Jennifer's car, so police do not feel it was for robbery or carjacking, but for Jennifer, herself. Bloodhounds tracked a scent from where her car was found back to her condo complex losing the scent on Jennifer's condo property.

Awareness will find Jennifer. Please think about everyone you know - if you believe someone you know or suspect someone you may know or might be involved, please call Crimeline or FBI immediately and share that information it may be nothing or it may be the missing piece of information that will help bring Jennifer home.

Part One

The Anthony Family

The Anthony's

In March 1981 twenty-nine year old George and twenty-two year old Cindy Plesea are married in Ohio.

The following November 20th the couple had their first child; a son whom they named Lee followed four years later on March 19th, 1986 by their daughter Casey Marie.

When George was twenty-two years old he joined the Trumball County Sheriff's department in 1974, where he worked for almost 10 years, but quit law enforcement at the age of 33 in 1985. This was one year before Casey was born.

The Anthony family eventually moved to Orlando in 1989, around the time Casey was three years old where George worked as (among other things) a security guard.

Cindy worked in the healthcare field for a company named Gentiva Health Services where she worked her way up to a nursing case supervisor.

As a child Casey was a bright, personable young girl with friends and what many thought was an ordinary American family. She was often described as a happy and outgoing child; however, friends say that a pattern of lying began when Casey was in high school.

Casey's High school photo

While Casey was in high school the people around her began to notice a change. She started going to parties, going to clubs, experimented with drugs and she began drinking. She also started lying. It was nothing too big at first, just little petty lies here and there. But slowly her lies began to escalate. Perhaps her biggest lie, at the time, involved her graduation.

In 2004 Casey would have graduated from Colonial High School. The invitations had been sent out. She had already begun receiving graduation gifts. Her mother, Cindy, was so proud off her daughter that she was preparing a huge graduation party for her.

In the days leading up to graduation, her mother started asking her questions. "Casey, where's your cap?" "Casey where's your gown?"' "What's going on?" "What are you not telling me?" "What are you hiding?"

At first Casey just blew off her mother and her questions. She came up with excuse after excuse, claiming nothing was wrong.

As graduation grew closer, Casey knew that she could not keep her secret much longer. And she was right. The day before Casey was supposed to get her diploma and graduate high school, Cindy got a phone call from the school saying, "Casey could not be part of the graduation ceremony." After that call Casey confessed to her mother that she did not have enough credits to graduate.

Cindy was irate. She yelled at Casey. "What are you talking about?" "What do you mean?" "Why?" Casey gave her multiple excuses blaming the school, when in fact it was because Casey wasn't showing up to class.

After Cindy calmed down, she told her Casey not to say a word to anyone. And they both went along with it, all the way to the graduation ceremony.

As her parents, brother and grandparents sat waiting for the commencement ceremonies to begin, Casey's grandparents started to become confused when they noticed Casey was not in a cap and gown like the others. When they asked Cindy why, Cindy explained that "the school had messed up, but not to worry."

Neither Cindy nor Casey called any family member to let them know Casey didn't graduate Casey did not return any of the graduation gifts that she had received. Neither Cindy nor Casey cancelled Casey's graduation party.

Casey never returned to school and never completed her missing credits.

Some people will ask themselves, "What kind of person would lead her family to believe she not only finished her requirements for high school, but would be walking into the ceremony with the rest of the graduating class?"

Caylee Arrives

When she was nineteen years old, Casey gave her family yet another shock.

During the summer of 2005, Casey's friends and family started to notice a change in Casey's appearance. Many believed that Casey was pregnant and when asked by her family, she denied the pregnancy and stated that she was a virgin.

In July Casey and her family went to South Carolina to attend her uncle's wedding. While they were there several people approached Cindy saying "I didn't know Casey was pregnant." or "Why didn't you tell me Casey was pregnant?" and so on. Cindy's response was either "Oh she's not pregnant, she's just retaining water." or "She's just gained a little weight."

Cindy was completely oblivious to the fact that her daughter was pregnant. After they returned home and Casey realized how many people had approached her mother with the same questions and concerns, Casey went to Cindy's work and admitted to her mother that she was seven months pregnant.

A few days later Casey and Cindy sat down with George and told him he was going to be a grandfather. And even though the pregnancy wasn't expected, George was elated He and Cindy began preparing their lives and their home for the arrival of their first grandchild.

Lee Anthony, Casey's brother, said he had his suspicions about his sister being pregnant. On one occasion Lee said he saw her stomach as she came out of a bathroom the two shared in 2005.

"When I went in, she was coming out. I could see her mid-section and she was showing."

Lee said he questioned Casey and their mother about it, but they both denied Casey was pregnant. Lee didn't learn the truth until just a few days before Caylee was born. He had been too hurt and angry about his family not including him in the truth that he refused to visit Casey at the hospital when she gave birth to Caylee on August 9th, 2005.

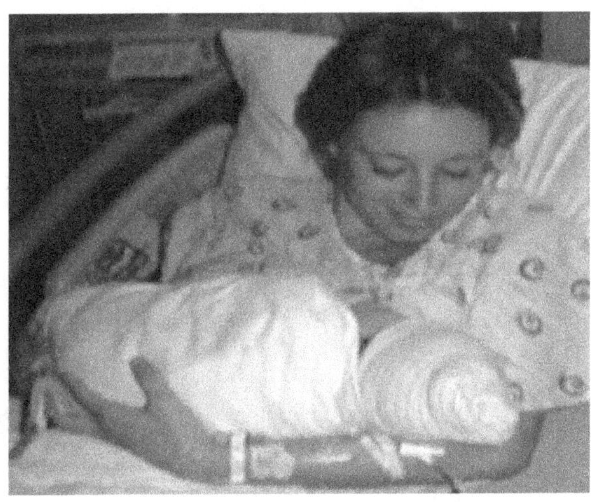

Casey and Caylee

The identity of Caylee's father is still unknown. There is a list of possibilities. Many have been removed from that list through DNA testing.

At the time of Caylee's birth Casey was engaged to a man named Jesse Grund. Casey allowed him to believe that he was Caylee's father. Caylee Marie Anthony was born on August 9th, 2005. Casey and Caylee lived with her parents and Grund took on the role of the father.

In a 2009 interview with *People Magazine*, Grund said it was "possible" that he was Caylee's father, but he didn't think the timing of conception was right. He later took a DNA test that proved he wasn't the father.

"For the first year or two of her life, I was dad," Grund told *People* in 2009. "I was the father figure in her life, and I loved her more than anything. She was an amazing little baby. I had never been a father before."

He told the magazine that he was disappointed to learn that Caylee wasn't his biological daughter. "I loved Caylee so much, and finding out she was someone else's daughter was hard," he said.

Grund later appeared on *Today*, where he begged Casey to start telling the truth.

"Casey, tell the truth. This isn't about you anymore. This is about Caylee," Grund said on the *Today Show*, speaking directly to his ex-girlfriend. "Stop dragging people's lives through this. Stop destroying people's lives and tell the truth. What happened to Caylee?"

Over the years there were several candidates and even one man Casey identified as the father, but there is still no definitive answer. The one common thread between many of the men is that they died in car accidents in 2007.

Here's a look at who the candidates for who Caylee's father was.

Anthony herself told some people that Jesus Ortiz, a high school classmate, was Caylee's father. It was later learned that a man named Jesus Ortiz died in a car crash in May 2007 in Orlando.

However, according to a website devoted to the Caylee Anthony murder case, an attorney for the Ortiz family said that they never even heard of Anthony. The statement read:

Miss Anthony never told the family Jesus was the father or that he might be the father. In fact, the family has never met her and does not know her. If the child is indeed their grandchild and alive, that is all they have left of their son, Jesus Ortiz. They would like to get to know the child if she is indeed still alive.

In June 2011, a lady named Donna Duggan told the media that he son Michael was the father. Michael Duggan also died in a car accident in 2007, but in Falmouth, Massachusetts. His mother said that she is "100 percent certain" that her son was the father.

Although Michael Duggan lived in Massachusetts, his mother says he often traveled in the south and worked for a moving company at the time Caylee was conceived. She said it was "routine for him to visit Florida" and his paternal grandparents lived near Orlando.

Donna Duggan said that she was only interested in learning the truth. She claimed that in the summer of 2007, her son told her that she already had a grandchild.

"We were talking about the upcoming birth of my other son's baby boy," Donna Duggan said. "I said I had really hoped for a baby girl grandchild, and that's when Michael told me that he already had one."

One of the lies Casey told police and even her own mother Cindy was that a man named "Eric Baker" was the father. She later called home frantically to tell her mother that Eric Baker had been killed in a car crash.

Casey's mother told the jury during the 2011 trial that Baker was married to another woman and had another child. Baker – like the other candidates – died in a car crash and Cindy claimed to have had an obituary that she lost.

Investigators never found the existence of an "Eric Baker" that was linked to Casey.

However, there was an Eric Baker who lived in Kentucky and died in a 2007 car crash, but his mother said they never heard of Casey Anthony before and he was too young to be the father.

A friend of Casey later testified that she confided in her that she became pregnant after having a one-night-stand with a man named Josh from Georgia, who worked at Universal Studios alongside Casey. According to Casey's pal, he also died in a car crash in 2007.

But the problem with that story was that Casey did not work at Universal Studios at the time that Caylee was conceived.

For years, George and Cindy were told by their daughter that she was working as an event planner at Universal Studios. That also turned out to be a lie. She actually did have a job on the lot *four years prior*, with a Universal subcontractor. It was said that her old job at Universal was taking photos of guests on the rides. After that, she simply pretended to still be employed.

The lie deepened as Casey made up coworkers, notably a friend named Juliette Lewis (yes, just like the famous Hollywood actress). Casey said that Lewis did a lot of volunteer work, prompting Cindy to drop by Universal to meet with Lewis about a fundraiser.

Cindy waited 90 minutes but Lewis never showed. Casey explained to her mother that Lewis had moved to New York. Later, Universal Studios said the company had no record of an employee named Juliette Lewis.

Casey even attempted to keep up the Universal job ruse during police questioning. At one point, officers accompanied her to the studio and asked to see her office. She led them around for a while before finally breaking down and admitting she no longer worked there.

The biggest shocker was when it was said that Casey thought that her own father could also be Caylee's father.

Baez first made the allegation that George had sexually abused Casey during opening statements at her 2011 murder trial. Baez stuck by this though, including in his book *Presumed Guilty, Casey Anthony: The Inside Story*. Baez wrote that Casey even thought that her father sexually assaulted her and impregnated her.

Casey said that it started with touching. She said her father named his penis "Baldy" and told her to play a game called "pet the bald-headed mouse."

"Pet it until it sneezes milk," she said he told her when she was 8 years old.

She told court-appointed clinical psychiatrist Dr. William Weitz that her father raped her "a few times a week" from the time she was 8 until she was 12. Then he did it less often, perhaps because she got her period and he was afraid she might get pregnant. Though her mother was a nurse, during her childhood Casey never once went to see a pediatrician.

These and other lurid details of Casey's alleged incestuous relationships with her father and later her older brother are all contained in court records related to her trial. Casey's attorney, Jose Baez, alluded to the allegations in the trial, and even asked George in court whether he had ever sexually molested his daughter. George testified that he had not, and the judge ruled the incest allegations to be irrelevant.

Many believe that in the details that were not introduced during the trial, there lies a plausible explanation not only of Casey's innocence, but of the circumstances of her daughter's death and the part George Anthony may have played in covering it up.

About the time George stopped the rape of his daughter Casey, according to her statements in court records, her older brother Lee started entering her room at night while she lay in bed and would fondle her breasts. He did this, she told Dr. Weitz, from the time she was 12 to 15. Casey said that after she turned 12, her father continued having sex with her, but far less frequently.

She never told her mother about what her father was doing. Once, however, Casey tried to tell her about the brother's sexual abuse. Cindy's response, according to her daughter, was to call her a whore.

George denied the allegations when he was called to the stand to testify.

Baez said the defense team had initially wondered if George or Lee could have been Caylee's father. Casey had suspected that too and, according to the book, she told a psychiatrist that she was worried about the possibility because her father had sex with her around the time she became pregnant with Caylee. The police later had a suspicion that Lee might be the father.

Apparently George also felt he might be the baby's father.

Some believe that George may have been the father because when the baby was born, photographs showed him in the delivery room on the receiving end as the baby was coming out. Many felt that this was not a normal thing for a father to do.

And in 2009 the vast majority of people had their doubts about George's claim of not raping his daughter. With the results of the DNA testing due to come in a couple days, on January 22nd, 2009, George tried to commit suicide. He left a text message that said in effect, "I'm sorry. Please tell Casey I love her."

Many people believe that George was afraid that the DNA test would prove that Caylee was in fact his daughter. And he was willing to end his life rather than go to prison for raping his daughter.

The DNA test showed that neither George nor Lee was the father of little Caylee.

After Caylee's death many of Casey's friends have stated that Casey didn't even want the baby when she discovered she was pregnant and talked about putting her up for adoption. But it is said that Cindy refused to let her.

The following two years were filled with more lies and countless nights partying while Caylee was left at home with George and Cindy. One of her favorite hangout was the Fusion nightclub on S. Orange Ave in Orlando.

Eventually the lies turn to stealing and in August 2007 Casey steals a check from her grandmother's purse and uses it to buy decorations for Caylee's second birthday party, about $50.

2008 was a continuation of 2007. Casey spent her free time partying with her friends and she still tried to convince her family that she was working. Caylee was by all accounts being raised by her grandparents. Casey appeared to be jealous of the bond that Caylee had with her grandparents. It was at this time that Casey created an imaginary Nanny named Zenaida Fernandez-Gonzalez, who she also identified as "Zanny". Although Casey had talked about her, Zanny had never been seen by Casey's family or friends, and in fact there was no nanny.Zanny, and it seemed as though Casey even started to create an imaginary life.

Some people believe that *"Zanny the Nanny"* could be, in fact, a code for the drug Xanax, which could have been used to knock out little Caylee while Casey went out at night and continued her partying lifestyle. When she was later asked about this, an upset Casey categorically denied it.

Casey had parents who would see to it that her daughter and she were provided for. She had a mother who excused her lies and behavior and sadly she believed she was able to do anything she pleased without a consequence.

March 17th & 21st, 2008

Somebody in the Anthony home did A search for "chloroform" on Casey's computer on March 17th and "how to make chloroform" on March 21st. Later this search would be the center of a lot of controversy in the trial.

Ricardo Morales, an ex-boyfriend of Casey, had a picture on his MySpace page depicting a poster with the caption "Win her over with Chloroform." During Casey's trial Morales said that the photo was on his MySpace page and that he had never discussed chloroform with Casey or searched for chloroform on her computer.

Later when the topic of the computer search came up in the trial Cindy said that she was the one who searched for the topic Chloroform. She said that she had searched for chloroform while looking up information on chlorophyll, a green pigment found in plants, which she thought might be making her dogs ill.

But her claim was undermined when her former boss told the Florida court she was still at work when the searches were made.

A chief compliance officer for Cindy's old company produced records which showed she was still logged into her work computer on the afternoons she claimed to be conducting the internet searches at her home.

DATE . . . . . .
TIME . . . . . .

GID	JOB_INFO	DATE_TIME
F1124	4176[illegible]/CMANTHON/W102937A	started on 03/17/08 at 07:02:02
F1124	4177[illegible]/CMANTHON/W102937B	started on 03/17/08 at 07:02:21
F1164	41767[illegible]/CMANTHON/W102937A	ended on 03/17/08 at 16:52:41;
F1164	4177[illegible]/CMANTHON/W102937B	ended on 03/17/08 at 16:52:51;
F1124	44968[illegible]/CMANTHON/W102937A	started on 03/18/08 at 07:16:02
F1124	4496[illegible]/CMANTHON/W102937B	started on 03/18/08 at 07:16:13
F1164	4496[illegible]/CMANTHON/W102937B	ended on 03/18/08 at 16:02:39;
F1164	4496[illegible]/CMANTHON/W102937A	ended on 03/18/08 at 16:02:40;
F1124	4846[illegible]/CMANTHON/W102937A	started on 03/19/08 at 07:59:51
F1124	4846[illegible]/CMANTHON/W102937B	started on 03/19/08 at 08:00:06
F1164	4846[illegible]/CMANTHON/W102937A	ended on 03/19/08 at 10:20:38;
F1124	4923[illegible]1/CMANTHON/W102937A	started on 03/19/08 at 10:20:35
F1164	4846[illegible]/CMANTHON/W102937B	ended on 03/19/08 at 17:26:21;
F1164	4923[illegible]1/CMANTHON/W102937A	ended on 03/19/08 at 17:31:22;
PF1124	5156[illegible]5/CMANTHON/W102937A	started on 03/20/08 at 06:45:37
PF1124	5156[illegible]2/CMANTHON/W102937B	started on 03/20/08 at 06:45:55
PF1164	5156[illegible]5/CMANTHON/W102937A	ended on 03/20/08 at 16:42:50;
PF1164	5156[illegible]/CMANTHON/W102937B	ended on 03/20/08 at 16:42:52;
PF1124	5487[illegible]3/CMANTHON/W102937A	started on 03/21/08 at 07:43:08
PF1124	5487[illegible]9/CMANTHON/W102937B	started on 03/21/08 at 07:43:20
PF1164	5487[illegible]3/CMANTHON/W102937A	ended on 03/21/08 at 16:37:31;
PF1164	5487[illegible]/CMANTHON/W102937B	ended on 03/21/08 at 16:37:41;

** END OF REPORT ***

John Camperlengo, of Gentiva Health Services, showed the court computer records which revealed somebody had used Cindy's username and password to log in early every morning and log out at around 4 or 5 p.m. every evening on her work computer the week she claimed she searched for chloroform at home.

The records also showed activity on her work computer in the afternoons of March 17th and March 21st, the same time the searches were performed on her computer.

During the trial Software analyst John Bradley states someone used the Anthony computer to search the website Sci-spot.com for "chloroform" 84 times on March 21st, 2008. But during cross-examination, he admits that automatic page reloading could account for that number and there was no way of knowing who performed the searches.

Prosecutors allege that Cindy made up the story of searching the word chloroform to try to protect her daughter, who they say searched for information on chloroform, 'neck breaking' and death in the months leading up to the death of Caylee.

Spring 2008

The spring of 2008 was the start of new things for Casey. It was around this time that she met Tony Lazzaro. He attended Full Sail 2007-2009. He eventually graduated with a degree in music business.

When he first met Casey he lived at Sutton Place of University Blvd. He lived with Cameron Campena. Later on his friends, Clint and Nathan lived off his couch. They paid no rent and he was just trying to being a good friend to them.

When he first met Casey, his schedule was not consistent. He'd have a class in the morning from 9 to 1 and an evening lab.

The school wanted the students to get involved with each other and recommended they do various projects with each other. He started a small company with his roommate Clint, focusing on making money from the nightlife, as DJs and promoters. They called their little company: DBC Entertainment. Their first engagement was with Fusion, which started at the end of May, 2008.

At the time that he met Casey he owned a '97 Jeep Grand Cherokee.

In May, he met Casey initially on Facebook. When he saw her picture on Facebook, he found her attractive and initiated contact. The first time they met in person was at his friend's birthday party at the end of May. He made it a Facebook "Event" and invited Casey along with a lot of other Facebook friends.

When he first saw Casey, he thought that she appeared to be a pretty girl and they "hit it off". That night went well and shortly after, he made plans to see her again. After that, they met more often. She brought Caylee the first time she came to his apartment. They went to the pool. This was June 2nd.

One time there was a party for Troy Brown, on the 4th of June, at Club Voyage. Casey drove Tony and two others to the party.

Casey told him that she worked at Universal Studios as an Event Planner. He remembered seeing her come in from "work" wearing a Universal badge around her neck.

Tony said that he saw Caylee a couple of times at his apartment and at the Millennia Mall. He later told the police that he was there to promote an event and hand out flyers. He also said that Casey did not help hand out flyers; she and Caylee went other places in the mall. When they met up, they ate at the Cheesecake Factory.

That was the last time he saw Caylee. They drove there in Casey's car. Casey brought him back to his apartment and left. He never saw Caylee again.

Tony and his roommates said that Caylee never spent the night at his apartment.

At the beginning of their relationship, Casey told him that Caylee's babysitter was called "Zanny". Whenever Casey stayed over she would tell everyone that either Zanny or her parents had little Caylee.

Casey told Tony that she was going to either live in the Anthony home with Amy Huizenga, because she told him that her parents were moving out, and if that didn't work out, they were going to move into an apartment. Casey never mentioned her relationships with her parents to tony.

On June 9th, Casey and Caylee, move out of Casey's parents' home, and in with her ex-boyfriend, Ricardo Morales, and a friend, Amy Huizenga.

On June 13th, Tony did a Hip-Hop Showcase at Fusion. It was the first time Casey was there with them. The showcase was a success and he had a few more coming up. After it was over, Casey returned to his apartment and spent the night for the first time.

In mid to late June, Casey starting staying at his apartment, all of their mutual friends say that Casey was basically living with him. The only problem was that Caylee was never there.

Sunday, June 15th, 2008

On June 15th Cindy visits Alex Plesea, Cindy's father at a Mount Dora Nursing Home around 11:00 a.m. She took little Caylee to visit her great-grandfather; during the visit, someone shot a video of Caylee sitting at a table, trying to read out loud from a children's book. The video shows a cute, playful little girl in a blue dress, with her brown hair pulled into a ponytail. Next to the book sits a pink sippy cup. The images may well be the last ever taken of Caylee.

After leaving the nursing home, Cindy and Caylee also went to visit Cindy's mother, Shirley Plesea. They had dinner with her at her house. She made Chili but Caylee didn't like it so she made her a peanut butter and jelly sandwich. Caylee played with Shirley's cat. Cindy and Caylee left somewhere around 4:00 p.m.

Shirley Plesea said Cindy voiced her frustrations that Casey was gone all the time with Caylee, and even though Cindy told Shirley that she was in touch with Casey daily but Casey refused to let her see or talk with Caylee.

Cindy stated that nobody was home when she and Caylee came back from their Father's Day visit and dinner with her mother around 4 p.m. George was already at work and Cindy didn't know where Casey was.

Later that night, Cindy and Caylee returned to the Anthony home on Hopespring Drive. After Cindy fed Caylee, the two were swimming in the backyard swimming pool. When Casey came home she wanted to go swimming also but Cindy said it was too cold and she was ready to take Caylee out of the swimming pool. After getting out of the pool, Cindy removed the ladder and closed the gate leading to the pool. According to Cindy and George, Casey and Caylee spent the night there.

But it all came to head in the Anthony home on the night of June 16th. Casey had stolen money and was arguing with her mother. She had stolen money before and when asked what made this time different Cindy replied that this time she stole from Cindy's mother.

Casey's grandparents had sent her a check for her birthday from an account used to pay for her Grandfather's care in a nursing home. Casey took the routing number and account number from that check and paid a cell phone bill totaling over three hundred dollars. When confronted by her mother apparently the argument was enough to make Casey take Caylee out of the house the next day. This was the beginning of the end for little Caylee.

George said he thinks Casey's car was in the driveway when he got home from work that evening. He said he knows for sure that his wife's car was there.

As George, Cindy and little Caylee slept, Casey spent most of her night on her phone, making calls and sending and receiving texts until 3:22 in the morning.

Part Two

The "31 Days"

Monday, June 16th, 2008

Caylee was last seen on June 16th, 2008. Neither the State nor the defense disputed that she passed away on this day.

We have put together a timeline of Casey's actions on that day based on the timeline presented in Casey's trial.

The only way to know what happened is to look at the events of June 16th.

The following is a reconstruction of the timeline of June 16th using the digital forensics cellphone and computer records and police interviews.

Casey was always on her cellphone. Therefore, the cellphone records could tell who Casey was talking to and, more importantly, where she was.

Whenever a cell phone is used either to make a call or to send or receive a text message it has to connect to the closest cell tower from the phones location to complete that action. (These are known as PINGS) Cell phone pings will help us track Casey's movements over the first three days after Caylee was last seen alive.

According to Casey's cell phone records, Anthony's cell phone pinged 20 different cell towers 754 times in the two-week period. Each time, her cell phone received or sent a text message or phone call.

Ninety-seven percent of the pings were to either her boyfriend's apartment near Winter Park, her friend's home in Orlando where she sometimes stayed, her parents' home off Chickasaw Trail and the Fusian Ultra Lounge, where she was photographed partying while Caylee was missing.

The other 3 percent of the pings, especially during three days in June have raised many unanswered questions.

Cindy testified that she left for work a few minutes before 7:00 a.m. while everyone in the home was still asleep. George said, "Generally I'd be up like at 7:30, 8:00 in the morning, shortly after my wife would leave."

It is believed that Casey woke up soon after her mother left for work. At 7:52 a.m. Casey logged into her MySpace account and researched "shot girls" costumes for Tony Lazzaro's night club events.

At 7:56 a.m. Casey's AIM account was used to chat on the computer. At 8:03:53 Casey sent the following text:"i'm finally moving into my house, at the end of the month. i'll have a roommate for a little bit. but at least my friend amy is like living with myself." Casey's AIM account username was "casey o marie"

Casey uploaded a photo to Photobucket of the interior of the Fusian Ultra Lounge at 9:27 a.m.

Casey texted Tony at 8:46 a.m. and did not have any further phone activity until 11:28 a.m. when Tony called Casey. The two spoke for about 19 minutes ending the call around 11:47.

After her conversation with Tony Casey had no cell phone activity between 11:47 a.m. and 12:53 p.m. Phone records show at 12:53 she texts again with Tony.

What happens around 1:00 is one of the biggest mysteries in this case next to how Caylee actually died. In a police statement that he made later George, recalled what he witnessed on June 16th.

Let's put it this way like 10 minutes to 1 that afternoon on the 16th is when I actually saw Casey and Caylee together. They're both leaving with backpacks and so my daughter said she was going to work and she was taking Caylee to the, to the nanny, to the babysitter.

Okay, my granddaughter had her white, uh, backpack um, I think it has little monkeys or something on it, like, like brown monkeys. And I know she was dressed in her little uh, blue jean skirt, the white tennis shoes...um.. she had a pinkish color top. One of those, uh, one has a sleeve on it. She had her little sunglasses on, they was white rimmed sunglasses. Her hair was in a ponytail that day, I remember that very, very well.

And my daughter had a like decent pair of like dress slacks on, top that she could be wearing to be going to work. There's not nothing unusual about the way she was dressed. I know she had a backpack full of stuff. [The slacks were] like a charcoal grey, like a pin stripe, like a pin stripe through it. [The top was] like a beige color, matter of fact almost like, not white but almost like and off white color top.

He said the situation was not out of the ordinary:

She just set it down and she says "Hey" she says. "I'm gonna be working a little bit late, uh, Caylee's gonna be staying with the nanny, I'm gonna back and stay there and I'll see you and Mom tomorrow afternoon." That's not nothing unusual, she's done that a few different times so. She said she already had, she says "I already talked to Mom, Mom knows I'm gonna be staying over." I said, "Okay. Just be careful and I'll see you tomorrow" type deal.

George later told detectives he was sure of the time because he was watching one of his favorite programs on the Food Network.

Cayce's Brother, Lee said that Casey left town with Caylee on Monday June 16th for work and vacation.

So Casey's father said that he saw his daughter and granddaughter leave his house at about 1 p.m. but at 12:50, there is further computer activity on the home computer associated with Casey's account. Either George has her phone and is pretending to be her online or this timeline is inaccurate.

But if they did leave at that time, the cell records show they did not go far. Casey's cell phone communicated that afternoon through the same three cell towers she could reach from her home.

At 1 p.m., Casey made a 14-minute call to her boyfriend, Tony Lazzaro. Some of Casey's supporters say that Casey called Tony from her car when she left her parents' home. We have two reasons why that scenario does not make sense here.

#1 Casey would have driven out of the range of the cell tower near her parents' home in the 14 minute time span.

#2 Casey is online on her home computer from 1:39 till 1:42.

At 1:44 p.m., she made a 36-minute call to her then-best friend, Amy Huizenga. This call would have ended at approximately 2:21 p.m.

With the statements of Casey's own defense team we can say that Caylee most likely drowned sometime during the phone call with Amy Huizenga between the hours of 1:44 p.m. and 2:21 p.m.

According to Casey's defense team during Casey's trial, Caylee drowned in the family's above-ground swimming pool sometime during this day and both Casey and George panicked upon finding the body and covered up her death. Baez had told the jury that Caylee was the victim of an accidental death and not a murder as the prosecutors contended.

Baez said, "Caylee Anthony died on June 16th, 2008, when she drowned in her family's swimming pool."

According to Baez, Casey and her father were home alone on the day the alleged accident occurred. The attorney said it was in the early morning hours of June 16th that George noticed Caylee was missing and he and his daughter began a frantic search. The looked under beds and in the garage. It was during that search that George decided to take the search outside, to the above-ground pool, Baez said.

"As Casey came around the corner of the pool she saw George Anthony holding Caylee in his arms," the defense attorney told the jury during the trial. "She immediately grabbed Caylee and began to cry. Shortly thereafter, George began to yell at her: 'Look what you've done. Your mother will never forgive you and you will go to jail for child neglect for the rest of your frigging life.'"

In his book, Baez said Casey wondered if her father "was doing something to her (Caylee) and he tried to cover it up." The line of thought here is that George was molesting Caylee and he killed her before anyone could find out. Many psychological experts say that this is not a common reaction to someone who is molesting a very young child. The same experts say that "if" George molested Casey as she claimed, then it would be very odd that she would bring her own daughter to her parents and leave her in the care of her father.

In court, George denied having any knowledge of his granddaughter's death.

George testified in court that, "I would have done anything I could to save my granddaughter."

George's attorney, Mark Lippman, said his client has no comment on Baez's book.

Baez, according to his book, remains convinced George knows a lot more than he has let on.

"George never saw himself as the bad guy. Instead, as is common with abusers, he saw himself as the victim of Casey's treachery," Baez wrote.

So, according to the statement by Casey's own defense lawyer Caylee died accidently in the family pool. And out of fear it is believed that Casey and her father tried to cover up the child's accidental death.

George testified that he left the home at 2:30 to go to work. Cindy said he usually left home at 2:00 p.m. Her statement to police was, *"He usually leaves to go to work around 2 you know at that time."* George worked in the security department at a Lexus dealership in Winter Park. His work was about a 30 minute drive from his home.

He arrived to work a little after 3:00 p.m. George worked 3:00 p.m. to 11:00 p.m. on this day according to his Security Forces time card.

There is no electronic information between 2:20 and 2:50.

At 2:51 someone does a search for "foolproof suffocation", misspelling the last word as "suffication". The user then clicked on several pro-suicide websites. (I personally believe it was in reaction to losing her daughter)

At 2:51 p.m. a Google search is made for the term "fool-proof suffocation," The user clicks on an article criticizing pro-suicide websites that promote "foolproof" ways to die.

At 2:52 p.m. There is additional activity on Casey's MySpace account. The computer forensics show that there was heavy computer activity on the Anthony's home computer between 2:00 p.m. and 3:00 p.m. and the cellphone pings show that Casey was at home. But here was no computer activity after 3:00 p.m.

At 2:52, Casey receives a phone call from Jesse Grund. Grund describes the conversation as abnormal. She told him her parents were getting a divorce and she had to find a place to live.

During this call Jesse said that he thought he heard Caylee's voice or Casey talking to Caylee.

At 3:04 George called Casey, supposedly from work. She clicked over and ended the call from Grund. According to Baez, George told her he took care of everything and reminded her not to tell her mother. This call lasted only for 26 seconds.

At 3:36, she tries to call Tony, he doesn't answer.

James Thompson later said that he had seen Casey and Caylee exiting Casselberry Walmart, 1239 State Road, Casselberry, FL around his lunchtime. (Approximately 4:00)

He made this statement on July 22nd, over a month after the date that he claimed seeing her.

He said that he recognized her because Casey and Caylee had been to his TechbayUSA store the week before. Thompson said Caylee seemed angry and was about 10 feet behind Casey exiting the store.

This sighting was investigated and determined to be a case of mistaken identity because at 4:11 p.m., Casey began trying to reach her mother, making four attempts in two minutes, according to her cell phone records. These calls were made in the area of the Anthony home about 25 miles from the Castleberry Walmart.

Cindy recalled the message that Casey left that evening.

But I had gotten a phone call, God I don't know what point in the evening, and said that um, she had a lot going on. And that she wasn't gonna come home they were gonna crash at Zanny's that night her and Caylee were gonna just stay at Zanny's.

At 4:18 her cell phone shows her leaving her parents' residence.

But why would George say that she left at 1:50 if it was proven that she stayed at the house until 4:18? Is it possible he just misremembered that day? He had a very detailed story about what everyone was wearing, what everyone said, what everyone was carrying. Either he accidentally fabricated the events that day or he intentionally fabricated what happened that day.

Casey then traveled north from her parent's home and called Lazzaro for one minute at 4:19 p.m. Two minutes later, she talked to Grund for a minute, and tried to call her mother again at 4:25 p.m.

In Baez's book, he says that after George left for work, she paced and cried and freaked out for about an hour before deciding she needed her mother and desperately called her.

So now we have some more unanswered questions here. Where was Casey after leaving her parents' home? Tony Lazzaro's home was at Sutton Place Apartments, on Ollie Avenue, in Winter Park. The drive from the Anthony's home was about 15 miles and could be driven in about 30 minutes. Casey's phone records show that there was no other communication from Casey's cell phone until a call was made to Lazzaro's apartment at 5:57 p.m.

And what was so important to Casey that she had to attempt to call her mother four times in a two minute period

Casey's boyfriend, Tony, would later testify that just hours after her lawyers claim that Caylee drowned, they both went to their local

Blockbuster video store at 7:54 p.m. to rent a movie. Caylee was not with them.

"She was the way she was every day – happy. Happy to see me. Having a grand old time."

What happened in the next hours is even more intriguing. Tony and Casey rented two movies for that night. One of them was "Untraceable" and the second was "Jumper".

Many people have said that these two movies show a connection with Casey and the killing of little Caylee. There are even numerous comments explaining what the two movie's plot lines are. And most of them are inaccurate. One even goes as far as to say that the movie "Jumper" is about a mother who drowns her 3 year old daughter in the pool and hides the body in the swamp down the road from her own home.

That is not the case. Untraceable is about a boy killing people via the internet and the more users that log in the faster the person dies, he does this because of his father's suicide being posted on television, And Jumper is about a guy who learns how to teleport himself.

They spent that night together at his apartment. The next day, he "played hooky" from Full Sail University because he "didn't feel like leaving my bed," he testified during the trial.

Lazzaro said that they "stayed in my bedroom" June 17th and Casey appeared happy to be there, giving no indication anything was wrong. But Casey had told her mother she and Caylee were staying with Zanny. She said the same for the 17th. But by June 18th, Casey knew Cindy wouldn't accept the same excuse. So she had to change the lie and added the conference in Tampa. She would bring Zanny AND there would be another woman there with a child the same age. She wanted her mother to believe that Caylee would have so much fun. Casey added to the lies over the days. And, Cindy was happy that Caylee was having so much fun at the theme parks.

In fact, Casey was staying with Tony and Caylee, in most likelihood, in the trunk dead.

So it looks like something happened between 2:20 and 2:50. Based on the fact that she's normal before she got off the phone with Amy and is acting weird by the time she gets on the phone with Grund. She's either reacting to something with the frantic phone calls to her mom and suicide searches or she's planning something at this time and is acting weird for that reason.

Either way, I think we can conclude that Caylee was most likely deceased by 4:18. (Note: personally, I lean toward accident because why would Casey frantically call her mom after committing first degree murder?)

The interesting thing about this electronic information is that it looks like both sides did some creative storytelling to avoid facing this computer timeline information. The prosecution claims they didn't have it. I don't buy it. The state *knew* Casey preferred *"Firefox"* and their excuse for why this information wasn't at trial was that they only looked at the internet provider *"explorer".*

Aside from that, the first thing I would look at as an investigator for the State Attorney's office or even the defense is the web information for that particular day. There's basically no way they didn't have it. I suspect the State didn't introduce it because they didn't want to have to explain why George is lying about that day.

Baez impeached George on his testimony about that day and poked some holes in it, but he had an ace in the hole with this computer info and chose not to use it because the 12:50 departure time for Casey was better for them in case the prosecution used the "foolproof suffocation" search.

If the State brought it up then the defense could argue that George did it. But even the prosecution had an ace in the hole with the "foolproof suffocation" search but couldn't use it because to bring it in would prove that George was lying and cast suspicion on him and away from their prime suspect, Casey.

So both sides knew George was lying about what happened and they knew Casey didn't leave at 12:50, but both pretended that was a legit timeline because it was better for their case.

So with what we know so far it can be determined that Caylee may have drowned in the pool while Casey was on the phone with Amy Huizenga, the body was discovered by George and Casey soon after that call ended and George disposed of the body on his way to work.

Even though many people refuse to accept that theory here is the evidence for that theory:

Her behavior as well as the way the body was disposed (19 feet from the road, just a few blocks from the house) all point to the death being unplanned.

We can also see that there appears to be a very distinct change in her behavior at a specific point in the day. We see this mainly in the gap in the electronic information that is between normal and abnormal behavior, this points to something unexpected happening in that gap.

The frantic calls to Cindy, It's the type of thing you'd do after an accident...not so much after you've committed murder.

The second theory of a drugging that ended in death is also inconsistent. The time of day would be bizarre for that type of thing. Why would she sedate her child in the afternoon on a Monday, particularly when she had no plans to go party that night. Also, this theory is inconsistent with her friend's testimony about her social habits. Also, George described her as being awake that day...she certainly wasn't sedated in his retelling, nor was she on any other day he could recall.

George is lying about the timeline that day. He claims Casey and Caylee left at 12:50. This doesn't protect Casey in any way, it only protects him by putting distance between himself and Casey. Of course, you might argue that he found out at a later date, but another issue to consider:

George stopped calling his daughter that day. Aside from the call at 3:04, he appears to be avoiding Casey completely that month. The previous month, they spoke about every other day, so this is a big change. On the other hand, Casey and her mother spoke frequently. He certainly wouldn't avoid Casey in anticipation of finding out about the death.

So now obviously, this leads to the question of why did they hide the death instead of calling police? There are a few possibilities:

Many say that either George was molesting Caylee or believed that Caylee was his child and wanted to cover it up. This was what the defense argued at trial, but personally, I lean away from this theory. I believe Jose put this in the trial for other reasons. Obviously this would explain a lot about the family's behavior (like why they hid her pregnancy).

People always want a reason why people act weird when often there is no reason for it at all. Maybe there was some sexual abuse, but I'm not sure it was related to the death. However, it's a theory so I thought I'd throw it out there.

Another theory that had been said over the years is that there was some neglect involved and they were afraid of being charged in the death. This is definitely a possibility. People always say there's no way they would cover up an unintentional drowning, but I'm not sure that's the case. We really have no idea how they would've perceived the situation and people really can get charged with these types of deaths.

We have heard in the news where there was a Pitbull mauling where the parents were in the home, but not in close enough proximity that they could hear the child and they were criminally charged. The computer and phone records place Casey on the computer and not watching her child for most of the day. It really is plausible that they thought she would be charged with the death.

Another possibility is that they just had a weird reaction to the death. Some people do sometimes pretend that nothing ever happened as a defense mechanism, particularly when you consider the history of this family. Their 19 year old daughter gets pregnant and they just pretend it didn't happen. It wasn't like they lied to people and hid it, no, she walked around with this huge belly and they just flat out denied it was happening. Even when people confronted them about it, they would deny it.

Some say that they just panicked over how Cindy would react. Both George and Casey seem to have some fears of how Cindy will react to things. And a lot of the lies seem to revolve around Cindy. I suspect George was worried that Cindy would leave him for not watching Caylee more carefully and Casey thought her mother would never forgive her. Both made statements regarding those fears after the death. I suspect it was a combination of these factors that led them to hide the death.

We do know that George wasn't entirely truthful with the Detectives investigating the crime. Whether it was an accident or premeditated I don't know. I do know that it's not a big stretch at all for a father to cover for his child.Tony and Casey went back to his apartment. His roommate Nate was there but he had his headphones on playing a guitar. Tony and Casey watched both movies that night. Casey had no cell phone activity after she checked her voicemail at 8:03 except for a text message from Amy at 11:17 saying, "I think I have cramps for the first time in 3 years. This sucks! I forgot how much it hurts."

Casey replied, "So I'm not feeling good so I'm just going to crash at the boys. I'll call in the morning"

Later George would say that when he arrived home that evening only Cindy was home. George said Casey told him when he seen her last at 12:50 pm earlier in the afternoon, that she had an event at her work that wouldn't be over until 11 p.m.-12 a.m. this evening. Casey told George that she and Caylee BOTH would be staying overnight at Zanny's.

Tuesday, June 17th, 2008

June 17th, George and Cindy notice that the gate to the swimming pool is open and the ladder is next to the pool. Cindy said that she put the pool ladder away Sunday evening 06/15 and that nobody swam in the pool on Monday 06/16. But on Tuesday morning 06/17 the ladder was back at the pool.

It was common practice not to leave the pool ladder up after the pool was used. And we know the pool ladder was up that day because Cindy discovered it, was very concerned, and told her coworkers about it. Later she even frantically called Detective Yuri Melich to tell him about this while he was questioning Casey.

Tony said he cared for Casey and the relationship was going well. (Or at least as well as a two week old relationship could go) They had no disagreements or fights. They spent that Tuesday together as well and Tony skipped school. Tony said that he preferred to spend his day with Casey.

This day, they stayed in his bedroom all morning and there was no change in her demeanor. She gave him no indication that there was anything wrong. Tony later said that he didn't recall her calling anyone in his presence.

Casey had no cell phone activity until 10:59 a.m. when she called to check her voicemail. Followed by an eight minute call to Amy and no activity after that call until 2:12 p.m. when she attempts to call George.

Casey apparently returned back to the family home at about 2:30 p.m.

Brian Burner, the next door neighbor returned from vacation the evening of June 16th and was home June 17th. He said that on June 17th, he saw Casey's vehicle backing into the garage.

He told the detectives that he had only seen Casey driving the car. He knew that the vehicle went all the way into the garage and this was the first time he had seen Casey do so. He had no recollection of the car leaving the house.

Then, around 4 p.m., the phone pinged a cell tower southwest of the family home at Lee Vista Boulevard and South Goldenrod. The location was near where detectives directed EquuSearch volunteers to look for signs of Caylee several weeks later.

At 5:20 p.m., Casey's cell phone pinged a tower near Blanchard Park at state Road 50 and Goldenrod. That site was also searched two months later in August by EquuSearch. Records showed that Casey's cell phone went silent during the time between 5:23 and 8:23 on June 17th, no text messages, no calls in and no calls out. Casey then turned up near her boyfriend's apartment. By then, around 8:30 p.m., Caylee had not been seen alive for nearly a day and a half.

Later the Orange County Sheriff's Department determined that by chemical evidence in the trunk of Casey's car indicates the decomposing body was there up to two and half days after death, so a key question for anyone looking for Caylee's body is, "Where did Casey go next?"

There were some parts of Casey's tale about Zanny, however, that had some connection to the truth. Detectives tracked down the real Zenaida Fernandez-Gonzalez and questioned her about her whereabouts on June 17th. She had visited the Sawgrass Apartments, looking for an apartment for her and her two daughters. That day, she filled out a card requesting more information, but never lived there. After looking at photos of Casey and Caylee, Fernandez-Gonzalez told the detectives she had never seen either of them. She also said she had never worked as a nanny or babysitter.

Another person who came into contact with Casey on June 17th was Christopher Stutz. He told Detective Yuri Melich that Casey came to see him at his parents' house where he lived in May 2008. At that time Caylee was with her. But, when she came to see him again sometime between June 17th and the 19th, Caylee was not with her, and she didn't mention her at all.

Detective Yuri Melich: And Caylee was with her?

Christopher Stutz: Caylee was with her and my parents saw her and uh, started interacting with them.

Detective Yuri Melich: Uh, also it says here June 17th uh, a dark colored Jeep Cherokee with New York plates uh....

Christopher Stutz: Without Caylee.

Detective Yuri Melich: And that was, or how did, how did you see her? Did she come to your house with that or?

Christopher Stutz: Yeah (affirmative), she drove over. Uhm, I had saw her I think it was the night before I saw her just randomly and so she decided to stop by the next day. We didn't really hang out or anything like that.

Detective Yuri Melich: How sure are you that it was June 17th?

Christopher Stutz: I'm pretty sure. My mother and I went over it because she remember Cay...uh, Casey coming over and we had just bought a treadmill.

Detective Yuri Melich: Uh-hum (affirmative).

Christopher Stutz: So it was either the 17th or 18th, or possibly the 19th. It's one of those three days.

Detective Yuri Melich: Okay.

Christopher Stutz: We're sure of that.

Detective Yuri Melich: Okay, so you've looked at a calendar and you're, you're pretty confident those are the dates?

Christopher Stutz: Yeah (affirmative), we went over that, yeah (affirmative), because she just bought the treadmill and uhm, she was using the treadmill when Casey came over.

Detective Yuri Melich: Did she just stop by to say hi? Did you guys talk about her coming over? How did that (inaudible)?

Christopher Stutz: Uh, she just stopped by to say hi. She was there for maybe an hour and a half, two hours.

Detective Yuri Melich: Was she with anyone else?

Christopher Stutz: No.

Detective Yuri Melich: And then including Caylee?

Christopher Stutz: Including Caylee.

Detective Yuri Melich: Did she say where Caylee was?

Christopher Stutz: No.

Detective Yuri Melich: Did you ask?

Christopher Stutz: No.

Detective Yuri Melich: Okay. Uh, what was her demeanor when she came to you on the 17th of June?

Christopher Stutz: Uhm, she was happy. She was distressed about her parents. She said that her parents were getting a divorce or getting split up.

Detective Yuri Melich: Oh.

Christopher Stutz: Because her dad was apparently cheating on her, or cheating on the mom. And so she's a little upset about that. But uhm, she barely went into that.

Casey also said she was buying a new house on Curry Ford Rd. They run $250,000, she said, for just her and Caylee.

He told the detectives that he saw her again in early July 2008, at Buffalo Wild Wings and she was upbeat and happy. And again she didn't say anything about her daughter being missing.

He even went on to say that Casey once told him that she didn't like to drink or stay out late because she didn't want to leave Caylee with her parents.

Matthew Crisp has been friends with Casey since 2002. He is a residential property manager (helps people find apartments) Casey called him on either June 17th or June 19th to help her boyfriend, Tony, find a new apartment. She never mentioned Caylee when they got together, and she seemed "joyful". When asked what "joyful" meant, he said, "exuberantly happy."

A few weeks later he met with her for lunch on July 7th at Subway. She told him that Caylee was in Sanford on a play date when he asked about her. Their conversation was happy and light.

Wednesday, June 18th, 2008

During his testimony at the trial, Brian Burner the next door neighbor said that Casey borrowed a shovel for about an hour and once again backed her car into her parent's garage. He was not 100% sure if the date was on the 18th or 19th of June though. He testified that he was outside doing yard work. Casey approached him about 1:20 or 1:30 to borrow a shovel to dig up a bamboo root that she claims she was tripping on.

He said that he gave her the shovel and Casey left his house and walked back into the Anthony's garage. He finished his work and went to see if Casey was finished with the shovel. When he arrived at the Anthony's home he saw that the garage door was still open and the car was still backed into the garage so he walked back to his house to take a shower and told his son about Casey borrowing the shovel. Casey returned the shovel to his son about an hour after he had lent it to her.

The only day, of the two days, that Casey could have gone to her parents' home and borrowed the neighbor's shovel, without George knowing, was on June 18th because George was at work that day.

On this day Casey made numerous calls to the Anthony's home and cell numbers prior to arriving at their home around 1:30. Her final calls were at 1:09 p.m. and 1:11 p.m. when she made her last attempts to call Cindy's cell phone and then the Anthony's home number.

Then there was no phone activity between 1:11 p.m. and 2:05 p.m.

Some people believe that she was calling to make sure that her parents were not home at this time.

George was not scheduled for work on the 19th so odds were that he would have been home. If Casey really needed a shovel to remove the alleged bamboo root she claimed she was tripping on, she could have just asked George on the 19th to get his out of the shed.

Brian Burner said Casey didn't appear to be muddy or sweaty and the shovel didn't have a lot of dirt on it. Brian Burner said he thought it was strange that Casey was concerned about a Bamboo root when it looked like she had moved from the home.

He said that he also saw her car again on the 19th or the 20th in the early afternoon between noon and three. He was in his house and the car backed in again. He said that he didn't know how long the car stayed there.

Casey's cell phone pings show that she was at or near her parents' home from 2:30 p.m. until 3:30 p.m. Casey's phone later pinged a different spot near the Econ Trail, south of Lake Underhill, records show.

Scientific evidence suggests that a body left its chemical signature in the trunk of Anthony's car after decomposing for less than two and a half days, which would be about the same time period that Casey was seen at the Anthony's home barrowing the shovel.

The defense claimed that Caylee drowned in the pool by accident and that George was the one who disposed of the body. If we consider the theory that Caylee did in fact drowned in the pool and Casey hid the body in the trunk prior to leaving her in the woods, then this "may be" why she backed her car in the garage.

Thursday, June 19, 2008

Casey's morning pretty much started like all of the others with nothing too exciting going on.

She started to get activity on her cell phone shortly after 11:00 a.m. when she and Tony started to text.

But it was the activity on her AIM account that afternoon that really put the proverbial nail in her coffin.

At 1:45 she sent a message to a user identified as; doorknob375 that read, "*ladies in free all night. guys, $5 cover. its a bad ass place*"

"*good! then i better see you tomorrow. really cute shot girls*" was the reply that she got in return.

Casey was telling her friends about the event that was going on the following night at the Fusion nightclub.

After the messages Casey contacted Matthew Crisp, leasing agent for Cranes Landing Apts. to set up an appointment for Tony to look at an apartment to rent. Matthew said both Tony and Casey came by later to see the apartment but Casey didn't have her ID so he could only show it to Tony but not Casey.

At 3:57 p.m. Casey made a Facebook Posting on Troy Brown's Facebook wall that read :"you, ric and dave should definitely come out tomorrow night. i'll give you a buzz later. i haven't see you in ages!"

At 9:09 p.m. she added, "until 2. i'll be there all night."

After posting the message Casey made a phone call to her parents' home.

Throughout the day Casey stayed in contact with her friends and not once did she make any comment that there was anything out of the ordinary going on with her life.

Friday, June 20th, 2008

The most damaging part of this story happened on June 20th. Casey is captured in various photos partying at the Fusion nightclub and participating in a "hot body contest". Many people are appalled by her actions because it was during this time that little Caylee is believed to be decomposing in a swamp not far from her grandparent's home.

June 20th was more focused on Casey promoting the "hot body contest" at the Fusion Nightclub than anything else.

At 11:29 that morning she was already in her AIM messenger account once again with "doorknob375" asking if he was going to show up that night.

casey o marie (11:29:08 AM): "you guys coming to hang out with me tonight?!"

doorknob375 (11:29:25 AM): "i dont even know yet, i havent talked to anybody"

casey o marie (11:29:45 AM): "well i'm going to text everyone. i say you do"

casey o marie (11:30:06 AM) "you know i'm relentless"

casey o marie (11:30:23 AM): "sean should bring some girls. there's going to be a hot body contest too"

casey o marie (11:34:18 AM): "i'm going to send out a big text now with the info." .

casey o marie (11:38:43 AM): "i want you boys to come out, seriously."

casey o marie (11:39:02 AM): "Cheap cover, you dont have to drive all the way downtown, and your happy ass should come up early and get some sushi!!!"

doorknob375 (11:39:41 AM): "i work till 9 tho. when does sushi end" casey o marie(11:39:54 AM): "at 11. dude its so good!"

Now to put things into perspective here; Casey does not only text doorknob375. During this time period she is also texting Troy Brown, Shawn Rimmer, Jeffrey Dale Hopkins, Jesse Grund, Sean Daly and Bj Jacke. And she even tried to call Robert Westenbarger also known as Rob at Arden Villa.

The rest of the day Casey spends calling and texting her friends. Many people assume that she is trying to spread the word about the night's activities lined up at the Fusion Nightclub.

But there was one call that was out of the ordinary, even for Casey. At 1:53 p.m. Casey calls the Lexus dealership where George works. There is no time length on this call so many believes that she called the dealership to see if her father was working. But she realized that it wasn't quite two o'clock yet and he would not be there so she hung up.

This theory is supported by the fact that exactly one hour later at 2:54 she calls the dealership back again. This time she is on the phone for five minutes. We do know that George was not working on this day.

The Anthony's neighbor Brian Burner said that he saw Casey's car backing into the Anthony's garage today *(third time this week)* in the early afternoon hours. He did not see Casey in the car, only the car. Burner said that this was after he shopped at Sam's Club, around 12-2 p.m. or 12-3 p.m.

Now to many this may not seem strange at all. But we will add that Casey was on the phone all morning either texting or calling her friends. "BUT" from 2:54 to 6:53 p.m. her phone is not being used at all. This is the time frame in which she is believed to be at her parent's home.

At 6:53 p.m. Casey once again starts texting and calling her friends all hours of the night.

Anthony Lazarro said he usually goes to the Fusian Ultra Lounge between 7 and 8 p.m., orders food and makes sure everybody gets there on time. On this night he allowed Casey to buy drinks on his bar tab and she run up $60 on booze. Tony later said that he was pissed and even argued with Casey for that.

Anthony Lazarro said he was busy that night at Fusian, making sure that there were no fights, nobody passing out, checking the shot girls, bartenders. Basically doing what a manager would do. He said that he wasn't able to keep any eye on Casey's drinking all night.

As the night went on the party atmosphere picked up inside Fusion.

Photographer Teddy Pieper was hired to take nightlife photos at Orlando clubs and they just happen to be working at Fusian on the night of the 20th.

The photos showing Casey were taken between midnight to 2:00 a.m. early in the morning of the 21st at the Fusian Ultra Lounge.

The pictures of Casey at the Fusian Ultra Lounge are now infamous.

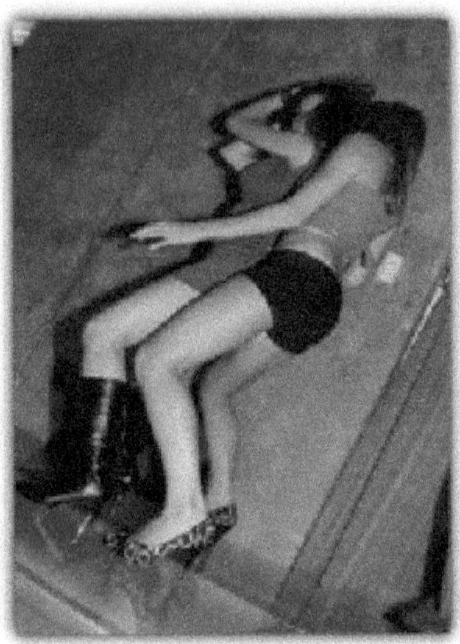

The emcee of the hot body contest later told detectives what happened that night.

Uhm, they were running short on girls that evening for the hot body contest. Someone had asked her, I'm not sure if it was Tony or one of the other promoters had asked her hey, would you do it?

So she changed. At that point she had like a skirt in her car or something. So she changed into that blue outfit at that point. Based at the realization that hey, I'm about to get on stage and do some dancing, she did proceed to pound some shots and some drinks before she got up on stage.

Melina Calabrese was a friend who knew Casey well and stated that there was something wrong with the pictures of Casey that night.

I would look at those pictures and I just didn't feel like [that was] the Casey I knew. She was trying too hard to be someone she was not. Those seem like she was trying too hard to, you know, smile for this camera and do these poses. Something about those pictures is just not sitting right with me.

Casey DID in fact win the "hot body contest". Tony Lazzaro's roommate Nate Lezniewicz revealed this fact in an interview after the trial. Nate implied Casey "won" by default only because she was Tony's girlfriend.

Casey did a good job at hiding her emotions from the people who were around her, most of whom were her new friends. But there were clues that something was amiss – besides the fact that a mother didn't have her child for a month.

At some point during the "31 Days" before her boyfriend left for New York, she awoke in the middle of the night when she thought everyone was asleep, sat up in bed, turned on her laptop and cried as she watched a video of Caylee reading her book while visiting her Great Grandfather.

Nathan Lezniewicz, a roommate of Casey's boyfriend, told detectives what happened.

Tony said that she [Casey] had had woken up before crying. Uhm, I guess it was, he had just told me this maybe a couple weeks ago that she had sat up one night [and] that he had woken up. I guess maybe between the hours of three and five he had woken up and she was sitting up in the bed next to him crying.

Tony, Casey's boyfriend, also recalled the event.

One time, a couple times that I had her, she had nightmares and she had these sweats, but I can't remember exactly what days those were.

Uhm, I remember, I would say it wasn't at night. It was in the morning. And she was already awake. And she was just on her laptop watching uh, this video and she was crying.

The video where I guess it shows like Caylee with the gr...her [great-] grandfather that was shown all over the news.

She was uh, uh, sitting up in my bed and like at, like at the end, like ... Indian style or whatever. And then uh, and she had the laptop in here, in her lap.

Casey's behavior throughout the "31 Days" was immature and Casey eventually recognized that according to a psychologist who testified at her trial.

She can't believe how immature and how she behaved. And again, I emphasize that I am seeing a Casey who has been in jail for close to three years when I start seeing her. So she, herself, when she looks back in time, has a real hard time understanding how she behaved the way she behaved.

Casey told him, "I'm embarrassed when I look at my behavior now. I can understand why others think the way they do."

The "31 Days" were not devoid of any criminal activity by Casey. She stole hundreds of dollars from her friend, Amy, and wiped out her bank account. It was only a matter of time before Amy found out. You can say that Casey was on a collision course with her own fate one way or another.

After the night out Tony said Casey slept at his apartment. He said she was drunk and babbling about how she could sing and that she could be a singer. He said he was just trying to get her to go to sleep and shut up.

Saturday, June 21st, 2008

Casey came in late the night before but she was up the following morning by 9:30 when she called and checked her voicemail. She then tried to call her parent's home but there was no answer.

She spent the rest of the day calling and texting her friends.

It was almost five o'clock when Casey finally spoke to her mother on the telephone.

Even though Casey had returned to the Anthony home numerous times in the past few days, when asked, Casey told her mother she was still in Tampa with her "imaginary friends."

However, her friend Maria Kissh is told by Casey that Caylee is with the nanny. Casey's lies fit the necessity of the audience.

Casey told her mother when she called her that Zanny, her roommate Raquel and Juliette were all taking Caylee & Annabelle to Busch Gardens. That's why they decided to stay one more night in Tampa and would be back Monday.

When asked about clothes for Caylee, Cindy said Casey told her that Zanny went shopping on that day and bought new clothes for her and Caylee. She went on to say, "Mom, Zanny always has extra outfits and clothes, shoes and things at her house."

Casey is creating a fictitious nanny that not only takes care of her daughter at all hours of the night, but also purchases clothing for both her and Caylee. And her actions are wrapping themselves around her imaginary nanny. She is going out partying and has a good time with her friends as if she thinks that her daughter is at her nanny's home and being taken care of.

Sunday, June 22nd, 2008

Sunday June 22nd started off early for Casey. This morning started off just the one yesterday.

Just after 9:30 she called and checked her voicemail.

Throughout the day Casey makes her regular calls and text messages to her friends. But in addition to these there are numerous calls between Casey and her parent's home.

In fact there were nine phone calls made throughout the day.

First call Anthony Home called Casey: 09:35 am 0 min

Second call Anthony Home called Casey 09:37 am 0 min

Third call Anthony Home called Casey 12:06 pm 0 min

Fourth call Casey called Anthony Home: 12:23 pm 0 min

Fifth call Casey called Anthony Home 12:27 pm 0 min

Sixth call Anthony Home called Casey: 02:37 pm 0 min

Seventh call Casey called Anthony Home 2:40 pm 1 min

Eighth call Anthony Home called Casey 09:57 pm 0 min

Ninth call Casey called Anthony Home 10:11 pm 6 min

If you notice that out of all of the calls only two times did someone actually answer the phone. The first time was at 2:40 p.m. when Casey called her parents back after missing a call from them at 2:37. But the call only lasted for 1 minute. (Maybe the call went to voicemail?)

The second time was at 10:11 p.m. when Casey called her parents back after missing a call from them at 9:57.

What puzzles most people is that these calls are made within minutes of each other yet nobody answers the phone.

Monday, June 23rd, 2008

Around four o'clock Casey called Tony Lazarro and told him that she ran out of gas near Hopespring Dr. Tony Lazarro drove to where Casey was and found her walking South on Chickasaw Trail with a backpack where he stopped to pick her up. She gets in Tony's truck and says, "Oh, I need to get gas. Drive back to my place."

Tony drove Casey to her parents' house on Hopespring. They went to the shed and it was locked. He broke the lock with a tire iron from his truck. He was concerned about it and Casey told him it was OK, it was her shed. They took two gas cans out of the shed and put them in his truck and went back to her car.

The Anthony's neighbor, Brian Burner recalls seeing a dark pickup truck like a Ranger; pull into the Anthony's driveway. He recalled seeing a white male, dark hair. He didn't see Casey but he heard her voice. Brian Burner said he did not see Casey's car.

When they pull up to Casey's car Casey insists on putting the gas into the car herself. After she emptied the cans she put the gas cans in the trunk. Tony said that he couldn't see inside the trunk when she opened it and there was no odor that he could detect.

After putting the gas in her car they then went back to his apartment.

Later that evening Casey told Cindy that Zanny & Raquel had an accident driving home, was taken to Tampa General Hospital. She told her mother that Zanny had a concussion, Raquel a broken arm. Casey said her, Juliette, Caylee and Annabelle were in Casey's car, and witnessed the accident.

Cindy asked Casey if she was coming home that night. She told Cindy she couldn't bring Caylee home today because she had to stay in Tampa with Zanny at the hospital. When Cindy questioned her as to why she had to stay Casey said that Zanny's sister couldn't go there and Juliette took Caylee and Annabelle back to the hotel in Tampa.

When Casey called her mother she would step outside to talk to her. Tony thought it was just a private matter with her mom. There would be no change of mood when she returned and she never discussed the call with him.

Tuesday, June 24th, 2008

George said he went to get the lawn mower out of the shed to cut the grass. It was 10:30 a.m. When he arrived at the shed he discovered the shed lock broke and the gas cans missing.

He then called police to report the break-in and report the gas cans missing.

Casey went back to her house later that day but didn't know her father would be home. George recalled the incident.

I got home about 2:25, 2:30, started to get ready for work and um, Casey pops in the door. I hear the garage door open, here comes Casey in. I think I startled her sorta being there cause my car was inside the garage. But she comes in, she says, "Hey Dad. How are you doing? I don't got much time, gotta go back to work for an event. She says she just came to get clothes George asked where's Caylee, Casey said with Zanny.

"Dad, I don't got time for it, I only got 10 minutes, I gotta get back to work."

Now we will note here that she tells her father that "I don't got much time, gotta go back to work for an event."

Well while she's in her room, she shouts out to me, "Oh by the way, I talked to Mom, I understand something happened here at the house." I said, "In reference to..." she says, "Oh the gas cans". And I said "yeah, isn't that something". "Oh Yeah Dad, that's terrible".

Now at this point she does not say to her father that she was the one that removed the gas cans the previous day. She plays along as though someone broke in and stole them

This investigator thing comes through and I, I know my daughter is not levelling with me. And I know this is what she's done in the past. I said, "Hey Case." You know in the back of your trunk in the car we got those metal wedges you put underneath the, your wheel, the car, if you jack your car up so it doesn't move. I said, "Hey I wanna get that one out of your car cause I already have one in the garage, I wanna get that other one just cause I'm gonna uh, go ahead and rotate your Mom's tires over this weekend, in case you're not home, I'd like to be able to do it."

Casey does not want her father to go into her trunk for some reason and tells him, *"Oh, Dad, I'll get it out for you." "Case, I got an extra set of keys, I'll go in the trunk and get it". So her and I got into a little verbal thing.*

George takes his set of keys and starts to go out to the car to get the wedges out of the trunk.

So as I'm getting ready to go out through our inner garage door before I open up the big garage door, she just blows right past me. "Dad, I'll get your thing". She said something very crude to me that I don't appreciate. So as I'm walking out the garage with her I'm walking at a pretty decent pace and she's almost running out to her car, she says, "Dad, I'll get it, I know where it's at". I said, "Casey, I'm capable of reaching inside the trunk of your car, unbolting that thing".

And she says, "Dad, I'll get it". As I'm walking, I just get back where the passenger rear tail light is to her car, she throw up in a turn, she says, "Here are your F-ing cans". I said, "Thanks a lot".

I said, "Now I look like a stupid ass, you know, I made a quick report to OCSO, now you got the cans, why do you have them?"

"Well I've been dragging, driving back and forth to Tampa to see Zanny."

And I'm like, "Wait a second, you're supposed to be working and now you're in Tampa?" "This don't make no sense to me".

REMEMBER: she told her father, *"I don't got much time, gotta go back to work for an event."*

"I'll talk to you and Mom later". She hurries up, she gets in her car, takes off. I had the gas cans because she handed them to me. I did not look in the trunk. Because the distance where I was at she's the one that just handed them to me and slammed the trunk right away."

Later during the trial George said that when Casey returned the gas cans to him, he had put duct tape on them to replace a missing vent cap. And prior to that there was no duct tape on them.

The duct tape on the gas cans are significant because the duct tape on them appears to be the same duct tape as that found on the mouth of Caylee's skeletal remains. The type of tape, prosecutor Linda Drane Burdick told jurors in her opening statement, is relatively rare.

So this would show that the tape found on Caylee's remains is similar to the duct tape that George owned and would be readily available to Casey.

After the gas can incident Casey called Jesse Grund. Later during questioning Jesse was so sure he heard Casey yelling at Caylee while they were on the phone, saying "Stop doing that. No." She told Caylee to get off the table. "Caylee no! Stop! No."

The very few supporters that Casey had, believed this proved that Caylee was still alive on the 24th. But when he was questioned again later Jesse said he wasn't 100% sure this was the day.

Later that evening Casey spoke to her mother on the phone. She lied to her and told her that Zanny stayed overnight at Tampa General Hospital. She went as far to say that she was vomiting, had a fractured rib and a laceration behind her ear. She even said that Raquel's mom was bringing Raquel back to Orlando to go to Jewett Orthopedic Clinic.

Cindy said Casey told her the reason she was in Orlando that day was she came home from Tampa to pick up Zanny's insurance information at Zanny's apartment. Casey said she had her own key to Zanny's apartment.

Cindy said Casey told her Zanny's sister had to bring Zanny's mother back to Orlando because the mother forgot her medications. Casey said she was stopping at home that day to get some things, and that's when George saw her.

June 25th - 30th, 2008

On to June 25th and 26th, she told Cindy that Zanny was released late and they were going to spend one more night at the hotel. By now it had been 10 days and Cindy couldn't wait to see her granddaughter.

Casey told her mother at different times during the month that the Caylee was missing that Caylee was at Disney World, Sea World, and was at Universal Studios. But unfortunately Caylee was already dead.

Also during these 31 days Amy Huizenga and Casey are working out the details for them to get a place together.

On the 25th while talking to Amy on the phone, Casey mentions that there was a horrible smell in her car (under engine) and she couldn't figure out what it was.

Casey said she thinks her dad ran over something with her car when he borrowed it.

When we look at this statement we have to ask ourselves if Casey is in her right mind. If Casey did in fact put Caylee in the trunk and her body started to decompose and give off a horrid smell, then why would she say that she did not know where the smell was coming from?

Maybe her plan was to plant the story about her father barrowing her car and hitting something to cover her tracks in case the smell was noticed later. If this was in fact the case, then Casey was lying to cover a lie that she may have to tell in the near future.

One of the fuel cans that Casey took from her father's shed had a gas and oil mixture which probably didn't help her fuel mileage when she put it in her car. Therefore, Casey's car ran out of gas again on June 27th.

She was driving back to her boyfriend's apartment after coming from her parents' house. The car ran out of gas at the corner of S.R. 50 and Goldenrod Rd. She had help to push it into the neighboring check cashing business Amscot.

Around 11:30 a.m. she contacted her boyfriend and he picked her up. She said that she ran out of gas and she'd take care of it later. Because she knew that he was busy with school and had schoolwork to hand in and was leaving for New York. So she chose to spend time with him rather than getting gas for her car.

She also messaged her friend Amy saying, "My car ran out of gas again."

Casey talked on the phone with Amy while waiting for Tony to pick her up. Casey told Amy whatever the dead thing was in her car was pretty dead. Amy said Casey was suggesting her dad ran over a squirrel.

When Tony arrived at the car, this is what he seen, "Her car was parked like this like kind of cockeyed. Like somebody pushed it in. So uh, she was standing out on the other side facing out the, the road on the cell phone with the groceries on the back of it. But she wasn't standing in front of the car. She was standing behind the car, by the trunk."

They weren't actually groceries from the store. It was from her house. (Bags of food that looked like she got from her parents freezer) She had some freezer pops and some like Tyson chicken, or something to make for dinner that night.

Uhm, and then pulling into the parking lot and she walked right up to the car with her bags. And I said, "I (unintelligible) what do to. Do I need to look at it?" Like, "Do you want me to look at it?" And she goes, "No, you know, my father will take care of it."

Tony admitted that he was a little irritated that he had to pick Casey up this day because he had to drop a project paper off at school. He said that he drove back to his apartment because he had to print some papers for his school project then he had to take the project papers to school and drop them off

Later, during the day branch manager Catherine Sanchez observed a white Pontiac parked by the business dumpster but she took no action.

But when she arrived at her work at 7051 East Colonial Drive (Amscot Financial) the next morning at 7:00 a.m. she observed the white Pontiac was still parked by the dumpster. She notified her corporate office who instructed her to call the law to make sure vehicle wasn't stolen.

Now you would think that Casey would have contacted her father like she said she would to tell him about the car being at the Amscot and out of gas. But instead at 2:11 she calls the J.C. Penny credit card customer service number. She hangs up at 2:27 and exactly 24 minutes later at 2:51 a security camera at J.C. Penny shows Casey and Tony. Casey makes a purchase of clothes for $84.00 using her mother's credit card.

Later when he was asked about this he said that he recalled that Casey bought some shoes and stuff at J.C. Penny to wear to Fusion Ultra Lounge.

The following day Casey called Jesse at 1:25 p.m. and told him about running out of gas the day before and wanted to borrow a gas can from him but he was on the opposite side of town and wasn't able to help her.

Cindy finally spoke to Casey on the phone on the afternoon of the 28th. Cindy said Casey said she (Casey), Caylee, Zanny and Jeffrey Hopkins were all together at Jeffrey Hopkin's hotel, the Hard Rock Hotel in Jacksonville.

There was a real Jeff Hopkins but, he later told the court, he only attended middle school with Casey and had run into her in a bar only once.

It was on the morning of the 29th, when she texted Amy looking for a gas can.

Casey: "Can I borrow you and your gas can today?"

Amy: "Storage hun. I was supposed to have my stuff out by now."

Casey: "Shit. I forgot"

Tony Lazarro said Casey, himself and his roommates all stayed at his apartment chillin' because he had to pack to get ready to leave for New York. Tony said Casey did not talk about Caylee at all.

Cindy started her vacation on the 30th. Cindy wanted Caylee for the week but Casey told Cindy a person named Jennifer Rosa was babysitting Caylee at Universal all week instead of Zanny.

She also told Cindy that Jeffrey Hopkins came to town and that she and Caylee spent 06/27, 06/28, 06/29 & 06/30 with him.

At 8:30 a.m. Catherine Sanchez, the Amscot manager, called Johnson Towing to come get Casey's white Pontiac still parked in the Amscot parking lot next to the dumpster.

Tony left Florida on the 30th of June. He drove himself and Cameron who was going to Ohio, to the airport in his Jeep along with Casey. Cameron's flight was around 10 a.m. and Tony's flight to New York was later but they both went to the airport at the same time. Casey was to bring Tony's jeep back to his apartment. There was no discussion that she could use his car. And he did not expect her to be using his car.

Gary Ridgeway, the tow truck driver for Johnson's Wrecker, was dispatched 8:50 a.m. to tow Casey's white Pontiac. He arrived at the Amscot at 9:06 a.m.

Mr. Ridgeway did not notice any damage to the car nor smell any odors but he recalled having a cold on June 30th, and couldn't smell anything period. Casey's purse and a child's car seat are found in the car's back seat.

Casey called Amy at 9:38 a.m. telling her to open Ricardo's apt door. Casey was standing outside the door and asked if Amy had a gas can but Amy told her again that her stuff was in storage so Amy suggested they go buy one at Target.

Both Casey and Amy went to Target to buy a gas can. Later when Amy was asked about this she said, "So we went to Target probably between eleven and one-ish that day. Uhm, bought a gas can."

They went in Tony's Jeep. Amy said Casey always insisted on driving Tony's Jeep even when Amy offered.

After she purchased the gas can she stopped off and purchased some gasoline and drove to the Amscot to get her car. Casey went to the Amscot and found out her car was towed because it was left abandoned for so long in the parking lot.

It doesn't seem like Casey intentionally abandoned her car at one of the busiest intersections in Central Florida. Apparently, she even left her driver's license and ID in the car. However, it doesn't seem like she was in a hurry to get it back either.

Amy said she had to go to work either 5 p.m. or 6 p.m. that day and that Casey stayed with her until she left for work. With Tony now in New York and her mother asking about Caylee, put Casey in a bad position.

So instead of going back to her parent's house she decided to spend the night at Amy's.

Tuesday, July 1st, 2008

Ricardo Morales woke up to find that Casey spent the night at his apartment. She was talking to Amy on his sofa when he saw her. Ricardo and Amy both said that Caylee was not with her.

Casey left Amy's apartment before ten o'clock that morning. Around 10:15 Jesse Grund received a call from Casey asking to use his shower. She told him she was at Tony's apartment and didn't have a key.

About a half an hour later Casey arrived at Jessie's without Caylee. She took a shower, watched TV with him and his roommate Rick Oswald until noon. She called Amy at 12:56 p.m.

Twenty five minutes later she calls the J.C. Penny credit card customer service number again. And later that same afternoon Casey got her nails done at J.C. Penny (Fashion Square Mall) for $31.93 and put it on Cindy's credit card.

At 8:00 p.m. Casey was at Miller's Ale House, Waterford Lakes at a welcome home party for Brandon Snow.

Jeffrey Hopkins said that he saw her at Miller's Ale House at Waterford Lakes that night. She said hello to him and then invited him to Fusan Ultra Lounge.

That evening Casey continued her regular routine of text messaging with Tony and her other friends. Casey now has Jeffrey Hopkin's number and adds him to her long list of texting friends.

Once again Casey spent the night at Ricardo Morales apartment with Amy Huizenga. And once again Caylee was not with her.

Wednesday, July 2nd, 2008

Casey was up early on the 2nd of July. Just after 7:00 a.m. she was already text messaging with Christopher Stulz.

But that may not be all that Casey was doing on that morning. Amy said that she discovered $400 cash missing on this morning.

Amy suspected Casey but she can't prove it. When she confronts Casey about the missing money, Casey tried to convince Amy that she hid the $400 while she was sleepwalking during the night.

Around noon Casey had gone to Cast Iron Tattoos and had the words "Bella Vita," Italian for "beautiful life" tattooed on her left shoulder blade.

The tattooist Bobby Lee Williams had known Casey for about seven years and said that she did not seem as though she was upset. After she paid for the tattoo she purchased pizza and shared it with the workers at the tattoo parlor.

On July 15th, Casey returned to the tattoo shop and made an appointment to get another tattoo on July 19th. Bobby asked about little Caylee and he was told that she was with her nanny. But that Casey would bring her into the shop with her on the 19th. Again, not exactly the behavior the detectives expected from the mother of a missing child.

Later that afternoon Casey calls the J.C. Penny credit card customer service number again. But she does not make any purchases at the store. Instead she goes to the Ross Department store that evening and makes a purchase in the amount of $37.23.

That evening Amy had to work until closing at her job. That night after Amy got off from work Casey, Troy, Amy and Melissa England go to the Voyage Night Club (Blue Room) and then to Mako's night club.

That night Casey slept at Ricardo Morales' apartment again. Casey showed her new "Bella Vita" tattoo to Melissa England and told her she should get a tattoo also. Melissa said no.

Thursday, July 3rd, 2008

July 3rd may be considered the beginning of the end for Casey. For the past two weeks Casey has come up with numerous excuses as to why Cindy could not see Caylee. And today Cindy finally decided that she was going to find her granddaughter.

Around 2:00 p.m. Cindy drives over to Universal Studios to see if she could find Caylee because Casey said somebody named Jennifer Rosa was babysitting Caylee at Universal all week.

At 2:49 Cindy sends a text message to Casey looking for Caylee.

Instead of calling her mother back on her cell phone, Casey calls her parents' home. And when she did not reach Cindy at home she texted her back.

The texts go back and forth for about 30 minutes. We are not 100% sure as to what was being said between the two. Then at 3:21 Casey makes a seventeen minute phone call to Cindy.

We can only guess at what was said between the two during this phone call. But once Casey hung up with her mother at 3:38 she immediately calls Jesse but does not reach him. She then calls Amy and talks with her for four minutes.

After hanging up with Amy she sends a text message to Jesse that may give us insight into what was happening between Casey and Cindy.

Casey texted Jesse and said, "If my mom or dad try to call you, don't answer. I will explain it later, but for right now just stay out of it." To make sure that he received her message she then called him and left a voice mail saying, "Something going on. If my family tries to call you don't say anything."

At 5:25 p.m. Lee sent Annie Downing a message on MySpace that Caylee was missing. When Annie read the message she immediately texted Casey to see what was going on with Caylee. Casey told Annie that Lee was crazy, and that Caylee isn't missing.

That evening Casey headed over to the Florida Mall to do some shopping at Team Choice and Anchor Blue.

Just before seven Cindy again sends Casey a text message and when Casey failed to respond she calls her. They speak for about ten minutes while Casey is shopping at Target at the Florida Mall. Casey checks out at 7:15 and in less than five minutes later she receives another text from her mother.

Between 7:19 p.m. and 7:36 p.m. Casey and Cindy exchange numerous texts.

Now to get a glimpse into the thinking of Casey at this point, you would think that the fact that her mother is now confronting her that she would be somewhat effected. But instead at 7:44 p.m. Casey texts troy Brown asking him, "You and Melissa are coming to dragon room."

The two send texts back and forth until almost 8:00.

Casey was under the impression that Troy was going to meet up with her at The dragon Room. But Troy had to work, and instead of hanging out with Troy Casey spent the evening with Melissa England and Casey never mentions Caylee all evening.

After the conversations with Casey, Cindy immediately contacted her son Lee around 8:00 and told him what had happened with Casey and that Casey and Caylee had not been home for longer than two weeks. Lee later testified that his mother asked him on July 3rd to help her find Casey.

Lee immediately contacts Michelle Murphy via MySpace. He told her no one had talked seen Caylee in weeks and no one had seen Casey in quite a while. .

Michelle Murphy found it odd that nobody seen Caylee or Casey since Casey had been posting new photos to her Facebook account.

Lee began searching online and found out on Facebook that Casey was supposed to be at some party at "The Dragon Room".

At 8:37 Cindy again attempts to call Casey but there is no answer. She hangs up and calls right back. From Casey's phone records we know that there is a two minute call and as soon as Cindy hangs up she makes a post on her MySpace account that read: "My Caylee Is Missing"

For almost three hours Cindy and Casey are exchanging text messages as Casey is hanging out at The Dragon Room with her friends.

Just after 1 a.m. Lee and Brian Lufkin headed to the Dragon Room with Mallory, who had agreed to meet them there. He also tried to text Casey. But Casey didn't respond. He asked Mallory to try and contact Casey without telling her that she was meeting up with him. But Casey was wise that Mallory and Lee were trying to find her.

At 1:15 a.m. Amy texted Casey regarding the money that came up missing at her house the previous day.

Amy: "Please tell me this hiding money is a joke! I can't find it anywhere."

Casey: "Are you serious? Im not joking thats not good at all. Did you check the car just in case?"

Amy: "No, I did check my suff in the garage."

Casey: "Where the hell did you put it? Thats crazy" .

Amy: "No idea dude"

Casey: "Jesus :-(do you want me to come back and help you look?"

Amy: "It's not going anywhere."

Casey: "Yeah. We just need to find it. Piece of mind right?".

Amy: "Si. Have fun. I was hoping it was a prank."

Casey:"Huny :-(god that sucks. It will turn up. No doubt. You going to be up or are you going to bed?"

Amy: "Who knows"

Casey: "I feel bad for not paying more attention."

Amy: "You didn't know. This is so unlike me."

Casey: ":-(im sorry love. Let me know if i can help"

Shortly after 1:30 Lee started texting Casey. Lee said that a friend of Casey's tipped her off Lee was looking for her.

As soon as Casey found out Lee was on the way to The Dragon Room she left. Casey was visibly upset when Lee called her that he was coming to get her and Casey wanted to leave. In retrospect, taking into account Melissa England and Troy Brown's testimony at the trial, Lee rather spoiled her evening!

When Maria finally arrived at The Dragon Room Casey had already left to avoid her brother Lee. Casey, Troy and Melissa left the dragon Room and went to another club called "The Lodge."

At 1:43 a.m. Lee made a phone call to Casey and asked her where she was. She told Lee that she was in Jacksonville. He said he knew that she was lying and that she was still in Orlando. She said she was out with a friend at a country-western bar.

During the calls, he also asked where Caylee was. Casey said, "Someone's watching her up here."

Lee later said that he didn't ask who the friend was.

When he told her he knew she wasn't in Jacksonville, she adamantly said that she was. When Casey was told that her family was worried about her, she said not to worry and that everything was fine. The conversation ended when he told her she needed to talk to their mother and she eventually hung up. He assumed Caylee was with Casey.

Casey and Lee sent text messages back and forth for the rest of the night with the last one at 3:24 a.m.

Lee said he was in the downtown Orlando area probably till 3:00 a.m. After trying to locate Casey in various nightclubs in the area he went to a few other bars that he thought that she would be at, but never found her.

After that night, Cindy told Lee to not pursue finding Casey anymore. He said that the next time he saw Casey was on July 15th after his father called him to go to his parents' house.

Friday, July 4th, 2008

Even though Casey was up late the previous night texting with Tony well after 3:30 a.m. she was up bright and early at 7 a.m. texting with Stephanie Kostakis (Special K). Followed by an 8:25 phone call to tony in New York that lasted until 9:42.

After Casey hung up with Tony Cindy called.

Cindy talked with Casey about Caylee seeing fireworks with her but Casey said that they were still in Jacksonville with Jeffrey Hopkins. Casey told her mother that she and Jeffrey were planning on moving in together when they get back to Orlando.

By noon Casey is back at Fashion Square mall and makes a purchase at Target in the amount of $12.71.

After her trip to the mall she spoke briefly with Jesse on the phone at 3:17 p.m. Jesse called Casey to try and get an explanation about what she meant the day before when she told him, "if my mom or dad try to call you, don't answer. I will explain it later, but for right now just stay out of it."

But instead of getting an answer she told him, "It was a long story and I will probably call you when I get drunk to tell you."

Amy Huizenga brought Casey to help decorate for William Water's 4th of July Party at 3:30 that afternoon. Then they went for party decorations, beer and food to Total Wine, on Colonial Drive, in Orlando. Casey didn't have ID as she left her purse and ID in the car when it ran out of gas at Amscot, so no sale at Total Wine.

Since Total Wine wouldn't sell to them, William had a friend pick up the stuff while he, Casey and Amy all went back to Will's house. After they arrive at Will's house, out of the blue Casey says, "You know I have a daughter?"

When she was asked about her daughter Casey said Caylee was at Sea World.

Starting at around 5:00 Cindy starts texting Casey and makes attempts to reach her on her cell phone.

Will's party starts and goes on until around 8:30 p.m. when Will's party friends along with Casey and Amy all went to Lake Eola to watch the fireworks.

William said while he, Casey and Amy were at Lake Eola that Casey was on her cell phone with Tony in New York. Apparently Tony was kidding Casey about staying in New York and not coming back to Orlando. Casey wasn't happy and didn't want to talk about it with Tony.

William Waters met Casey at a party over the 4th of July. He overheard Casey having the conversation on the phone with Tony. She seemed angry, but when she went back to the party, her anger was gone and she appeared "carefree."

The two started talking and after Casey and Amy left the party and went back to Ricardo Morales' house, she texted with William right up to almost 3 a.m. (even as she was on the phone with her boyfriend Tony)

Saturday, July 5th, 2008

It was an early Saturday morning for Casey. After ending her previous night well after 3 a.m. she was up and texting BOTH William Waters and Tony at 6:39 a.m.

Amy said Casey was giddy because Tony Lazarro was coming home from NY today, Casey clicking away at her laptop while talking to William Waters on the phone same time.

After William and Casey texted on the phone in morning, she showed up at his place at 9:30 a.m. and they hung out at his place until around 11:00 a.m.

While she is at Williams's house she makes a post on Tony's sister's Facebook page at 10:12 a.m.

"i'm going to prove to your brother how much of a dork i really am.... i ABSOLUTELY can't wait to see him today hope you guys had fun while he was home.<3"

Had she told him that at this very moment that she was sitting in another guy's apartment that she had just met the previous night he may not consider her a "dork" but something much worse.

From around 10:30 till about 11:00 Casey and her mother exchange numerous text messages.

After leaving William's apartment And Amy text:

Casey: "What did you forget this morning?"

Amy: "My pouch."

Casey: "That sucks. Glad its not that far."

William later testified that he was with Casey from around 12:30 p.m. till about 4:00 p.m.

William and Casey ate lunch at Zaxbys. Casey told him she and her best friend who also had kids were getting a place together and having her nanny move in as a live-in.

Next door to Zaxbys was a Target Store so William and Casey went there. Casey told William that she was going to Valencia College. William asked about Caylee, Casey said told him Caylee was with the nanny.

William and Casey went to IKEA Orlando where they window shopped for several hours.

Casey said she was looking for a place on the east side close to her school.

Casey was in Amy's car and told him this was because something was wrong with her car. She seemed upbeat during their time together, didn't mention that her child was missing.

During this time Casey exchanged numerous texts with Tony and had a brief phone conversation with him just before 3 p.m.

At 3:45 Casey also had a short phone conversation with someone from the Anthony's' home.

The day ended for Casey and William around 4 p.m. They made a date for dinner and a helicopter ride a few days later but she never showed.

After her time with William Casey stopped at Best Buy at the Fashion Square Mall to buy a CD for Tony. For some this may seem like a romantic gesture, but Casey talked to William on the phone while she drove to airport to get Tony, including while at a CITCO car wash and even while she was on the airport escalator.

William said that Casey got to the airport and I was like, "Alright, 'bye. You know I'm, I got things to do. I got uh, my motorcycle to work on."

And then five minutes later she called him back again. William said that she was like, "Well Tony's not here yet," blah-blah-blah. I'm like, "Okay," huh. That should have been a telltale sign right there that somebody needs attention.

Casey picked Tony up at the airport early evening. All she brought with her was a CD she bought for him. She told him she got the Jeep washed.

That night Tony and Casey went to Buffalo Wild Wings, on Alafaya Trail for UFC Fight Night. Tony met Casey's friends, Sean Daly and Annie Downing.

Tony said from July 5th Casey was staying at his apartment full time. He said 2-4 times she would wake up sweaty in bed from nightmares. When he would bring up the nightmare in conversation later she would just say that it was pertaining to their relationship.

At no time was Caylee ever at Tony's apartment after Casey was staying there full time.

Sunday, July 6th, 2008

On Sunday morning Casey received a text message from her mother at 9:48 a.m. From Casey's phone records we know that she never replied to the text message.

It was common for Cindy to have little Caylee on Sundays. And some would speculate that the reason for her text message was to see if Casey was going to bring Caylee by today.

After an hour with no reply Cindy once again sent a text message to Casey. This one arrived at 10:40 a.m.

And once again the text message goes unanswered. Some of Casey's supporters claim that Casey may have just been asleep and never knew that her mother has sent the two messages. But her phone records indicate that at the time of her mother's messaging Casey was using her phone to text and call Troy. So obviously Casey is avoiding her mother intentionally.

Finally around noon Casey decided to call her mother.

The first attempt Cindy did not answer so she decided to hang up and try to call the Anthony's house phone.

The phone records showed that the call was answered (maybe by the answering machine) but only lasted 1 minute.

Six minutes later she again attempts to call her mother's cell phone. This time Cindy answers and the two have an eleven minute conversation.

Cindy recalls that Casey told her that she woke up (Jacksonville) and her car was missing. She found that Jeffrey Hopkins took her car to a shop for an oil change, have the brakes done and to get a new gas sensor.

This was the perfect excuse for Casey to use for not being able to bring Caylee to her mother's home that day.

After Casey hangs up from her mother she spends the next hour text messaging with Troy. Jesse said Troy was trying to talk with Casey on July 6th at 12:52 p.m. about the Puerto Rico trip plans that month. But Casey texted back that she was busy with her boyfriend Tony. Jesse said Casey told him she did all the Puerto Rico trip planning, flight, food, expenses, etc.

Troy tells Casey that he and Melissa are going to go bowling. Casey said that she would like to go bowling with them but she never shows up.

Later that afternoon Amy and Casey have another text conversation regarding the $400.00 that came up missing at Amy's house.

Casey: "Hello love. What's the verdict? Any luck?"

Amy: "No luck. Everything is clean at it's still gone."

Casey: "Find JP's keys?"

Amy: "Nope. But I found my sweater and a shirt of Troy's"

Casey: "Ha ha geez. I'm sorry hun. I'll help you look before you leave. Might as well"

Amy: "Did you and tony want to go to Voyage tonight and check out that 100 bar tab thing?"

Casey: "Potentially. Any cover?"

Amy: "I don't think so. We never have to pay so I'm not sure. But I don't think so."

While Casey is text messaging she receives some phone calls from her parents' home which she ignores. Then at 5:45 she tries to call her mother's cell phone but there is no answer.

Ten minutes later she attempts to call her parent's home but again there is no answer.

In the meantime Tony went to Winn Dixie to do some food shopping, and then back to his apartment. After he put away his groceries he then went to the airport to pick up his roommate Cameron.

Shortly after 8:00 p.m. Casey receives another call from her parent's home that goes unanswered.

Cindy then sends a text message to Casey who then returns her text. The two do not have any more communication for the rest of the night.

At 9:47 Amy sends Casey a text message saying, "So I'm guessing it's a no on Voyage since I haven't heard from you. Have a great night tho!"

After an hour Casey still has not replied to Amy. Then at 10:52 Amy sends Casey her final text message of the night. "Oh, Will gave me your poster from Ikea to give you"

There is no activity on Casey's cell phone at all that evening.

Monday, July 7th, 2008

At 8:11 a.m. Casey texted Amy: "Sorry I didn't text you back! I couldn't find my phone. Stupid silent settings. Blah. You know Will went back and bought that.. Oh, that boy! Call me later love."

Amy: "It's all good. He is a sweetheart. And I got an appointment for 3! And for tom I think we need to head to the airport at like 6am. Is that ok?"

Casey: "Yes ma'am! Works for me. Glad you got your appt. Definitely good. Will is too damn sweet I swear."

While she is at Tony's apartment texting Amy she is also texting William Waters.

Casey: "What time do you work?"

Amy: "5 but I have to try and get out of it cause I have to move my car today or they will tow it."

At this point you would assume that this statement that Amy makes about her own car being towed would make Casey remember that her car had been towed and that she needed to contact her father to retrieve it.

About 12:30 Casey decided to just call Amy and the two spoke for about 16 minutes.

Then about 2 hours later the pair is back to texting

Later that afternoon around 5:00 Matthew Crisp ran into Casey at Subway at University & Goldenrod, driving Tony's SUV. Matthew asked, "Hey how's the munchkin?" Casey said Caylee was good and that she was on a play date with one her mother's friends in Sanford.

Matthew said they talked about their 4th July activities and Casey talked about when her boyfriend Tony was out of town.

After Casey leaves Matthew she goes to Target at University and Goldenrod.

As Casey was leaving Target she receives a text message from her mother. She returns a text and about an hour later she receives a call from her parent's home. But she decides to ignore it.

We don't know what the text with her mother said. But what we do know is that right after the call that she declined from her mother, Casey makes a post on MySpace saying: "On the worst of worst days, remember the words spoken, Trust no one, only yourself." "Everybody Lies, Everybody Dies"

Cindy makes two more attempts that evening to text Casey, one at 7:56 and the second just an hour later at 8:47. But both of her messages are not answered.

She makes one last final attempt to contact Casey when she called her at 11:00 but Casey did not answer.

Tuesday, July 8th, 2008

At 5:45 a.m. Casey sent a text message to Amy, "You on your way?"

Amy texted Casey back, "Yup"

Amy was heading to the airport to catch a flight to Puerto Rico. Amy said she left her place around 6:15 a.m. so she could stop at 7-11 across the street from Tony's apartment to get gas. She wanted to make sure her car had a full tank of gas for Casey when she was gone.

Casey drove Amy to the airport to catch her 8:10 a.m. flight for her week vacation trip to Puerto Rico. Casey said her car was in the shop (claimed faulty gas gauge from running out of gas) so Amy loaned Casey her 1997 Red Toyota Corolla for Casey to use for the week.

Casey dropped Amy off at the Airport around 6:30 a.m., and then headed back to Tony's apartment. (It is believed that somewhere during this time frame Casey found Amy's checkbook in her glove compartment and stole Amy's check book)

As Casey drove back to Tony's apartment she tried to call William Waters. He didn't answer, but within a minute of Casey hanging up he called her back.

The two talked on the phone as Casey drove back to her boyfriend's apartment.

Shortly after 9:00 a.m. George called Casey. The two spoke for about five minutes.

After hanging up with her father Casey sends a text message to Amy, "Hope you found some potential latin lovers ;-)"

Followed shortly by a Facebook Posting on Amy's page that read, "oh puerto rico....has stolen my friends. we shall be reunited shortly"

At 10:42 a.m. Amy texted Casey once she landed in Puerto Rico: "always. Its unfortunate I dont generally find spanish men attractive." Followed by, "safe and on the ground!"

Casey texted back: "Nice! Glad youre safe! Cant wait to get my happy ass down there"

At noon Casey is seen at target by security cameras cashing one of Amy's checks for $111.01

Ten minutes later Casey texted Ricardo Morales that she had other plans and couldn't meet him at Chili's for lunch. He had a five hour layover and wanted to get together with Casey during his layover between returning from Boston and then flying to Puerto Rico.

Most of Casey's afternoon that day was spent texting back and forth with Amy about her experience in Puerto Rico.

She also communicated with Tony and William throughout the day.

At 3:43 p.m. Casey tried to call her parent's home but nobody answered.

Around 6:30 Cindy sends a text message to Casey and she replies.

This was followed two hours later around 8:30 by an unanswered call from the Anthony's home phone to Casey.

An hour later Cindy sent yet another text message to her daughter and instead of ignoring the message Casey decided to call her mother. The two spoke for about 25 minutes.

Shortly after Casey hung up from her mother she went on her laptop and uploaded a picture that read, "Why do People kill people who kill people to show people that to kill people is bad?"

July 9th & 10th, 2008

July 9th was just another day for Casey. She spent the day texting and calling her friends.

July 10th also started off just like any other day. Casey woke up and sent some text messages to her friends. (Mostly to William Waters)

She sent a message just before 9 a.m. to Amy saying, "So im looking at a couple more places today and finding a flight tonight :-)"

She even went as far as to add a little smiley face at the end of the text. But two hours later she was back inside the Target store writing another check this time for $137.77 with Amy's stolen checkbook.

Now this is bad. But what Casey does next will show us the mentality of this woman.

At 11:09 a.m. (not even 30 minutes later) Casey attempts to call Amy but does not get in contact with her. She is calling Amy as she is walking into ANOTHER Target store to purchase items with Amy's stolen checkbook.

While buying groceries and writing a check for $155.47 stolen from her friend Amy, she was also texting and talking on the phone with William Waters.

A mother of one of Casey's friends (Mark Hawkins) saw Casey at the Waterford Lakes Target. She said Casey was by herself, appeared normal and happy as usual.

After Casey left the Target store she tried again to call Amy but she did not answer the phone. Casey then attempted to reach Ricardo who was in Puerto Rico with Amy and also did not answer.

Right after Casey hung up the phone from attempting to reach Ricardo, Amy called her. The two had a six minute phone conversation, and I am sure that Casey did not tell her about her shopping spree on Amy's checking account.

Casey spent the rest of the afternoon calling and texting Mark Hawkins and William Waters.

William and Casey had a reserved date to meet at 6:30 p.m. to go on a helicopter ride at Saw Island. After several attempts to contact Casey, she finally texted him back, said she couldn't make it, she said that she was with "Na-Naw".

At 7:42 p.m. Cindy calls Casey and the two talk on the phone for 19 minutes. Cindy recalled Casey told her that she and Jeffrey Hopkins were out to dinner, they were going to pick up her car and that they would be home to Orlando on the 12th.

About ten minutes after they hung up Cindy texted Casey: We don't know what that text said but Casey never replied to it.

Also on that day, Troy called Casey to see if she was or wasn't going to Puerto Rico. Casey said the reason she couldn't go to Puerto Rico on vacation with the others was because she needed to find a place to live and was searching to buy a new car.

Friday, July 11th, 2008

Casey spent the morning of the 10th texting Troy.

Sometime that morning a notice was delivered to the Anthony's home from the towing company informing them that they had Casey's vehicle. The notice was left on the front door of the residence. Cindy and George didn't find the notice that day about Casey's car being towed because the notice was on the front door that they don't often use.

Around 2:30 Casey uploaded a file to her computer that read, "You can spend minutes, hours, days, weeks or even months over-analyzing a situation; trying to put the pieces together, justifying what could've, would've happened.. or you can just leave the pieces on the floor and move the fuck on."

Casey spent the remainder of her afternoon texting William and Mark Hawkins.

And it seems as though there may be a little something going on between Casey and William because when Casey texted William asking if he was going to the Susi Bar (Fusian Ultra Lounge) William declined the invite.

William told Casey: "No. Why would I want to hang out with you and then Tony is supposed to be there at one o'clock."

After that text exchange the two did not have any more contact with each other for the rest of the night.

At 7:30 p.m. Casey texted Amy (in Puerto Rico): "Ill still call you later..but I don't know if im going to be able to come out there at all. Im going to decide tonight and ill let you know either way. If I do ill be out there early tomorrow morning"

Casey spent the remainder of her evening send out texts to her friends. Probably inviting them out to Fusian Ultra Lounge where she was working as a "Shot Girl".

At 8:49 p.m. Casey called her mother at her house: Cindy later said Casey called her asking why she hadn't called her all day. Cindy told her what was the point since Casey said she was coming home on the 12th. Cindy said she didn't call because she was tired of getting excuses as to why she could not see Caylee.

Casey spent the rest of her evening partying at Fusian Ultra Lounge)and finally ending her night well after 2 a.m.

Saturday, July 12th, 2008

This morning Casey sends an email to a man named Shawn Jarrett. This email was discovered after Casey's arrest by the Orange County Sheriff's Office Forensic Investigators after their search found e-mail message fragments sent between Casey and Shawn Jarrett. Casey said she didn't go to Fusian last night but stayed home to smoke, eat and watch horror movies with Tony's roommate Nate.

Casey spent most of her day texting and calling her friends.

Cindy was expecting Casey and Caylee to be back home today. At 1:47 p.m. Cindy tried to call Casey. But like so many other times she refused to answer the call.

Cindy waited to hear from Casey but when it was almost 4:00 she decided to send her a text message that read, "R u coming home 2day?"

Again Casey did not reply.

An hour later Cindy sent another text that was just, "???"

Forty-five minutes later Casey returned the text.

Cindy said that Casey told her that Jeffrey Hopkins was supposed to follow her back to Orlando from Jacksonville that morning. Casey's next excuse was that Jeffrey's mother was getting married and that she was in Jacksonville and was going to stay longer to attend Jules Hopkins' surprise wedding. She was actually staying at the home of her boyfriend Tony.

Later that evening Casey decided to go shopping at Winn Dixie where she wrote a check for $92.62 from Amy's bank account.

Cindy texted Casey again that night at 11:01 but Casey waited until after 1:00 a.m. to respond.

At this point it seemed as though there may have been more between William and Casey than just friends. William sent Casey a text message that night that read, "Hey sorry 2text u but we r going 2 vixon. hit me up n the morning i will c there i am leaveing sun up hit me when u wake up i have friends that have a house on the beach"

From the numerous texts and phone calls between the two it seemed as though neither one of them cared that Casey was dating Tony at the time.

William even finished his night with a 1:30 a.m. text that read, "U looked sex"

Sunday, July 13th, 2008

Sunday morning Casey was up early and posted a message on MySpace to a friend with the user name "Little One" at 7:36 a.m.

Casey wrote to Little One, "you little hoochie! where are "our" new pictures????"

And it seemed as though William was alos up early. Because just before 8:00 a.m. he sent Casey a text message that read, "Get ur butt up. And grab ur board"

About 8:15 Casey texted Chris Stutz wishing him a Happy Birthday, then texted to see if he had plans for the night, he said no that he had to go to work in the morning, Casey never texted back.

At 9:34 a.m. Casey wrote to Chris Stutz on MySpace, "happy birthday love!!!!"

Casey and Cindy exchanged a few texts and then around 11:30 a.m. Casey logged onto her AIM account where she started to instant message her friend with the username Doorknob375. The two messaged back and forth for about 20 minutes.

doorknob375: "late night?"

casey o marie: "eh, not really just haven't been sleeping well"

casey o marie: "can't wait to get into my own place"

doorknob375: "when is that happening?"

casey o marie: "probably within the next week"

doorknob375: "oh true, you and tony?"

casey o marie: "no sir just me and the kid"

casey o marie: "possibly in winter park villas. i've looked at alot of places".

casey o marie: "its off semoran, just before university"

casey o marie: "i'm also looking at places near where my parents live"

doorknob375: "is it an apartment?"

casey o marie: "i didnt ever want to live in an apartment, but i dont know if me getting a house is the best idea... not right now"

doorknob375: "so what do u do when u work? with the kid that is"

casey o marie: "I have a nanny. i love her." .

doorknob375: "how much do they charge?"

casey o marie: "we've been friends for over 6 years. definitely someone i trust"

casey o marie: "I pay her a lot more than most nanny's make. its worth it though."

doorknob375: "where does tony live?"

casey o marie: "she's a friend. between myself, and one of my coworkers, it's her main source of income"

casey o marie: "he's off of university really close to full sail"

casey o marie: "he's going to be moving off of goldenrod and university soon though, within the next month, to cranes landing"

doorknob375: "Why arent u guys living together???"

casey o marie: "we've only been dating for 7 wks"

doorknob375: "Why arent u guys living together???"

Rather than answer this question Casey decides to send her mother a text message instead.

doorknob375: "Wheres the other guy. the spanish guy?"

casey o marie: "Ricardo and i arent really even friends anymore"

casey o marie: "We stopped dating in march, right around my birthday. yeah, seriously."

doorknob375: "Still have feelings for him?"

casey o marie: "Ha definitely not"

casey o marie: "the other way around actually"

casey o marie: "I didnt have the same feelings, he said i led him on. i never really ever saw him as more than a friend. it sucks, but i was honest"

doorknob375: "And it bit him i the ass. are you happy now?"

casey o marie: “I am very happy now”

After this last message doorknob375 does not respond any longer.

After Casey’s arrest the Orange County Sheriff’s Department found a fragment of Yahoo mail that has come to be known as “can't sleep”:

The estimated date that this email was written was on 07/13/2008. This is based on a quote within web mail, “Anheuser Busch bought by foreign company” which was in the news on 07/13/08.

The email said:

“can't sleep, stupid hot flashes wake me up then I start thinking about you and Caylee. Dad said he went to work at 9am and got home at 630p, he said he did not come home in between. I don't know who or what to believe anymore.”

The email goes on, “You told me everyday that you were going to call me and you haven't but you choose to call when you know I won't be home. What the hell is going on? I've tried not to bug you to death but I still haven't gotten to see pictures of Caylee or gotten to speak to her. It's been over a month now. Am I ever going to see her again? Are you still with Jeff? Are you going back to work”?

Cindy goes on to write, “I'm not sure how much longer I can continue on this day to day course. I'm going freakin nuts not knowing what's going on with you. I had a breakdown at work, can't take much more.”

Well if Cindy was not already confused enough, what she found on her front door did not help.

Cindy and George were doing yard work Sunday and found the notice from the Post Office to pick up a registered letter on their front door.

Monday, July 14th, 2008

Casey woke up Monday morning at Tony's apartment. The first thing she did when she woke up was to log onto MySpace. The first thing that she did after she logged in was to send a message to William Waters. It read, "will.i.am i miss you :("

After finding the letter from the Post Office to pick up a registered letter, Cindy had to go to work early and George just started a new job at Andrew's International so neither of them could pick the letter up on this day

At 7:35 Casey receives a text message from her mother saying, "Remember me?"

Most of Casey's day was spent texting with William.

Just before 3:00 Casey logs back into her AIM account and starts messaging with doorknob375

casey o marie: "Boo that sucks. i went and worked out in the fitness centre at tones apt thismorning. i feel like an animal. haha"

casey o marie: "I just wanted an excuse to see you, duh"

casey o marie: "I'm getting a puppy when I get my new place . You need a beach day. You need a beach day with a really bad ass chick"

doorknob375: "Wheres the badass chick at?"

casey o marie: "Right in front of ya."

doorknob375: "Oh you wanna go on a date with me at the beach while you have a boyfriend, that looks grrrrrrrrrreaaaaaaaat"

casey o marie: "Hahahaha. It wouldnt have to be a "date" . But you need a friend, I miss my friend. Its a win, win"

doorknob375: "How did you get over me? Was it Mr Ricardo Morales montoya gonzalez?"

casey o marie: "Haha. It helped . I've had a constant crush on ya for a long time" doorknob375: "We didnt even hang out that much"

doorknob375:"I'm sure you wouldnt want anything with me right now, i'm in the worst state of mind to commot to somebody"

casey o marie: "Shit, even outside of a relationship, I'm probably not in the best spot either. haha"

casey o marie; "I'm pretty hung up on tony, and realistically, if he moves back to new york next year, my relationship will end.sucks to know that inevitably, unless I were to drop everything, I'm going to lose someone close to me."

doorknob375: "Then why dig a deeper hole? I couldnt do that to myself"

casey o marie: "Thats why I'm torn right now."

casey o marie: "If he gets offered the jobs he's supposed to, I couldnt keep him here"

casey o marie: "Not when he's worked so hard to get where he's going"

casey o marie: "A lot can happen in the next year. He'll be graduating from full sail this time next year."

doorknob375: "Whats his job?"

casey o marie: "After such a short time of dating, I feel stronger for him, than I have ever felt for anyone else. He's doing music business at full sail. He's already been offerred a couple of jobs back in new york."

casey o marie; "I dont want to set myself up for heartbreak. But at the same time, I dont want to throw something away that could be so great"

doorknob375: "I dont know, if you know its a dead end.... Havent talked to him about it with him?"

casey o marie: "Its not a guaranteed dead end, but the likelyhood of us staying together, just seems so dim.. We talk about it all the time. He even told me, he would ask me to leave with him, in a heartbeat."

casey o marie; "As nice as it is to hear, I have no desire to live up north. Love to visit new york, but that just doesnt seem my style"

casey o marie; "I never thought I would even consider moving for someone, unless it was someone I was already married to, or in the process of marrying, you know? Thats a big commitment. Its a huge deal"

casey o marie: "I'm glad that I have all this time to think it over, if it comes down to it, but there is always that lingering thought that it may not work out because of that."

casey o marie: "Its sad, but him and I both agreed that it is the inevitable road block ahead."

casey o marie: "Absolutely. Its hard. I feel like i'm setting myself up for failure"

casey o marie: "I feel like i'm working towards something great. And i'm all sorts of confused. haha"

doorknob375: "Its either horrible heartbreak, or a horrible lifetime regret"

casey o marie: "Exactly. I could deal with the heartbreak. I couldnt deal with regret. Love is too complicated."

doorknob375: "Why bother?"

casey o marie: "Because i'd rather have my heart broken a thousand times, than to never know what its like to love someone"

It was now 3:33 and Casey decided to try to call her parent's home. But nobody answered.

Half an hour later Casey finishes her AIM messaging with doorknob375.

casey o marie: "However if youre going to take a risk on something, of all things, why not let it be love? It is by far the most damaging and rewarding thing in the entire world"

doorknob375: "The person that can make you the happiest in this world, is the same person who can make you the most miserable" casey o marie: "Its a powerful thing, to hold someone elses heart in your hand"

doorknob375: "I'm listening to this disturbed song, enough. from the new albumn, you should youtube it. Listen to the lyrics"

doorknob375: "when your own have died, And theres no more pride, when your soul is frozen, Its had enough, When a heart is broken, A thousand times, with every moment. Is that enough?"

casey o marie: "I'm listening to "everyday is exactly the same" by nine inch nails. Haha"

casey o marie: "Holy crap that song is amazing!!!! I love disturbed"

casey o marie: "I know!!!!. Sevendust is my all-time fave"

doorknob375: "If my heart is broken like this a thousand times in my life, I better be immune. My old rangers used to say that about gun shot wounds hahaha."

doorknob375: "I have jury duty monday

casey o marie: "Boo that sucks"

casey o marie: "I've yet to actually go to jury duty. I get called every year, but never have to go"

casey o marie: "I always call the night before, and my number doesnt get called. Doesnt bother me"

Casey finishes her messaging and logs off AIM just before 4:30 p.m.

Casey receives a call from Cindy just before 6:00 p.m. But Casey does not respond until an hour later at 6:11 p.m. when Casey sends Cindy a text message.

This is followed by another text from Cindy at 8:30 p.m. that read, "Can u call me soon? ill be going 2 bed soon." But like every other time this is ignored.

Casey spends the rest of the evening calling and texting her friends.

At 11:33 p.m. Cindy tries again to call Casey but it is again ignored.

30 minutes later Casey receives a MySpace Alert that read, "New Message from Cindy! Go to MySpace alerts"

Just then she receives a text message from Amy saying, "The flight is in at 1130. Ill call in the morning.

July 15th & 16th, 2008

First thing Tuesday morning Casey sent a text message to her friend Shawn then returned Amy's text from the previous night, "I got it. Youre in around 230. Ill see you then!"

Casey spent the remainder of her morning texting back and forth between Tony and William.

Just after 11:30 a.m. Casey receives a phone call from Jamie Realander, who works at Fusion.

Jamie called Casey to talk about the incident that happened last week on the 11th at Fusian. She just found out Caylee was Casey's daughter. During this call Casey never said Caylee was in danger, hurt or missing, only that her birthday was in August. Casey said she was going to her job at Universal. The two spoke for 23 minutes.

George didn't have to go into work until later in the afternoon so he went down, picked up the register letter at the post office. George called Cindy between 11:30-12 to tell her that the letter was from a tow company.

Cindy was confused because up until this point she was under the assumption that the car was in Jacksonville with Casey.

On this date the only people that Casey physically spoke to on the phone (according to her phone records) were: William Waters, Amy, Tony, Mark Hawkins, Erica Gonzalez, Jamie Realander, Directory Assistance, and a call to 1-866-361-4999. We don't know what the purpose of this call was but when it is called a recording comes on and says, "We're sorry but your service has been temporarily suspended."

The reason that this information is important is because Casey told the investigators after her arrest, *"On Tuesday July 15, 2008, around 12 p.m., I received a phone call from my daughter, Caylee. Today was the first day I have heard her voice in over 4 weeks."*

Around noon George called Cindy from Johnston Wrecking Towing to tell her that they both needed to be there along with vehicle's title. George also told Cindy they needed $480 in cash for the towing and impound fees.

After Cindy spoke with George she got the title and stopped at the bank to get $500 cash to cover the tow and impound fees.

Simon Birch, the facility manager at Johnson's Towing, said that after the car was there for a couple weeks he was curious and went to look at the car. He said that he recalled smelling a foul order coming from the vehicle.

When Cindy arrived at the towing company she was upset about the charges and asked for a discount. Cindy spoke with Simon Birch about the charges but he refused to offer her a discount.

When the investigators later spoke with Simon Birch he said that "he walked with George into the tow yard to get the car. George told him that his granddaughter had been missing and that his daughter refused to allow him or Cindy to see her."

What makes many people take notice of this conversation is that at this point Caylee was not technically missing. As far as either of them knew (or believed to have known) is that Caylee was still with Casey in Jacksonville. Why he said that Caylee was "missing" is a mystery to many people.

Simon and George walk back to where the car was parked.

Simon said George used a key to unlock the Pontiac's driver side door. When the door opened, a very foul odor came from inside the car. Mr. Birch recognized the odor as the same odor he smelled in a car stored on the lot where a dead man was inside of for five days.

George told investigators later that When he got within three feet of the car and he could smell what he described as "the worst odor that you could possibly smell in this world." (He said that he had smelled that odor before and to him it smelled like a decomposed body)

George then asked Simon to walk around to the rear of the car with him.

Simon asked, "Why?"

George replied, "There's a smell coming from this car and I just need to know where it's coming from."

George said that as he walked to the back of the car and before he put the key into the keyhole he did whisper to himself, "I hope it's not my daughter or my granddaughter." He said that he felt that in his heart.

Simon stated that both he and George went to the trunk to try and locate the source of the odor.

When they opened the trunk lid flies flew out and the stench was horrific.

Inside the trunk, George and Mr. Birch found a white garbage bag inside the trunk. George being a former law enforcement officer knows what the smell of a decomposing body smells like. So he knew that the smell could not have been that trash in the bag.

Simon opened the garbage bag and seen papers, a pizza box, and maggots. He threw the garbage bag over a fence and into the tow lot's dumpster. The smell did not seem to dissipate after they removed the garbage bag from the trunk.

Simon said George said the gas gauge read empty so he went back to his car and returned with a gas can.

During the trial George testified that the odor was so powerful, George said he could not drive it home from the impound lot without rolling down the windows.

"I did worry for my daughter and granddaughter," George testified, noting that he had not seen Casey or her 2-year-old daughter Caylee since June 24th when she returned the gas cans. "I didn't want to believe what I was smelling."

George drove Casey's car home from Johnsons and Cindy followed in her own car. George parked Casey's car in their garage then removed the battery so that Casey could not come later and take the car without them knowing.

After they brought the car home, Cindy told George to go back to work. Because he had an event at work and he was pretty livid at the moment.

Cindy told him, "I'll, I'll handle everything with Casey."

Cindy searched the car, in addition to Caylee's car seat, baby doll, some of Casey's things that were in the car were; a work bag in the front seat, pair of gray slacks, boots and shoes in the back seat. Cindy said that Casey's gray slacks smelled so she washed them.

Cindy was under the impression that Casey and Caylee were in Jacksonville with Jeffrey Hopkins on June 27th through the 30th, the weekend Casey's car was at Amscot and then towed. So it was confusing to her why Casey's car had been towed to Johnson's wrecking yard.

Cindy's co-worker, Debbie Bennett said Cindy came back to the office around 1:30-2:00 p.m. and was in the hall by the receptionist desk telling her that they found Casey's car at the tow yard and that Caylee's baby seat, baby clothes and baby doll were all still in the car.

Debbie said that she was also concerned because Caylee's stuff was in the car. She suggested Cindy call the police. She also suggested that Cindy to call Universal Studios to see if Casey had been to work or not. Cindy said she was going to wait for Casey's explanation.

Debbie also talked with Cindy's supervisor, Debbie Polisano, who also talked with Cindy and she suggested that she go home and take care of whatever was going on in her family. But Cindy didn't leave.

While George and Cindy are trying to understand what is going on with Casey and Caylee. Casey is busy writing a check for $250.00 from Amy's bank account at Bank of America at 2701 South Conway Road, Orlando.

After leaving the Bank of America, Casey heads to Cast Iron Tattoos where she talks to Dan Colamarino (Dan and Casey were friends) to make an appointment for that coming up Saturday the 19th for her and one of her friends. At the time Dan said that she was driving a Maroon four door. Casey told Dan that she borrowed the car to pick up friends flying in from Puerto Rico because their baggage wouldn't fit in her car.

When Dan asked her why she did not go to Puerto Ricco with her friends Casey said it was because of financial reasons. He also said that he hadn't seen Caylee in almost six months so he asked about Caylee and Casey said she would bring Caylee in for her appointment on July 19th.

After the tattoo parlor Casey picked Amy up at the airport in Amy's car. Amy wasn't 100% sure if Casey told her on the way home from the airport about Caylee calling her on the telephone.

Amy later told investigators, "I feel like that's when she had told me that she was really excited that Caylee had figured out how to use a phone and that she had called her."

Amy drove Casey to Tony's apartment, and then drove herself back to the airport to get Ricardo. Later Amy went to Florida Mall to look at buying an IPhone.

At 4:02 p.m. Casey wrote at on Amy's Facebook page, "so glad you're home. i better not see you online. life is on hold until tomorrow".

At 4:27 p.m. Cindy sends a text message to Casey, "Call me asap major prob"

Casey returns the text at 4:44 p.m.

Cindy replies to Casey, "Call me"

At this point Casey does not call Cindy. She assumes that Cindy wants her to call regarding Amy's camera that is being shipped to Casey's parent's house.

So she sends a text message to Amy saying, "I think your camera is at my parents. Ill check later to be sure"

Amy texted Casey back about half an hour later saying, "Its not. I must have put down the wrong address bc it came back there. Im just having it sent to the boys house."

Casey replied, "Oh ok. My mom had texted me something about it"

Cindy arrived home from work between 5:30 - 6:00 p.m. and she found Amy Huizenga's resume inside Casey's car in Casey's work bag (purse?). She found Amy's phone number on a paper under Casey's purse and she called Amy immediately to tell her what was happening and to find out if she had heard anything from Casey.

While at the Mall getting an IPhone, Amy received a call from Cindy looking for Casey. Cindy offered to pick Amy up at the mall and they both headed to Tony's apartment to find Casey.

During the drive to Tony's apartment Cindy filled Amy in on all of Casey's lies that she had said in the past few weeks.

While on the ride with Cindy to Tony's apartment Cindy told Amy about the smell in the trunk of Casey's car. Amy thought it was the smell Casey told her was from the engine but Cindy said that the smell came from the trunk.

Amy said Cindy's reaction to the smell was that it was so pungent that they really thought Caylee and Casey were in the trunk of the car. Cindy also told Amy that Caylee's baby doll and car seat were also in the car.

During this ride, Amy found out the truth from Cindy that George never had a stroke and they weren't getting a divorce. Amy then told Cindy about her $400 that came up missing and that she suspected that Casey had taken it. She also hoped to get it back from her.

Cindy told her "No, honey that money's gone. You'll never see it again."

Cindy continued to tell Amy about Casey stealing money from her and from her grandmother.

Cindy said, "Do you know where Casey works?"

Amy said, "Universal?"

Cindy said, "I'm not even sure she has a job."

At 5:42, 5:59 and 6:26 p.m. Casey called 1-866-361-4999. The message when you call this number is, "We're sorry but your service has been temporarily suspended due to a past due balance. Enter the wireless number you are calling about."

While Cindy and Amy were driving to Tony's apartment, Casey was busy spending more of Amy's money.

AT&T texted Casey at 6:30, the text read, "AT&T FREE Msg: #QPSCAC237316569. Bank Acct debit authorized for $574.60 on 07/15/07 and successfully posted to Acct 04985420-001-04"

NOTE: Casey paid for this from Amy's bank account.

When Cindy and Amy arrived at Tony's apartment Nathan (Tony's roommate) said he was waiting for the All Star game on TV so it was around 6:30 - 7:30 p.m. Nathan said Casey answered door then went out in the hall to talk with her mother. Cindy was hell bent on seeing Caylee and she was furious with Casey. She confronted Casey about all of her lies and demanded to see Caylee, Casey refused. All she would say is that Caylee was safe.

Cindy kept saying, "You are taking me to Caylee now." And Casey was like, "She's fine. She's with the nanny." Amy said Cindy was like, "You're taking her to me now."

Casey's response was that Caylee was probably already getting ready for bed and did not want to disrupt her.

But Cindy wanted to see her granddaughter. So they drove around in Cindy's car while Cindy tried to convince Casey to take her to where Caylee was.

Cindy started to get an eerie feeling that something wasn't right in Casey's voice.

Tony said he was playing Xbox and this was the day Casey was supposed to get them tickets to see the Batman movie but that fell through. After Cindy arrived, she told Tony, "I hope you have lot of money because she'll take you for all you have."

Cindy, Amy and Casey all left Tony's apartment together. Cindy drove Amy to Ricardo Morales apartment where she was staying. Once Amy was home, she checked her bank account and that's when she discovered that her balance was no at zero and that her checks were missing.

After the three women left, Tony called Amy using Casey's cell phone because he had no clue what was going on so Amy told him. Later they met in person and talked more.

The 9-1-1 Calls

Just after 8:00 Cindy tried to call George on his cell phone to tell him what was happening. George missed the call but immediately attempted to return her call, and only got her voice mail.

Cindy drove Casey to the Orlando police department on Pershing but unfortunately at that time the station was closed. They informed her that when she got back home to call them.

Cindy called 9-1-1 on three separate occasions that night. Here are the transcripts from those calls.

The first call was made at 8:08 p.m. as she drove from the Orlando Police station back to her home.

Operator: Hello

Cindy Anthony: Hi, I drove to the police department here on Pershing but you guys are closed. I need to bring someone into the police department. Can you tell me where I can? The closest one I can come too.

Operator: What are you trying to accomplish by bringing them to the station?

Cindy Anthony: I have a 22-year-old person that has um grand theft sitting in my auto with me.

Operator: So the 22-year-old person stole something?

Cindy Anthony: Yes

Operator: Is this a relative?

Cindy Anthony: Yes

Operator: Where did they steal it from?

Cindy Anthony: Um, my car and also money

Operator: OK. Is this your son?

Cindy Anthony: Daughter

Operator: OK, so your daughter stole money from your car?

Cindy Anthony: No. My car was stolen. We've retrieved it, today we found out where it was at. We've retrieved it, I've got that. And

I've got affidavits from my banking account. I want to bring her in. I want to press charges.

Operator: Where, where did all of this happen?

Cindy Anthony: Oh, it's been happening.

Operator: I know, but I need to establish the jurisdiction is what I'm trying...

Cindy Anthony: Oh well I live in umm in Orlando

Operator: Yup, but what address did these thefts occur at?

Cindy Anthony: Um, well I guess my residence.

Operator: What's that address?

Cindy Anthony: 4937 Hopespring Drive

Operator: That's actually going to be in the jurisdiction of the sheriff's office, ma'm, not the Orlando Police Department.

Cindy Anthony: Alrighty...

Operator: Let me transfer you over to the communication section for Orange County.

Cindy Anthony: Ok, now so...is the Orlando Sheriff's Department the one on 436? Is that open this afternoon or this evening?

Operator: Um, the substation you're at off Pershing, if it's Orlando Police...we're open primarily in the day, but that's not the sheriff's, that's the city police which does not have jurisdiction for your address.

Cindy Anthony: I know the sheriff's department on 5th, I mean on 436.

Operator: What I'm gonna do is I'm gonna transfer you to the sheriff's communications section and you can...determine that.

Cindy Anthony: OK.

{Dial tone}

{Phone dialing}

{Phone ringing}

Cindy Anthony talking to Casey in the background: My next thing will be child (inaudible) thing and we'll have a court order to get her if that's what you wanna play. We'll do it and you'll never...

Casey talking to Cindy in the background: That's not the way I want to play.

Cindy Anthony talking to Casey in the background: Well then you have...

Casey interrupts Cindy: Give me one more day.

Cindy to Casey: No I'm not giving you another day. I've given you a month.

George: finally got a hold of my Cindy at 8:35 and she asked when he would be home. He told her about 10-10:30.

On that night George worked for Andrews International Security Company and was working at the fashion square mall for a movie.

Cindy told George what was happening and that she had called the police. Shortly after they hung up George left work and drove home. The mall was approximately 25 minutes to the Anthony's home.

Cindy and Casey return home at 8:44 p.m. meeting Lee in driveway. Cindy overhears Casey tell Lee that Caylee's been missing 31 days. Cindy goes inside of her home and calls 9-1-1 again. Telling them that she wants Casey arrested for stealing the car, money and possible missing child.

Dispatcher: 9-1-1 what is the address of your emergency?

Cindy: 4937 Hopespring Drive

Dispatcher: 4937 Hopespring

Dispatcher: 911, ok what's happening?

Cindy: I have someone here that I need to be arrested... In my home

Dispatcher: they're there right now?

Cindy: I have a possible missing child of a three year old that's been missing for a month

Dispatcher: a three year old...

Cindy: yes

Dispatcher: have you reporter that

Cindy: I'm trying to do that now ma'am

Dispatcher: k... What did the person do that you need arrested

Cindy: my daughter

Dispatcher: for what

Cindy: For stealing an auto and stealing money. I already spoke with someone. They said they would patch me through to the Orlando Sheriff's Department have a deputy here. I was in the car... I was going to drive her to the police station and no one's open. They said they would bring a deputy to my home when I got home to call them.

Dispatcher: so she stole your vehicle

Cindy: yes

Dispatcher: when did she do that?

Cindy: on the 30th. I just got it back from the impound. I'd like to speak to an officer. Can you have someone come out to my house?

Dispatcher: ok, ok I got to ask you these questions so I can put them in the call ok

Cindy: ok

Dispatcher: 30th of June?

Cindy: yes

Dispatcher: how old is your daughter?

Cindy: 22

Dispatcher: what's her name?

Cindy: my name

Dispatcher: her name

Cindy: her name's Casey Anthony C-A-S-E-Y

Dispatcher: And your name?

Cindy: Cynthia Anthony

Dispatcher: Cynthia can I get a phone number that I can reach you at?

Cindy: 4078084731

Dispatcher: and you say you have the vehicle back?

Cindy: yes... I have the ahh statements

Dispatcher: she's there right now

Cindy: yes. I got her. I finally found her after a month. She's been missing for a month. I found her but we can't find my granddaughter.

Dispatcher: how tall is Casey?

Cindy: ahhh 5 foot one and a half

Dispatcher: thin, medium or heavy build?

Cindy: thin

Dispatcher: color hair?

Cindy: brown

Dispatcher: what color shirt is she wearing?

Cindy: white

Dispatcher: what color pants

Cindy: (sighs) they're shorts, they're plaid, they're like pink and teal and white... Black plaid

Dispatcher: does she have any weapons on her?

Cindy: no

Dispatcher: is she not telling you where her daughter is?

Cindy: correct

Dispatcher: ok we'll have a deputy out to you as soon as one is available ok

Cindy: thank you

Dispatcher: thank you

Cindy: bye

Dispatcher: bye

At this point Casey has not informed her mother that Caylee was actually kidnapped.

Cindy kept pacing between the hallway, Casey's bedroom and the garage as she waited for the Sheriff's deputy to arrive.

During this time Casey was in her bedroom and Lee was also in there talking with Casey.

Lee thought to himself that nothing was making sense to him. Why couldn't they just go get Caylee and bring her home? There was no reason for Casey to fight with their mother at this point. Casey and Cindy continued to fight despite Caylee being "missing" at that late hour.

Casey began by telling Lee that Caylee was sleeping at the nanny's and that she didn't want to interrupt her sleeping routine. Lee offered to go pick her up, but Casey declined and said it was a bad idea. Lee asked his sister what she was going to say when the police arrived. What reason would she give them for why they can't just go and pick up Caylee?

Lee later said, "She just looked at me with no reaction... Then at that time she told me that she had not seen Caylee in 31 days, that she had been kidnapped and that the nanny took her."

Lee said that he was given the name Zenaida Fernandez Gonzalez shortly afterwards and that it was a name that he had never heard before. He reiterated that Casey was specific about the number: 31 days.

It was at this time that Cindy went to Casey's room and she seen Casey sitting on the floor crying.

And that's when she overheard her tell lee that Caylee was gone for 31 days and that the nanny had taken her.

Cindy then went into the bedroom and started yelling at Casey.

"What do you mean she's been gone? Why didn't you tell me?" Cindy screamed.

Cindy swore at her and then she hit the bed and ran out of the house and into the garage and called 9-1-1 again, it is now 9:47 p.m.

Cindy's first two calls to 9-1-1 were not fruitful. It was her third call that finally made the police take notice.

When Cindy calls 9-1-1 she is distraught.

Dispatch: 911 what's your emergency?

Cindy: I called a little bit ago. The deputy sheriff's not here. i found out my granddaughter has been taken. She's been missing for a month. her mother finally admitted she's been missing.

Dispatch: ok. What's the address you're calling from?

Cindy: 4937 Hopespring Drive. We're talking about a 3 year old little girl.

Dispatch: 4937 what?

Cindy: Hopespring H-O-P-E-S-P-R-I-N-G Drive Orlando. My daughter finally admitted that the babysitter stole her. I need to find her.

Dispatch: your daughter admitted that the baby is where?

Cindy: that the babysitter took her a month ago. That my daughter's been looking for. I told you my daughter was missing for a month. I just found her today. But I can't find my granddaughter. She just admitted to me that she's been trying to find her herself. There's something wrong. I found my daughter's car today and it smells like there's been a dead body in the damn car.

Dispatch: okay. What is the 3 year old's name?

Cindy: Caylee. C-A-Y-L-E-E Anthony.

Dispatch: Caylee Anthony?

Cindy: yes.

Dispatch: okay. is she white, black or Hispanic?

Cindy: she's white.

Dispatch: how long has she been missing for?

Cindy: I have not seen her since the 7th of June.

Dispatch: what is her date of birth?

Cindy: um. 8. 8-9, 2000. Oh god she's 3. She's 2005.

At this point George arrives at the house and finds Cindy standing in the garage crying and talking on the phone to the 9-1-1 dispatcher.

George asks Cindy, "What's going on?"

Cindy to George: George: Caylee's missing.

George: what?

Cindy to George: Caylee's missing. Casey says (Zenaida) took her a month ago. She's been missing for a month.

Dispatch: okay. I need. um. I understand. Can you. Can you just calm down for me for just a minute. I need to know what's going on. Okay. I'm gonna try and...

Cindy: (inaudible)

Dispatch: is your, is your daughter there?

It is believed that at this point George tells Cindy to call 9-1-1.

Cindy to George: I'm on the phone with them.

Dispatch: is your daughter there?

Cindy: yes.

Dispatch: can I speak with her? Do you mind if I speak with her? Thank you.

There is a short pause in the conversation as Cindy walks back into the house to Casey's bedroom. As Cindy is walking into the house she is talking with George.

Cindy to George: I called them two hours ago and they haven't gotten here. Casey finally admitted that (Zanny) took her a month ago and has been trying to find her.

Dispatch: ma'am, ma'am.

Cindy to Casey: it's the Orange County Sheriff's Department. They wanna talk to you.

At this point there is some mumbling heard in the background. Some say that they hear Casey say, I don't have anything to talk to them about."

We have listened to this part of the 9-1-1 call and we are unable to determine what is actually being said.

Cindy to Casey: answer their questions.

At this point in the call Casey gets on the phone and talks to the dispatcher. And unlike her distraught mother Casey is as calm as can be. Her tone is as if she was just on the phone and ordering a pizza.

Casey: hello.

Dispatch: hello.

Casey: yes.

Dispatch: hi. What can you... can you tell me what's going on a little bit?

Casey: I'm sorry?

Dispatch: can you tell me a little bit what's going on?

Casey: my daughter's been missing for the last 31 days.

Dispatch: and you know who has her?

Casey: I know who has her. I've tried to contact her. I actually received a phone call today. Now from a number that is no longer in service. I did get to speak to my daughter for about a moment about a minute.

Dispatch: okay, did you guys call and report a vehicle stolen?

Casey: um. Yes, my mom did.

Dispatch: okay. So is the vehicle stolen too?

Casey: no. this is my vehicle.

Dispatch: what vehicle was stolen?

Casey: um, it's a 98 Pontiac Sunfire.

Dispatch: okay, I have deputies on the way to you right now for that. So now your 3 year old daughter is missing? Caylee Anthony?

Casey: yes.

Dispatch: white female?

Casey: yes, white female.

Dispatch: 3 years old? 8-9-2005 is her date of birth?

Casey: yes.

Dispatch: and you last saw her a month ago?

Casey: 31 days, been 31 days.

Dispatch: who has her? Do you have a name?

Casey: her name is Zenaida Fernandez-Gonzales.

Dispatch: who is that, Babysitter?

Casey: she's been my nanny for about a year and a half. Almost two years.

Dispatch: why... why are you calling now? Why didn't you call 31 days ago?

Many ask the very same question as this dispatcher did, "Why didn't you call 31 days ago?" That's the key question that has haunted this entire case.

Casey's reply is:

Casey: I've been looking for her and have gone through other resources to try to find her, which was stupid.

Dispatch: can you... can you give me the name of the nanny again? Like spell it out for me?

Casey: Zenaida. Z-E-N-A-I-D-A.

Dispatch: last name?

Casey: Fernandez.

Dispatch: Fernandez?

We will note that up until this point there is no sound of concern what so ever in Casey's voice. She sounds calm and collective compared to Cindy who is obviously distraught on the phone talking to the 9-1-1 dispatcher. But once she notices the Sherriff's deputy's car in her driveway you can hear the tone change in her voice and she starts to cry.

Casey: hyphen Gonzales. I think the officers are here.

Dispatch: the officers are there?

Casey: yes.

The Arrest

When the police arrived Cindy was incredibly upset.

The scene inside the house is total turmoil. Cindy and Casey are at each other's throat. Cindy is frantic and worried sick. She's confronting Casey and trying to get the truth out of her.

Deputy Andriana Acevevo was the only female officer and second deputy to arrive at 9:52 p.m. at the Anthony home on Hopespring Drive. Deputy Andriana Acevevo said that Cindy was upset while George was calm and quiet. (which didn't make much sense to law enforcement officers at the time)

The deputy also said that Casey was fairly quiet just like her father.

The deputies on the scene contacted Sergeant Reginald Hosey, who arrived at Hopespring Drive at 10:23 p.m.

For a time it was unclear what they were responding to. For Sgt. Reginald Hosey it appeared it was both a domestic dispute and a missing child.

Judging from the interaction between Casey and her mother, Cindy, the sergeant thought Casey was merely trying to hide Caylee from a grandmother seeking custody. He thought if he could separate Casey from Cindy and reassure her that he didn't have a court order and was not about to take Caylee away from her, he would have a better chance at getting her to tell him where Caylee was located.

Sergeant Hosey walked Casey down the block for a moment of solitude to try to get her to shed some light on the situation:

He later testified that he did this "...just to reassure her...we didn't have any court orders to take the baby from her, we just wanted to make sure the child was ok...she was constantly talking about her and her mother not getting along and it was more so that she wanted to keep her mother from getting the child from her."

Deputy Ryan Eberlin first received the dispatch call at 10:18 p.m. to report to Hopespring Drive regarding a stolen vehicle. He arrived at Hopespring Drive at 10:42 p.m. He first spoke with Lee upon arrival then the other family members.

Lee said that while he was waiting to make his statement, he sat in the garage with Casey by her car. He said he couldn't be there any longer than a minute and had to keep going back inside because the smell was so bad.

Casey told him that, "Two dead squirrels crawled up under the hood of the car and they died in there."

Cindy called Amy at 11:00 p.m. telling her Caylee was missing for a month. Amy told Cindy that Casey emptied her checking account. When Cindy asked Casey about Amy's account and Casey admitted to the fact in front of her mother and police.

At 11:38 p.m. Amy made a post on her Facebook page that read: "A person who I thought was my friend stole money one night while I was sleeping and made up a story about how I got up in my sleep and put money away for the trip I was going on (I got back today, it was a great trip!). I bought that, she's my friend, but after today I know it was her. I let her use my car while I was gone and my check book was in there. Account cleared out. Hopefully I'll be able to get that back... but yeah... overall... about a grand. Which isn't even the worst (for me it is...) apparently her kid has been missing for a month. She claims the nanny stole her and was too afraid to tell her mom. So, as bad as all this is, there is a little girl out there (hopefully) that I'm way worried about. Anyway, how are you?"

Around 11:00 p.m. Lee offered to go and get Casey's cell phone at Tony's apartment. But instead an officer went to Tony's and returned with the cell phone and started calling all the contacts in Casey's phone looking for little Caylee.

At 11:50 p.m. Deputy Andriana Acevevo left Hopespring Drive with Casey in a marked patrol car for the seven mile (9 minutes) trip to the Sawgrass Apts. Casey was in the cage portion of the vehicle. Casey said she didn't know the apartment number at the Sawgrass where she last left Caylee so that was the reason they took her to show them where the apartment was located.

Deputy Acevevo said she did pat Casey down because rules state that it should be done for anybody transported in her vehicle. Her own policy is to place the person in back seat. Casey gave directions to Sawgrass through an opening in the cage window.

Deputy Acevevo said that three law enforcement officers (Deputy Rendon Fletcher, Sergeant Reginald Hosey and Deputy Ryan Eberlin) remained on the scene at the time she took Casey to the Sawgrass Apartments to find Zenaida.

Deputy Rendon Fletcher followed a short time later in a separate vehicle because he needed to stay at the Sawgrass Apartments to obtain any additional information.

Around midnight Lee went to Tony's apartment at Sutton Place to pick up Casey's Laptop and her belongings. The Laptop really belongs to Cindy but Casey was using it.

When Lee arrived at Tony's, the Laptop was on the kitchen counter. He turned it on, the display read the last time it was shut down it was shut down improperly and some of the data was lost. And then within a second or two the screen turned blue.

Lee said, "Casey's Yahoo e-mail, everything predating July 15th was deleted. There's no saved e-mails, There's no spam, there's no inbox messages, there's no sent mail there's nothing. Somebody had to log into her Yahoo account to delete them."

Lee also said that Casey's MySpace messages were also deleted on July 4th dating back to April 2008.

Besides Casey's Laptop, Lee also retrieved a large leopard print duffle bag of clothing, a white backpack w/pattern symbol, a large purse w/female items and a slender black bag used for the Laptop and some paperwork.

Lee said Amy's checkbook was apparently in Casey's bag also but it was removed and sitting on Tony dresser. Tony told Lee that Amy was coming to his apartment the next day to get her checkbook that Casey stole.

Jesse got a call from his friend Jeff at 12:05 a.m. and told him that the Orange County Sheriff's had called him from Casey's cell phone. Jesse called Casey's cell and the Orange County Sheriff's answered and advised Caylee was missing.

Deputy Acevevo said they arrived at the Sawgrass Apartments at 12:05 a.m. and they left the Sawgrass at 12:14 a.m., returning to Hopespring at 12:25 a.m. Casey never left Deputy Acevevo's vehicle and just pointed to where apartment #210 was. The trip there and back took only 35 minutes.

Twenty minutes after Casey returned to the Anthony home Sergeant Reginald Hosey contacted the Orange County Sheriff's Department because the case was not in the jurisdiction of the Orange County Police Department. Yuri Melich was notified by Sergeant Reginald Hosey, given information that a child was missing for 30-31 days and reported by the grandmother. At the time Yuri Melich was working in Missing persons and child abuse cases.

Deputy Acevedo and Sergeant Hosey later testified that George remained calm and quiet while Cindy was running through a range of emotions; at times upset, sad and angry. Casey also appeared calm and quiet.

During the trial Defense Attorney J. Cheney Mason asked Sergeant Hosey about Casey's lack of emotion further.

"When you walked with her (Casey) she had a flat affect?"

Sergeant Hosey replied, "Yes."

"You know what that means don't you?"

Sergeant Hosey replied, "Yes I do."

It was almost 2:30 a.m. when Lee brought back a black vinyl bag back from Tony's apartment that Casey had cosmetics in. Cindy dumped the stuff in the bag on the garage floor; there was cash, two credit cards: one for J.C. Penny and the second one from Sears. George said Cindy grabbed the cash and credit cards.

Lee also found 22 receipts of financial transactions of Casey's that Lee later gave to Casey's attorney.

Yuri Melich received a second call at 2:30 a.m. with some additional information regarding the case and he arrived at 4937 Hopespring Drive at 3:30 a.m.

Detective Yuri Melich interviewed Casey for the first time at 4:11 a.m. at Hopespring Drive in a room known as the computer room.

Casey told Detective Melich that she dropped Caylee off with Zenaida Fernandez Gonzalez at the Saw Grass Apartments on Conway and Michigan. She said she's known Zenaida for four years this Christmas. She said that she had met Zenaida through a mutual friend, Jeffrey Hopkins.

Casey said that she got off work at Universal Studios (Statement shows 06/09/08 but 31 days is 06/15/08), she drove to the Sawgrass Apartments to get Caylee, knocked on Zenaida's door but there was no answer. She said that she tried calling Zenaida but the phone was no longer in service.

Casey said she waited on the apartment steps for a while then went to J. Blanchard Park and other places looking for Zenaida. Casey said she tried calling Zenaida's mother Gloria, but Casey can't find her number. By 7:00 p.m., she went to her boyfriend Tony's apartment where she felt "safe."

Casey said Zenaida had a prior apt on Glenwood but she had been at the Sawgrass for the last 3-4 months. Zenaida also lived with her mom for a while (Off Michigan). Casey said she told her co-workers Jeffery Hopkins and Juliette Lewis about Caylee being missing.

The detective asked Casey why she didn't call police prior to today.

Casey said, "I think a part of me was naive enough to think that I could handle this myself, which, obviously I couldn't."

Casey also said that she was doing her own investigation to find Caylee, going to places like Fusian Ultra Lounge and a couple other Orlando bars where Zenaida hung out and asking if anybody had seen her.

Detective Melich, "Did you cause any injuries toy our daughter Caylee."

Casey replied, "No sir."

Detective Melich, "Did you hurt Caylee or leave her somewhere..."

Casey interrupts him and says, "No."

Detective Melich, "And you're worried if we find out, that people are going to look at you a wrong way?"

Casey replied, "No sir. I just want my daughter back."

She said she lost a 2nd cell phone that has Zenaida number in it that the number was not saved to the SIM card. She told the detective that she had left phone on her desk at Universal but she said she hasn't been to work for the last 3-4 days.

After the interview ended Detective Melich gave Casey the option to change her original story or stick to the one on her statement, Casey replied: "It's the story I'm gonna stick with yes."

The detective knew that Casey was not telling him the truth, he just didn't know why.

When the interview was finished Casey left with Yuri Melich in an unmarked patrol car about 5:00 a.m. George said she got into the front seat of an unmarked vehicle and were gone for 2-2-1/2 hours and returned when it was daylight about 7-7:30 a.m.

Yuri Melich took Casey to show him the places where Zenaida lived, where she dropped Caylee off, etc. A marked patrol vehicle followed them.

While Casey was out driving with Detective Melich somebody was using the Anthony's desktop computer searching for keywords "Zenaida" on Reunion.com at 6:21 a.m.

Casey first took him to 301 Hillside. Casey said Zenaida once lived there but now it was a senior only facility.

Their second stop was the Sawgrass Apartments, they drove through the parking lot and she pointed out Zenaida's apartment. The manager at the Sawgrass Apartments said apartment #210, the apartment where Casey claimed she had been dropping Caylee off for the last three or four months had been vacant since February. (It's been vacant 142 days)

Casey then led Melich to the Crossings at Conway where Casey said Zenaida's mother lived.

The detective couldn't find anyone who knew Zenaida, nor was there any record of her having ever lived at any of the locations.

The police know from the get go that this is not normal behavior of a mother who is missing her child.

At 6:50 a.m. Tony sends a text message to Casey, "Where is Caylee?"

When Casey does not reply he sends another at 6:58, "Y wouldn't u tell me of all people I was ur boyfriend that cares about you and ur daughter. Dosnt make sense to me. Why would u lie to me thinking she was fine and with your nanny?"

When Yuri Melich brought Casey back to Hopespring Drive at 7:00 a.m., George came to the window of his vehicle concerned that Casey was holding information back.

After Detective Melich dropped Casey off at her parents' house he then went to Universal Studios.

There, Melich discovered that Casey had been fired in April 2006. He found out that Jeffrey Hopkins had also worked there, but he left in 2002, and no one named Juliette Lewis had ever been employed at Universal. Casey had also claimed that Zenaida had been a seasonal employee, but the company could find no record of any past or present employee by the name Zenaida Fernandez-Gonzalez.

Melich decided to call Casey from Universal and put her on speakerphone so that Universal's representatives could hear what she said. The detective again asked about her employment at Universal. Casey again said that she had her own office, but unfortunately she couldn't remember the building's number or describe the exact location.

She even went as far as to give Melich her office telephone number, including her extension, but the company representatives said that the extension did not exist. Casey also claimed that her supervisor was named Tom Manley. But Universal said that there was no Tom Manley ever employed at Universal. When Melich asked if she had a company ID, Casey said she did but that she had lost it.

At 7:04 a.m. Tony sent another text that read, "Who is this Zanny nanny person"

Around 9:30 a.m. The orange county Sheriff's Office removed the 1998 Pontiac from Hopespring Drive, George gave them permission to search and process the vehicle to help find Caylee.

At 9:39 a.m. Jesse sent a text message to Casey to find out what happened. Casey sent him back a text message advising him that Caylee had been missing for 32 days, and that, in a second text message, "Her nanny took her."

Jesse Texted Casey back, "Thirty two days? Is that a misprint?"

Matthew Crisp told the detectives that he also receives a text from Casey. It says, "Caylee is missing. She has been for thirty-two days now. Please, if you have any information call me on my cell or at home."

His response was, "Is this serious?" Uh, "I believe having, we had lunch since then uh, and it never came up."

Uh, her response to, to my text message was, "It's a long story. Posting on My Space and Facebook shortly. Please pass it on. Uhm, I recall sending a text message back stating; uh, "I will" Uh, and, and with that she said, 'Thank you." Uh, that was uh, the last text message was at 9:46 a.m.

Between 11:30 a.m. and 11:45 a.m. George went to work just to tell them he was taking time off to look for Caylee. On his way back home he got a call from Yuri Melich around 11:30 or 11:45 a.m. telling him two officers were going to be picking Casey up for questioning and that she might not be coming back.

Detective Yuri Melich sent Sergeant John Allen and Detective Appie Wells to pick up Casey and take her to Universal Studios, a 30 minute drive from Hopespring Drive.

When Casey arrived, the park's security personnel wouldn't let her on the property because she didn't have an employee ID. They checked their computer data base of employees and they did not show her as an employee.

They then asked Casey what her supervisor's name is. Casey gives him a name and then the security guard then looks in the computer again and says that that is not an employee here either. So he finally asks her for her phone extension. At this point she gives him a phone extension and he looks at her and says to her, "That's not a phone extension here."

She then tells the detective that she could take him to her office.

So they let her through just to see what she would do.

Then she leads them on this elaborate journey through offices and then through an entire complex. While she's walking down these halls she's waving and smiling to people who she sees along the way saying cheerfully, "Hey, how are you doing?"

The workers are mystified as they have no idea who this person is.

During the walk the detectives are starting small talk with her, asking her about her aspirations to be a personal trainer.

According to Melich's report, "She walked with purpose and acted like she knew where she was going."

She takes them all over the final building until she gets to an end of a hallway. Then she stopped, turned to Melich and placed her hands in her back pockets and puts a big smile on her face and says to him that she did not work at Universal Studios and that she had been lying to him.

They already knew that she was lying but they wanted to see how far she would take it. They wanted to get a feel for exactly where her psyche was.

In reality this really worried them, because Casey would latterly take them to a dead-end hallway before giving up the truth. And this made them realize that she was going to be a very tough nut to crack if they were to get the truth about what happened to Caylee.

Casey was certainly not acting like a mother who was trying to help the police find her daughter. In fact, she was purposely leading detectives astray, forcing them to spend hours chasing down false leads and not looking for Caylee.

Melich asked to borrow a conference room, and he and the two other detectives sat down with Casey for a second interview.

Once inside Detective Melich told Casey, "Obviously I know and you know that everything that you told me is a lie, correct?"

Casey replied, "Not everything that I told you."

Detective Melich, "Okay. Ah, pretty much everything that you've told me. Including where Caylee is right now."

Casey, "That I still, don't know where she is."

Detective Melich, "Sure you do. We need to end it. It's very simple we just need to end it."

Casey, "I agree with you. I have no clue where she is."

Detective Melich, "Sure you do."

Casey, "If I knew in any sense where she was this wouldn't have happened at all."

Many people look at this one statement that Casey made that day and say that she is telling Detective Melich that she knows more than what she is leading on.

Her statement is, "If I knew in any sense where she was this wouldn't have happened at all."

She says, "Where she *was*" and not "where she *is*".

The second thing that that she says, "This wouldn't have happened at all."

What wouldn't have happened?

Most individuals at this point would start to confess. But for Casey that never happened she stuck to her story and it just became more elaborate as to what happened.

She stuck to her story that she had dropped Caylee off with Zenaida, even though Melich told her he had spoken with the manager and no one lived at The Sawgrass Apartments by that name. She refused to change her story even though he told her that apartment #210 had been empty for several months.

Casey did admit that not all of what she had said to the detectives was true, but she was adamant that not everything had been a lie either. She said that some of it was true. She claimed she was doing everything she could to help them find Caylee.

"I'm scared," she said. "I don't know where my daughter is. The last person that I saw her with is Zenaida."

The detectives wanted to know why Casey had led them to Universal Studios of all places. They asked her how that was supposed to help them find her daughter.

"Honestly, I wanted to come and try to talk to security," Casey said. "Maybe pass around a picture of Caylee."

The detective asked Casey, "I want you to tell me how lying to us is going to help us find your daughter."

"It's not going to," Casey admitted.

It seemed as though the more the detectives pressed Casey for the truth, the more she repeated her fake nanny story.

Casey said she even tried TWICE this morning to send an e-mail to Zanny but the e-mail just bounced back. Casey said if she could get to her computer she might find Zanny through instant messaging. Later when the orange County Sheriff's office searched her computer they did not find any such email attempts.

The detectives confronted her with the phone call that she claimed that she received from Caylee just the day before.

Casey told the detectives how Caylee called her at noon on the 15th.

They asked her, "What did Caylee say?"

Casey replied, "She said, hi mommy."

Casey said Caylee started to tell a story talking about her shoes and books and she seemed perfectly fine. She said that she asked her to give the phone to another adult, she was willing to do it, but the phone hung up.

By the end of the interview, the detectives had gotten nowhere.

At 4:30 p.m. the Orange County Sheriff's Department arrested Casey. She was charged with child neglect, false statements, and obstructing a criminal investigation (and later charged for Murder).

At 6:13 p.m. Jesse Grund found out Casey had deleted over 200 photos of Caylee on Facebook.

Part Three
The 21 Weeks of Searching

July 17th

That same day Casey appears in court, during which time the judge denies her bail.

The judge did make a statement to Casey at her arraignment hearing.

He said, "It appears to the court you care so little for your child you did not even report her missing until five weeks later and only because the child's grandmother insisted. Your two year old child is still missing and it appears that you have shown no regret or concern in all of your actions. Miss Anthony the court would say to you, 'Where is Caylee Anthony' but I can't force you to answer that question. But that is the question I leave. Do you understand?

Casey simply replied, "Yes sir."

The forensics deputies from the Sheriff's Office search Casey's car and takes several items of evidence.

They suspended their search in the backyard of George and Cindy's house late Thursday night (the 17th) until at least 8:00 a.m. Friday the 18th.

On Thursday night, search dogs and digging equipment were brought in to search the property. The sheriff's department said they're just trying to rule things out.

"This is part of the investigation, said Carlos Padilla from the Orange County Sheriff's Office. Right now we're trying to rule out any possibilities. You know again during an investigation you try to confirm or rule things out, so right now, according to the detectives handling this, they're trying to figure out if the child had ever been back there after she went missing."

Detectives also removed items from the home and took a shovel from a neighbor's home.

The detectives also seized Casey's car and sent it to a forensics bank after finding evidence of possible human decomposition in the trunk.

A dog trained to locate human remains alerted his handler to them in two locations: the trunk of Casey's car and a corner of her parents' back yard.

On first pass by the dog, Gerus, around Casey's white Pontiac Sunfire. Gerus started indicating in the rear of the vehicle. His handler could tell he smelled something.

As the dog came around the front of the car, his handler asked that the trunk be opened. When Gerus came around to the trunk, he put his front paws inside, and then lay down—a signal to his handler that he had detected the scent of remains.

Casey's car and the open truck where cadaver dogs also hit on the scent of human decomposition

Gerus also alerted in the southeast corner of the Anthony back yard. However, after technicians had examined the area and scraped the surface of the land, he returned the following day and the dog did not alert in the back yard.

Some people believe that when the neighbor observed her backing into the garage and she barrows a shovel that she was going to bury Caylee in the back yard. The sheriff's department did find what appeared to be the beginning of a 12 inch wide hole about five inches deep that was being dug in the area around where the dog alerted. Some believe that she decides that's not a good place to hide her and puts her back in the trunk; remember the dogs hit on the backyard because Caylee's decomposing body was placed on the ground.

Casey then drives away again; with Caylee now back in the trunk with the laundry bag and some of Caylee's favorite possessions.

This scenario also explains why Gerus detected human decomposition in the trunk and on the ground in the backyard.

They suspended their search in the parent's backyard Friday afternoon.

George & Cindy's back yard

Another photo of the Anthony back yard

The play house and the spot where cadaver dogs hit on the scent of decomposition

That evening after her arrest Casey called her parents' home from the jail.

In the 13 minute long conversation, Casey told her mom she did not want to talk to her and asked for her brother, Lee, after about two minutes. Casey then asked Lee for Tony's number. She also informed Lee that she did not want any of her family members coming down to her first bond hearing.

A frustrated Lee then handed the phone to Casey's friend, Christina.

For the remainder of the phone conversation, Christina tried to get information from Casey about Caylee's whereabouts. But Casey said that she tried to tell investigators everything she knew, but that they won't listen to her.

On Friday July 18th, while the Orange county Sherriff's Department was searching for Caylee, Casey hires Jose Baez as her legal attorney. She heard about him from some of the other inmates in the jail with her. He was not a well-known lawyer dealing with murder cases. He was more experienced in the field of regular criminal cases. At one time he even had an online business selling bikinis.

Jose Baez was treated as an incompetent lawyer. The State prosecutors laughed at the notion that Casey was going to get good representation. But people underestimated Jose Baez. And as the state will soon learn, there is a danger in underestimating your opponent.

As questions are being raised as to whether Casey had anything to do with her daughter's disappearance Baez writes a letter to the Orange County Sheriff's Office about Casey's willingness to cooperate with law enforcement.

In addition, Baez said he plans to reveal evidence that will exonerate Casey once they get their time in court.

He said that Casey has undergone psychological counseling while behind bars, but mental illness is not a factor in her defense.

Baez said Casey's first priority is finding her daughter, despite some sensationalized media reports.

"She's doing her best to keep it together and to assist in any way she possibly can because now is not the time to lose it, said Baez.

He also said, "She needs her composure and her ability to think so it can best help Caylee."

Baez said he is outraged that Casey is still in jail considering she has not been charged in connection with her daughter's disappearance or harming her in any way.

Cindy and George began handing out fliers at the Publix at Lake Underhill Road and Chickasaw Trail at 10:30 a.m. Saturday the 19th, hoping anyone will have information on the girl's whereabouts.

The group that met at Publix also included strangers who just wanted to help.

The family also released new home video of Caylee reading with her family, hoping it will help in the search.

Cindy told everyone that Caylee was last heard from on Tuesday. She said that she briefly spoke to Casey by phone, but when she asked to speak to an adult, the line was disconnected.

Many people close to the family felt that Cindy believed this story about Casey speaking with Caylee on the phone to keep any hope of Caylee being found alive.

After just a few days missing a reward of $225,000 is now being offered for information leading to the safe return of Caylee.

Cindy said she believes Casey when she told her the missing 2-year-old might be with her babysitter, even though the sheriff department's investigators do not believe that the woman even exists. The sheriff department's investigators searched for DNA samples of Caylee: toothbrush, hairbrush, etc.

"No one can imagine why you wouldn't go to the police. Well, I can imagine a reason," Cindy said.

According to Cindy her daughter's behavior, including her lack of emotion and conflicting stories, all support the idea she is holding back information to either protect Caylee or the family.

Cindy was asked if she and the family planned to attend Cindy's hearing Tuesday afternoon. Cindy said she did not think so.

The family plans to do more media appearances to focus on finding Caylee, and not on Casey.

"I trust her attorney to do what's right for her," Cindy said. "He knows her intention is to get her home, but I don't want to lose hours not spreading the word."

Friends of the family continue to pass out fliers. Their base of operations is still at the Publix at Lake Underhill Road and Chickasaw Trail in Orlando.

The group has fliers in both English and Spanish, and is hoping businesses will take media CDs to help them print out fliers, because the family is in desperate need of supplies like paper, ink buttons—anything to spread the image of Caylee.

"We want her home as soon as possible, as safe as possible, and I plead to whoever may have her: Drop her off here. Send her to the tent. I won't ask questions; I just want her home safe," said a friend of Caylee's family.

Casey's lawyer Jose Baez said that Casey is fully cooperating.

Jose Baez said the perception that his client is not cooperating with police in the search for her missing daughter is just wrong.

Baez said that Casey has never refused to speak with police, and she wants to get out of jail so she can also help search for Caylee.

Baez said he is carefully monitoring what Casey is saying in an effort to only protect his client.

Baez also said a hearing has been set for 1:30 p.m. Tuesday for the judge to rehear arguments for bail.

According to Baez, Casey is only being charged with a third-degree felony and misdemeanor, and a second-degree misdemeanor.

He said it is unusual for someone facing such charges to be denied bond.

On Tuesday the 22nd, Casey had her day in court to try and get a bond for her charges.

Even though Cindy wanted to spend this time searching for her granddaughter she was the first person to testify at Casey's bail hearing.

She was in tears as she saw her daughter for the first time since her arrest.

When Cindy asked the date of the last time she saw Caylee, Cindy said for a long time she was sure it was June 8th, but after seeing video of Caylee reading a story book over and over again, it came to her that the video was shot on father's day on June 15th.

Cindy also testified that a woman named "Zani" had been babysitting Caylee for more than a year, but she had never met or talked with the woman because she never came to the house.

She also said that she thinks she knows why her daughter is not telling the whole truth about Caylee's disappearance.

"I know Casey as a person. I know what she is as a mother," Cindy said. "I know there is only one or two reasons why Casey would be withholding something about Caylee, and I believe that it's something someone is holding over her, and threatening her in some way."

When Casey's brother, Lee took the stand, he said that on the night that his mother called the police, he had pleaded with his mother not to make the call until he had the chance to talk with Casey and get her to confide in him.

Lee said that before authorities were called on July 15th, Casey told him and their mother she knew where Caylee was, and would take them to her the next morning. He said he was able to get Casey alone for a short time, and she admitted to him, “I have not seen my daughter in 31 days.”

During the hearing, deputies on the stand released new information, saying Casey’s car was found abandoned in late June at an Amscot store on Goldenrod Road and Colonial Drive.

Detective Yuri Melich, said that when they recovered the vehicle at the Anthony's residence, “there was a very bad smell in the car.”

Search teams said they found what appeared to be Caylee's hair and some dirt in the back seat, along with a foul odor, but they said that they have not been able to confirm exactly what the smell was.

“Briefly, just before I came into the Child Abuse Division, I was a homicide detective for two years with the Orange County Sheriff's Office, and in my experience, the smell that I smelled in that car was the smell of decomposition,” Melich said.

Crime scene investigators are continuing to look for the source of the smell, according to Melich.

“One of the areas that they focused on now is the trunk of the car, because they found hair samples in the trunk of the car that are similar in length and color to that of Caylee,” Melich said. “They also found a stain in the trunk of the car that came under black light that's questionable.”

The FBI reported that the hair showed signs of decomposition (hair banding). Which is the presence of a darkened band at the root portion of the hair, this postmortem hair banding is a sign of decomposition.

Melich also said that the Sheriff's Office received a tip from a hairdresser who said Caylee had bruises and marks on her, as well as a photo from another witness that showed a cut under Caylee's eye.

Later even George met privately without his wife with the detectives investigating the case. He said that he wanted to speak with them without anybody in his family knowing that he was coming to talk to them.

When he sat down with the detectives he said, "Where this is leading, I don't want to think about that but I had bad vibes the very first day that I got that car. I can be straight with you guys and I hope it stays in the confines of us three."

During that conversation where he seemed to have poured out a lot of things to the detectives, he got sick. He had to go into the bathroom and vomit.

Melich also said a witness (Jesse Grund) came forward who said he had heard Caylee in the background of an extensive phone call he had with Casey on June 24th or 25th. Jesse told the investigators that at one point during the conversation, Casey told Caylee to get down from the table.

The sheriff's investigators said Casey has been lying to them about what happened, including where she worked, and even where she dropped off her daughter.

When the topic of the babysitter was brought up Baez said that the babysitter has ties to several cities outside the area, including Miami, Gainesville and Bradenton, Fla., Charlotte, N.C., and Brooklyn, N.Y.

The defense attorney would not say why those cities are pertinent to the investigation.

Baez also told the judge that Casey has been cooperating fully with the Sheriff's department investigators.

However, Casey's mother has said that she thinks Casey is sending subliminal clues to Caylee's location through the statements she originally made to police.

Casey, herself, has appeared to shut down and isn't saying much to anyone except her lawyer.

The hearing took about three hours and at the end the judge ruled to give Casey a $500,000 bond. In addition to the bond, if she is released Anthony would have to have a GPS device attached to her. He later modified the conditions to include home confinement.

Casey's attorneys were asking for her bond to be set at $10,000 on the felony and two misdemeanor charges. (Casey has been charged with child endangerment, making false official statements and obstructing a criminal investigation a third-degree felony, third-degree misdemeanor and second degree misdemeanor)

Judge Stan Strickland said he could not set bond at such a low price, because of the circumstances surrounding the case.

Jose Baez said after the bond hearing that a $500,000 bond is the same as to no bond because her family doesn't have that kind of money. Jose Baez files an appeal with the Fifth District Court of Appeals, in Daytona Beach.

Casey remained in jail Wednesday despite being granted the $500,000 bond.

Later, Judge Strickland makes the now universally acknowledged statement that the "truth and Casey Anthony are strangers".

The following day, July 23rd, Amy is interviewed by police; she tells them she wants to press charges against Casey for stealing her checkbook and writing checks on her account. She also tells them Casey told her that her car smells as though something died in it.

Casey's family are talking with bond agents about ways to get together the $50,000 cash and $500,000 security needed to get Casey out of jail so she can help in the search for Caylee.

The Find Caylee Trust Established

The Anthony family is refusing to call Tuesday's bond hearing a setback.

They said that new efforts are under way to locate Caylee.

George said that to ensure that they properly handle donations to help in finding Caylee, a trust has been set up at all Sun Trust banks.

A law firm is in charge of dealing with the money for the search. George said the trust money would be used strictly for flyers and billboards and that none of it will be used for Casey's bond.

The Anthony family wanted to make it clear that, although they still don't know where they will find the $50,000 needed to get Casey out of jail, no donations will be taken from the efforts to find Caylee.

The Kid Finders Network tractor trailer-size mobile billboard showing Caylee's picture was in the Publix parking lot on Lake Underhill Road again on Wednesday. George was also there to give out the latest contact information to anyone who might have a lead.

"Anyone that would donate to the Find Caylee Anthony Fund for my granddaughter, none of that is going to be used towards Casey's bond. We will not do that. That is totally separate," he said.

The family has also set up a 24-hour call center at a professional building office that was donated. They hope the call center will help find a lead and the person responsible for Caylee's disappearance. The family is using the assistance of the Never Lose Hope Foundation to run the call center.

Jose Baez tried to speak in defense of Casey on national television Wednesday night.

Jose Baez faced some tough questions from CNN's Nancy Grace about why his client has not been more forthcoming with information.

Grace: "Why didn't your client report her missing immediately?"

Bacz: "Well, her reasons and explanations for those are confidential and I can't reveal them at this time."

Grace: "You know that doesn't make any sense."

Baez: "Well, you know, I'm sorry it doesn't make any sense to you, but you don't know what our defense may be."

Grace: "Your defense to what?"

Baez: "Any charges that may arise where she is prosecuted. I have to protect my client and it's something I must do and took an oath to do."

Grace: "You're hiding behind the attorney client privilege."

Baez: "I'm not hiding behind anything."

Grace: "You are."

At one point, Grace said she had sheriff's deputies on the phone to try and arrange a meeting with Baez, but they were never put on the line.

Thursday, July 24th, The Orange County Sheriff's Department released the two 911 tapes regarding the search for missing Caylee.

Casey's attorney said the family cannot make the $500,000 bond needed to get Casey out of jail.

On Thursday evening, Jose Baez said he will file an appeal with the courts in regards to the bond amount.

Baez said that Casey does not pose a flight risk.

George and Cindy said if and when Casey gets out of jail, she'll be staying with them at their home. The family also believes once home, Casey will be more forthcoming with information.

There are three holds against Casey that must be satisfied before she can be released. Two of those holds have not been released, but one is believed to be a requirement she give up her passport. The third is the requirement she be held on house confinement under electronic monitoring.

As of noon on Thursday, Casey was still behind bars waiting for her family to raise the $50,000 and $500,000 security needed for her bond. She is also not talking to authorities.

While the sheriff's office is conducting a criminal investigation, the family has launched their effort in finding Caylee with a call center.

More than 15 people are manning the phones for a possible lead in the case. The call center was set up by the family to call everyone they can.

People who get a call will hear a pre-recorded message from George, and then anyone with information, can then be directly connected with the call center staff.

George said, so far, 100,000 people have been contacted by the family's call center, in hopes of finding clues in the case.

But he also admitted that he felt the investigation may have to go outside Florida's borders.

He said, "I'm not going to impede the investigation, what might be going on at the moment, in which I hope there's one going on. All I can do is tell you that there's been some credible things that have been passed on to us, that we feel credible, anyhow in our heart, not speaking emotionally but common sense wise and gut feeling, that there's something going on in another state that we believe needs some attention drawn to it."

Casey's attorney Jose Baez said that he has also hired a private detective to assist his team in Casey's defense.

The Orange county Sheriff's Investigators said that they are following a lead that Caylee may have been sighted boarding a flight at Orlando International Airport.

Cindy said she got a call from a woman on Tuesday who said she saw a girl who looked like Caylee at the airport. The woman said she asked the girl what her name was and that the girl replied

"Caylee Marie Anthony," pronouncing her last name without the "h" like Caylee did.

The caller said she was 99 percent sure the girl was Caylee, but investigators have yet to say if there is any validity to that claim.

Cindy said that the woman who provided the tip was supposed to be meeting with detectives to help create a composite sketch of the woman who was with the girl at the airport.

Unfortunately this turns out to be one of the many false leads that always happen in high profile cases like this.

Casey's attorney and the Orange County Sheriff's Office detectives met in a closed-door meeting on the evening of Friday July 25th, at the Orange County Jail. But everyone is remaining tight-lipped about the outcome of the discussion. It is believed that it is in connection with some sort of unspecified deal involving immunity or limited immunity.

Earlier Friday, Casey's brother, Lee, visited his sister Friday for the first time since her arrest.

Records from the Orange County Jail showed that her brother Lee visited her at noon for 45 minutes Friday.

Lee said the family is getting a crash course in the legal system because they haven't been through this before.

He also said his sister is not mad at investigators anymore and is even willing to talk to them.

Casey's parents also visited after Lee for 45 minutes at 1 p.m.

During their meeting, Casey told her mother specific information about the family's safety.

"We haven't had any major threats or anything like that, but she warned us of certain people to stay clear of, said Cindy.

Cindy would not share those names, or how they might know the Anthony family. All Casey told her mother was that she's positive a number of people are involved in Caylee's disappearance.

Cindy was asked if she believes her daughter got involved in something dangerous, or a situation that was out of her control. Cindy would not comment.

Cindy said her daughter told her she has reason to stay tight-lipped, and only has specific detectives in mind she feels she can trust.

"I'm sure she'll get with her brother, and her focus is getting her in front of people that can help in the investigation that she feels comfortable with that maybe these people don't have connections with." said Cindy.

Lee is working with Casey, her lawyer and investigators to meet with the detectives she specifically named.

"Casey did say there were a few people she was involved with already, said Lee. "You know, that asked her questions, or came to the house that evening. I mean, we had probably a dozen different officers and detectives and things like that at the house. So I'm pretty sure she has a certain comfort level with some, for whatever those reasons are."

Cindy told the local news station on Saturday afternoon that Casey fears multiple people could be involved in the toddler's disappearance.

"She forgives you, and just please bring Caylee home, where she belongs," said Cindy.

"And the message for Caylee is, Mommy loves you with all her heart. You're the most important person in her world, and wants you to stay brave. Very soon you'll be home with all of us."

This is the message Cindy says Casey wants to send out to Caylee, and those who might have her.

Cindy said that she got the message from Casey the previous afternoon during her visit at the Orange County Jail.

"We came to find out yesterday, that we could have been seeing her all along, and I think they felt bad, and facilitated us seeing her yesterday," said Cindy.

By this time the backlash against Casey is growing, especially since the 911 tapes and jailhouse phone calls were released to the public.

Family members said people are criticizing Casey at the information booth set up at Publix parking. Some people have even made threats against Casey's life through the call center and the information booth, according to George.

Meanwhile, family members are hoping to get more information out of Casey once she's released from jail.

"We said that again yesterday", said George. "It's like Casey, you know, where's she's at. Tell us. We can get this thing worked out. That's all we need. That's all we need."

Casey's family is now in the process of setting up a fund to help pay for the cost of Casey's defense. At some unspecified date in the month of August, ABC pays $200,000 to Jose Baez for photographs and home videos of Caylee in order to help fund Casey's defense.

Jose Baez sees how much negative publicity for his client is coming out of the release of the 9-1-1 tapes and all jailhouse recordings. So to stop this from happening again he attempts to block these records being released by filing a motion with the courts.

On July 29th, a Judge denies his motion to ban the release to the media all jailhouse recordings, 911 tapes and visitor logs. Florida public records law mandates record requests by media be honored promptly. *(Over the next three years thousands of pages of audio, video, forensic information and legal documents detailing the criminal investigations will be released.)*

While Baez was in court regarding this motion, State prosecutor Linda Drane Burdick offers him "limited use immunity" for his client if she wishes to participate in locating Caylee. This relates to the July 25th closed-door meeting at the Orange County Jail with the Orange County Sheriff's Office detectives.

On July 30th, Jose Baez's bond appeal is denied by the Fifth District Court of Appeals, in Daytona Beach. He had asked for Casey's bond to be reduced to $10,000.

Baez said he is now continuing his plans to appeal her $500,000 bond to the Florida Supreme Court.

Also on the 30th, the FBI interviewed the Anthony family.

On Thursday July 31st, Cindy weighed in on her meeting with the FBI during another appearance on CNN's "Larry King Live".

Cindy said her meeting the previous day "went well", but she would not say what information she told them.

Cindy told King she thinks she knows who has the toddler, but was on the defensive again about the day she called 9-1-1.

"I said whatever I needed to do to get the authorities to come help me," Cindy said. "I worked on whatever I could to get them out there, so I'm not a liar. I just stretched the truth a little bit. The car wasn't where it was supposed to be, so I said it was stolen, because I didn't have any reason to come to my house. That doesn't make me a liar or a murderer, and that doesn't make my daughter either, just because she had some mistruths."

Meanwhile the Orange County Sheriff's office is making national headlines for its investigation into the disappearance of Caylee Anthony.

Carlos Padilla, with the Orange County Sheriff's Office, said Casey is the last person to have had contact with Cayley, but she refuses to sit down with law enforcement.

"We truly believe she has info that could help us find her little daughter," Padilla said.

Padilla sat down with People magazine for this week's cover story, which will be released Friday.

The national attention in this case means investigators have a lot of interviews to watch. Padilla said investigators are watching those interviews as a way to connect the dots and get a picture of what happened.

"Keep in mind, we have a whole unit and also have civilian personnel taking down tips and turning them over to police," Padilla said.

In the article, Padilla said there is no evidence to prove the toddler is dead at this time.

He also said several suspects have been ruled out, including Casey's boyfriend, who has been fully cooperative. Padilla said that Caylee's biological father is dead, but he would not say who the father is.

According to Padilla, DNA results, including evidence collected from the trunk of Casey's car and her parent's backyard is expected to be in by late next week.

Casey is now limiting her visits at the Orange County jail to just her immediate family. The request did not say why she is limiting the list, but she is only allowed three visits a week.

A new phone call recording was also released on the 31st, between Casey and her brother Lee. The two talked about some sort of letter that's in the works.

Lee: "How is that letter coming?"

Casey: "Umm, well, when I get a chance actually to write a little bit more, I should be able to do that in the next little bit because I have quote rec time."

The call was made Wednesday, and while no specifics were discussed (possibly because both knew the call was being recorded) Lee did press Casey for information.

Lee: "You know, I know there's some people you've referred to in the past, and you know I'm just curious if anything has changed with who I can trust and all those type of things."

Casey: "Well, as far as I'm concerned here, I don't really know on that level. I guess, understandably, just being out of contact, but um, as far as I'm concerned, nothing has really changed on that level."

Lee said he's talked to everyone Casey has mentioned to him, but didn't elaborate on who they were or what they might know.

He did tell Casey he wasn't able to make it to her court hearing Tuesday because he was "working on other stuff."

Later when Lee visited Casey in the jail they had yet another conversation where the detectives felt that the two were being cryptic in their conversation. They obviously knew that their visits were being recorded so they tried to hide what the conversations were.

Lee asked Casey if there were any meanings behind the passwords that was using for her social media accounts and if they would conclude to any of this?

Her answer was, "yes."

He then said, "I will let you elaborate if you want to or I can move on if you want to it's okay."

Her response was, "Move onto something else we'll cover that by other means."

The password that they spoke about was "TIMER55".

The prosecutors speculated that it stood for the fifty-five days between the last day that Caylee was seen alive (June 16th) and when Caylee would have turned three years old (August 9th.)

Casey knew that when Caylee's birthday came around she wouldn't be able to avoid Cindy any longer. Cindy would have insisted on seeing her granddaughter for her third birthday. So "TIMER55" may have represented that countdown.

Speaking on NBC's "Today," Cindy says she won't explain what she meant when she said that "pieces of the puzzle" are coming together regarding Caylee's disappearance.

Cindy said she doesn't want to jeopardize Caylee's safe return by publicly revealing information told to her by her daughter.

As July 2008 came to a close prosecutors called Casey a person of interest in what they say appears to be a homicide investigation of Caylee.

The state attorney's office is trying to decide out if any formal charges will be filed against Casey.

If that happens, she will be entitled to another bond hearing in an Orange County court.

August

On August 1st the Orange County Sheriff's investigators took two large bags of evidence from the Anthony home.

The investigators were only in the house for about five minutes, and then left with two large brown paper bags containing gasoline cans, which are being checked for forensic evidence.

The Orange County Sheriff's Office wouldn't comment on what was taken, but said the family is cooperating.

Sheriff Spokesperson Carlos Padilla said his office has been receiving a lot of tips, and detectives are looking into them.

Casey's parents met with investigators and the FBI, and both agencies agreed that they're using every resource to find Caylee.

They said the biggest obstacle in the case is Caylee's mother Casey.

"Casey has the key to this. Casey was the last person to be seen with the child and we still believe that Casey knows more than what she's telling us and she's the only one who can tell us something that can turn this around," said Deputy Sheriff Carlos Padilla from the Orange County Sheriff's Office.

Detectives also said the name Zenaida is not as uncommon as they first thought.

Meanwhile, they say that they are awaiting DNA results from other evidence taken from the Anthony's home and from the trunk of Casey's car.

George would not comment earlier on the bags, or a visit he and Casey's mother made to the Orange County Sheriff's Office Friday morning.

Also on that night, dozens of people turned out in Daytona Beach for a benefit to help raise money to assist in the search for Caylee.

Friday's event at Speed Park Motorsports was designed to help all the missing children in the state of Florida.

All the donations will go to the Kid Finders Network, which also was on hand to take photos and fingerprint kids.

As for the Anthony's, they said they were touched to see all the people who wanted to help, and said their ordeal is teaching things about themselves they never knew before.

George also said he learned a lot Friday night about several other missing children, and not just his granddaughter.

George paid Casey a visit at the Orange County Jail Sunday morning.

As he arrived at the jail George told reporters he simply wanted to have a conversation with his daughter, to find out how she is doing. He also said he was prepared to ask Casey some tough questions about where Caylee could be.

"She's got herself in a tough spot," George said. "Maybe there's something she can say to me today that can help me find my granddaughter. It just might happen. I just don't know."

George said he is trying very hard to bring Caylee home by her third birthday, on Friday. They had already planned a trip to Disney and a party before the girl was reported missing.

A Sunday night vigil for Caylee came just hours after her grandfather visited Casey.

For the third week in a row, the vigil was held at the Anthony family home on Hopespring Drive.

Cindy had some choice words after someone called her to say that a 9-1-1 dispatcher in Pennsylvania told a caller that Caylee was dead. "I'm telling everybody, get off your asses and look for my granddaughter. I don't care if this is on the news or what, but she is out there. She's out there and God knows what I'm talking about."

Investigators said Monday they are still waiting for the results of FBI lab testing on some evidence they collected in the case, but said they may not release those results based on what they reveal.

There have also been reports someone involved with this case may be asking for immunity. But so far, investigators and the State Attorney's Office will not confirm that.

On Tuesday, August 5th, The State Attorney's Office filed formal charges against Casey.

Casey has been in jail on a felony child neglect charge and a misdemeanor charge of filing a false police report. She was formally charged with those crimes by the State Attorney's Office.

Casey is still not charged in the disappearance of Caylee, who has not been seen in weeks. However, prosecutors called her a person of interest, and said she is not cooperating.

Cindy said that the charges are actually good news.

Cindy said, "It's a good thing, look what they charged her with. They didn't charge her with anything but voluntary child neglect and withholding evidence. If they had anything concrete on her, I think they would have used that today."

Cindy was scheduled to visit Casey at the jail, but said that after consulting with attorney Jose Baez and her family, she decided against it.

She told reporters that she felt if she visited Casey in jail, it could jeopardize Caylee's safety because the visits and conversations are recorded and made public. Cindy believes that something she says could put Caylee's safety in danger.

Meanwhile, Casey's brother, Lee, has a visit scheduled for Thursday the 7th. But when he arrives for that scheduled visit she refuses to see him.

Meanwhile the Anthony family is now looking for two personal assistants in their search for Caylee.

On their MySpace pages, the family posted two volunteer positions: one to assist George and the other to assist Lee.

The job has some stiff qualifications though.

The posting states volunteers need to be available 24 hours a day, seven days a week, and says the assistant must be willing to travel, even out of state.

Each position would have various tasks.

George's assistant would help coordinate volunteer efforts, while Lee's would be responsible for running errands and updating Web pages. The family is also seeking volunteers to continue to hand out fliers.

Again on August 7th, Investigators served a search warrant at the Anthony home, and removed a number of clothing items belonging to Caylee, which her mother said had been in Casey's car. Unfortunately some of them had been washed by Cindy, because they had a "foul odor."

Deputies also confirmed during a press conference that the last time Caylee was seen by anybody other than Casey was on June 15th, based on video and pictures on Casey's computer of Caylee on Father's Day.

Investigators also said a call Casey said she got on July 15th in which Caylee talked to her probably never happened. Phone records showed that there were no calls to Casey's cell phone at that time.

On August 8th, local news stations start to report that investigators suspect Caylee may have drowned in the family swimming pool on June 16th.

August 9th, 2008 would have been Caylee's 3rd birthday. Unfortunately the day came and went with no solid leads.

The following day Cindy and George had a scheduled visit with Casey. When they arrived at the jail they learned that Casey cancelled the visit. This would be the second time in three days she has refused to meet with her family.

On the afternoon of August 11th, meter reader Roy Kronk is in his van when he needs to urinate. He walks onto a small patch of swampy land near the Anthony family home. Although a lot of the swampy terrain was underwater from a recent tropical storm, Kronk saw something about 25 to 30 feet in the distance that caught his attention.

Later that night Kronk called the local police to report what he saw: something white that didn't look like it should have been there."

On each of the next two days, Roy Kronk made a follow up call to police to see if they found what he had seen in the woods. Finally, on the third day, (August 13th) an officer drove out and met Kronk at the site where he had seen the object.

According to Kronk the officer stood in one place, looked left, then right, took a step and slipped down into the mud. For the next 30 minutes, according to Kronk, the officer "chewed him out" for making him come out to that location that was made muddy by Tropical Storm Faye.

Exactly four months later, Roy Kronk again went into the same woods to relieve himself. This time he came across the skull and skeletal remains of a young child. They belonged to Caylee Anthony.

And instead of being credited for his tenacity while attempting to aid in the solution of the Anthony mystery, Kronk became a scapegoat and a suspect. The defense team's theory of defense for Casey alleges Kronk stole the child's body from they-don't-know-where; kept it stored in an unknown place; and dumped the remains in the woods so that he could "find" it and claim the $225,000 reward.

On the 12th, George said that he believes Caylee was kidnapped, and that the kidnappers are being watched.

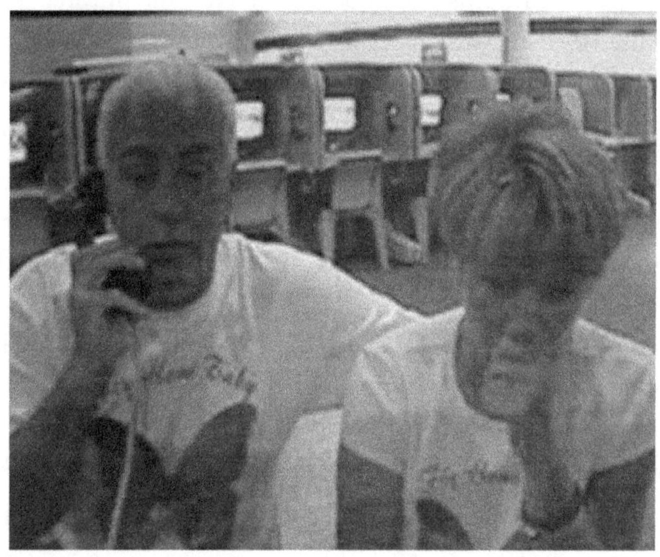

During one of George and Cindy's visits Casey was smiling sadistically and laughing at Cindy when Cindy was crying and she remarked to her father about Cindy, "why is she crying already?" as she laughed.

On August 16th, California bounty hunter Leonard Padilla announced he and his nephew, bail bondsman Tony Padilla, would fly to Orlando and post Casey's $500,000 bond. Padilla said they wanted to "find the baby." And they thought that by having Casey out of jail that would help bring Caylee home.

His theory was, *"I'm gonna bail her out. I'm gonna sit her down and she's gonna tell me the truth. I'm gonna take care of it."*

The next day Leonard Padilla arrived in Orlando. Leonard and Tony Padilla posted the bond necessary for Casey's release on the 20th.

Casey walked out of jail 10:30 a.m. on the 21st after being fitted with an electronic monitoring device. Things didn't go completely smoothly during her release after Casey's attorney Jose Baez shoved a photographer that got too close.

Baez said, "We stopped for a brief moment, and she told me in my ear, she wanted me to take the umbrella down because she said to me 'Jose, I'm innocent. I'm gonna walk out of this place with my head high.'" Casey said that the umbrella ruined plans for her to show her face.

Leonard Padilla said that he believed that Caylee is still alive and that Casey just passed her off to one of her friends and asked her to watch Caylee and that she would be back in a couple of days. But that person for whatever reason is down the road with the baby.

He told a group of spectators outside of the court, "I find it hard to believe that a mother of three year old child would harm her."

On the 26th, hundreds of documents are released. Some of these documents revealed that Cindy called Casey a sociopath and a "mooch," and that a friend said Casey wanted to put Caylee up for adoption, but Cindy would not let her.

Also on the 26th, George and Cindy hire attorneys Mark Lippman and Jennifer Craddock.

The following day, Linda Drane Burdick offered Casey a limited-immunity deal if she will lead them to Caylee. If she takes the deal, the specific information that Casey provides could not be used against her by prosecutors. The offer is only good until September 2nd.

The Orange-Osceola State Attorney's Office would not publicly discuss details of the inquiry, but spokeswoman Danielle Tavernier said that Casey has been "invited to our office to shed light on the disappearance of the victim in this case."

That same afternoon an Orange County sheriff's official said that Air-sample tests from Casey's abandoned car show that the trunk once held a decomposing human body.

Casey's family members publicly dismissed the strong odor in the car, saying it must have come from a spoiled pizza. But during the July 15th phone call in which Cindy reported the disappearance, she said it "smelled like there's been a dead body in the damn car."

Samples of air from the car were sent to the University of Tennessee Forensic Anthropology Center near Knoxville, where researchers gather data on how bodies decay and other information to help law-enforcement agencies determine time of death.

Evidence from the trunk also has been sent to the FBI's forensic lab for DNA testing, but the results have not been announced yet.

Casey's attorney said detectives had not given him information about the anthropology center's findings. He said the information leaked to reporters and the resulting speculation "was very disappointing and shocking to us."

About 2:45 p.m., sheriff's Sargent John Allen, the supervisor on the case, and three FBI agents arrived at Jose Baez's office, where the lawyer was meeting with Casey and Cindy.

Casey was wearing big sunglasses and a T-shirt with Caylee's picture on the front of it. Casey left Baez's office about 20 minutes later. She rode alone in the back of a vehicle driven by a bounty hunter associated with the man who helped bail her out of jail.

Two hours later Cindy walked out with Baez, giving no comment to reporters. The two climbed into Baez's car, and he drove her home. She left her Toyota sport utility vehicle, which has "Missing" posters about Caylee on the doors.

Sargent Allen and three FBI agents with him also left without commenting.

Baez would not give any details about the meeting but said that no plea deal was discussed.

When asked how Casey was doing, the lawyer replied: "This doesn't help any. . . . We are doing the best we can."

Earlier in the day, before news of the air samples and the possible legal deal, the California bounty hunter who secured Casey's release said she has made no effort to help him find Caylee.

"She has not communicated with us at all," Leonard Padilla said. "She has no interest in communicating with us."

Padilla, whose nephew posted Anthony's $500,200 bail last week, said that if he knew then what he knew now about the case and that Casey wouldn't cooperate with him he probably would not have helped get her out of jail.

Padilla said he still thinks Caylee is alive and that Casey handed her off to someone. But he dismissed the story that the toddler disappeared in mid-June after being dropped off with a baby sitter named Zenaida Fernandez-Gonzalez, which Casey has told detectives.

"We don't believe Zenaida Fernandez-Gonzalez exists," Padilla said. Casey "got an invisible friend that's called Zenaida," he said. "She's got a world that she lives in that's apart from ours."

On August 29th, as news crews stood in front of the Anthony home the Orange County Sherriff's Department arrived on the scene with their lights flashing. As the news cameras rolled, Casey is arrested again on charges of writing four checks worth nearly $650 on Amy Huizenga's checking account without permission. Orange County police said the charges are "unrelated to the investigation." The new charges include uttering a fraudulent instrument, petty theft, and fraudulent use of personal information. Deputies said they had surveillance video of Casey using the forged checks.

Jose believes that the sheriff's Department waited until they knew that the national news media would be present and going live on the air before arriving at the Anthony's home to arrest his Client. So that they could march her in front of all these cameras and it would be live. And because they swooped in on the house like a SWAT team to arrest her on very minor charges, he is accusing the

Sheriff's Department of using this as a media tactic and making a spectacle of this event.

At this point Casey had an attorney that was representing her. And while they were not able to question Casey without her attorney present they hoped that she would make a spontaneous statement that they could use against her later.

And arresting her again puts Casey back in front of the detectives with the hopes that she would slip and say something.

A new bond for Casey set at $3,000. The original posted bond had been revoked, so Casey would have remained in jail even if the new bond was posted.

At the time of the arrest, there is a demonstration against Casey outside the family home.

Deputies also served Casey, George, Cindy and Lee Anthony with criminal witness subpoenas to appear in court sometime in November.

Cindy and George contacted Texas EquuSearch. They are a Mounted Search and Recovery Team. They arrived in Central Florida on the 30th to help search for Caylee. Texas EquuSearch Mounted Search and Recovery Team are a volunteer horse mounted search and recovery group for lost and missing persons.

The month of August ended with the Sheriff's Office confirming that the hair found in the trunk of Casey's car belonged to Caylee.

September

On Tuesday, September 2nd, Casey officially refused the offer of limited immunity from Linda Drane Burdick. The offer was only good until September 2nd.

The next day Casey made bond on the new check fraud and theft charges that were filed against her Wednesday by the Orange County Sheriff's Office.

The McDonald Bail Bonds agency posted the $2,700 bond late Wednesday. Therefore, Casey will not have to appear in court Thursday morning.

However, she will not be released from jail because her more than $500,000 bond for child neglect charges has not been posted. And until that amount is posted she must remain in jail.

Casey's parents are expected to meet with Casey via video visitation on Friday at 9 a.m. Her brother is expected to visit Saturday at 1 p.m.

For the first time we learn that Chloroform was found in the trunk of Casey's car, according to a report in the Orlando Sentinel.

The chemical is capable of putting someone to sleep, and it can be deadly if too much is inhaled.

On Wednesday George and Cindy met with high profile defense attorney Mark NeJame. NeJame won't say what they discussed, but said for now, he has not been hired as their attorney.

He said the family is frustrated with the public and media for not focusing more on searching for the missing toddler.

The following day Mark NeJame said he has taken them on as clients.

NeJame said that they have lots of legal questions.

He said they also want him to help to get the focus back to finding Caylee, and away from people making judgments on them.

"My heavens, who's trained to deal with such a thing? To lose your granddaughter and then to wake up in the morning with a camera under your nose and to go to bed at night with a camera in a tree looking at every move that you're making. There's no opportunity for them to handle this, and they need help and they've asked for our help, and we're happy to provide it," said NeJame.

NeJame said he is in no way representing Casey.

NeJame would not go into detail about how the Anthonys will be paying for his legal fees.

Crews also spent the day Wednesday continuing their search for Caylee's body near Orlando International Airport.

Late Wednesday afternoon, a team with a group called the Body Hunters searched an area near Orlando International Airport after they said one of their dogs hinted on a smell in the woods.

The group, which claims to also have psychic abilities, found a rolled-up carpet in the area.

As of right now, there are no indications it is connected in any way to the case.

Some people believe that after Casey failed to bury Caylee in the family's backyard she then left and went to the area near the airport. But for whatever reason she changed her mind and left yet again. (Leaving the decomposing scent of Caylee behind.)

A separate group, Texas EquuSearch, also continued their hunt for Caylee.

The group's founder was going to be pulling his team out of Central Florida, citing frustration with the family over the lack of information that they are providing his team in the case.

However, they agreed to stay after Sheriff Kevin Beary offered more money and equipment to keep things going.

"We, in this community know what fuel costs are all about so, Tim, you'll be getting that check for $5,000 tomorrow morning so we can continue the search for Caylee. And again, we need credible information. That's all we've been asking for the whole time. If somebody has that information, they need to be contacting the Orange County Sheriff's Office." Beary said.

Beary is also pleading with more members of the public to volunteer to help in the search for Caylee. On S eptember 3rd, 2008, roughly fifty thousand people visited Walt Disney World in Orlando, while all of twelve people showed at the EquuSearch command center to search for Caylee.

After a sluggish start, the number of volunteers searching for Caylee quadrupled by Thursday.

They've been searching with special equipment near the Orlando International Airport, and not far from the Anthony home, looking for any clues that could help with the case.

"He flipped the coin for us and lit a fire under the search and it exploded the way we anticipated it would explode when we came into town, we're getting cooperation from them and it's warming my heart." said Mandy Albritton of EquuSearch.

EquuSearch and the sheriff's office are looking for volunteers to keep looking Friday, Saturday, and Sunday.

Volunteers are asked to meet at the command center on TPC Boulevard (about 5 miles from the Anthony's home) before 8:30 a.m. The searches will go until dusk.

It was announced Thursday that an anonymous person put up the $50,000 cash to post Casey's original bond on felony child neglect charges.

It is reported that two bond agencies in Kissimmee will work together to post the entire $500,000 amount.

Casey's lawyer, Jose Baez, issued a statement Thursday saying: "The individual posting the bond prefers to remain anonymous, and is doing it because of the belief that Ms. Anthony's constitutional rights have been grossly violated."

The release also said neither Baez nor Casey will be working again with bounty hunter Leonard Padilla, who originally posted Casey's bond.

Casey is expected to leave jail sometime Friday morning, and will be on home confinement with an ankle monitor.

Jose Baez arrived at the Orange County Jail with two bodyguards just after 10 a.m. Friday to get Casey out.

Minutes later, Casey and the group left amid media frenzy in a black sport utility vehicle without saying a word.

Unlike Casey's prior release on Aug. 21st, the facility used police tape to better control Anthony's exit.

Casey was fitted with an electronic monitoring device. Under the terms, she will have to remain on home confinement at her parents', George and Cindy's, home.

The protests at the Anthony home reached a boiling point Friday night after Casey was released from jail earlier in the day.

The Orange County Sheriff's Office was called in after neighbors started fighting with protesters.

The protesters were demanding Casey be returned to jail.

Will all of the commotion on Hopespring drive the neighbors of George and Cindy are reaching their boiling point.

Upset over the number of protesters and media invading their neighborhood every night, they have now made an appeal to their homeowner's association.

The neighbors said they are trying to restore some peace and quiet to their community.

The homeowners association is asking a judge to restrict the time, place and manner in which protesters can gather. They want the crowd to move away from the Anthony family's front yard and go to the entrance of the neighborhood, which is off Chickasaw Trail.

Sheriff's deputies were on hand Thursday afternoon, but only to keep the peace, not to remove protesters.

The lawyer for the homeowner's association said, "The noise is out of control, there have been field trips driving by to see the Anthony home, people have been rifling through trash, school buses can't get to the children in the morning and waste management has had a problem with picking up the trash."

The lawyer for the homeowner's association said that the Sheriff's Office has done a great job handling criminal situations, but more needs to be done.

The lawyer for the homeowner's association said, "But the Sheriff's Office, being bound by the public assembly law, they don't have a tool at their disposal that they can help, maybe, prevent some of the physical confrontations or altercations, or screaming—everything that amounts to a nuisance, basically, that's interfering with our association's homeowners' quiet enjoyment of their property."

If things weren't bad enough at the Anthony's residence, deputies seize a handgun from the trunk of George's car the next day.

Having a gun on the property violates Casey's bail but since she appeared to be unaware of the gun, she was not taken back into custody. George says he planned to use it to force Casey's friends to tell him what happened to Caylee.

During the first week of September EquuSearch temporarily called off the search for Caylee, citing environmental conditions and concerns following Tropical Storm Fay that passed through central Florida just a few weeks earlier. Some areas of the state received up to 25 inches (64 cm) of rain, causing serious flooding. Native wildlife, including alligators, was seen in flooded neighborhoods after high water forced them from their habitat.

Many of the areas that EquuSearch planned on searching were just too flooded for their searchers to safely search.

On September 10th, it is reported by a FOX affiliate news station that the whole family allegedly refuses to take a lie detector test offered by both the FBI and local authorities.

The California bounty hunter Leonard Padilla who posted Casey's first bail was the one who reported the incident to the station. He said that Casey, as well as her parents and brother were all given the opportunity to undergo a polygraph,

Padilla said he was present when her family was approached about the lie detector test.

Casey's parents George and Cindy and her brother Lee initially agreed to take a polygraph, according to Padilla. They changed their minds only hours later, and Lee delivered the news to Padilla and his crew.

"We thought, well here's an opportunity for you and your mom and dad to kinda clear yourselves," Padilla told the news station.

There was no word on why the family had a change of heart.

On Thursday, fraud charges were filed in court against Casey.

The Orange County State's Attorney's Office charged Casey, with grand theft in the third degree, three counts of fraudulent use of personal information, three counts of check forgery of a check and three counts of uttering a forged check.

The charges stem from allegations that Casey used checks belonging to friend Amy to buy groceries and other items.

Amy is accusing Casey of using checks from a checkbook left in hers car, which she let Casey borrow.

Orange County Sheriff's Captain Angelo Nieves said investigators also found evidence that Casey used the checks in question.

He also said they had videos of Casey using the stolen and forged checks, but the videos might not be released to the public because they could be used to help establish a timeline in Caylee's disappearance.

Investigators said Casey wrote the first check on July 8th out of Amy's account. The check was written for $111.01

Investigators said Casey then forged a check using Amy's identification on July 10th at the Target on North Goldenrod Road. That check was in the amount of $137.77

A third check, according to investigators, was also forged on July 10th at another Target store, this one on North Alafaya Trail. That check totaled $155.47.

When all three checks are added together, they total more than $300, which allowed investigators to charge Casey with grand theft, a third degree felony in the state of Florida.

Casey is now facing a total of 10 charges connected to check fraud.

It is still unclear when Casey will go to trial on the check fraud charges, but because of all publicity this case has generated, there is still some speculation that there may be a change of venue.

On Friday the Orange County Sheriff's Department released audio recordings of authorities interviewing Casey after she reported her daughter missing.

This has a local expert in voice stress analysis worried.

Susan Constantine told the Orlando Sentinel she believes she heard deception in Casey's voice when she gave a long answer to a yes-or-no question.

"Too much information is a true sign of lying," Constantine said.

The analyst added Anthony's answers seem rehearsed, and she believes Casey's words did not coincide with the tone of her voice.

The weekend at the Anthony's home was in turmoil with the protestors that made their daily pilgrimage to the Anthony's home on Hopespring Drive.

Cindy got into a shouting and swearing match Saturday night with protesters who called Casey a baby killer.

The protesters appeared to come onto the Anthonys' property, screaming and cursing, while Cindy was trying to post "No Trespassing" signs that had been torn down earlier in the day.

George called the Orange County Sheriff's Office to report the incident.

The child of one of the protesters appeared to be hurt when his arm got caught in a car door by his mother as they went to leave.

Day 62 in the search for Caylee wrapped up with the weekly Sunday night vigil outside of the Anthonys' home.

The vigil was marred with protestors outside the home. Some were chanting "baby killer" while others yelled at Cindy to come after them. Some stated George "knows how to push a woman."

The neighbors are already fed up with all of the commotion and to make matters worse, there was a delay in the injunction for the Anthony family's Home Owners Association.

The Chickasaw Oaks Subdivision asked the ninth district court to keep protestors out of the neighborhood; however, the court has not acted on the homeowners request by Monday.

There is no word on when the judge will take up the case.

On Monday, the Department of Children and Families (DCF) said that they are starting an investigation into the mother who slammed her kid's arm in the door of her sport utility vehicle.

DCF said they used the license plate in the video to track the mother down so they can talk to her as part of their investigation.

Casey turned herself in five days after the Orange County State's Attorney's Office charged Casey, with grand theft in the third degree, three counts of fraudulent use of personal information, three counts of check forgery of a check and three counts of uttering a forged check.

On the 15th, Casey was arrested Monday following a meeting with her home confinement officer. She was with her attorney, Jose Baez, at the time.

Casey will be spending the night in jail. She will not be bonding out, according to Allen Moore, a spokesman with the Orange County Jail. Her first appearance was before a judge early Tuesday morning.

She was released the next day after appearing in court on $1,250 bond, and again fitted with an electronic tracking device and returned to the Anthony's home.

During the final week of September, 591 pages, including text messages and interviews with family and friends are released.

Followed the next day by a Kissimmee, Florida woman with the same name as the one Casey gave to police, Zenaida Fernandez-Gonzalez, files a lawsuit against Casey for defamation.

By the end of September Caylee has been "officially missing" for eleven weeks (77 days) and Casey is still not cooperating with the Orange County Sheriff's department to find her daughter.

October

On October 1st, Jose Baez enters a not guilty plea to the check fraud charges on Casey's behalf. It was also on this date that the Orange County Sheriff's Office officially changes her status from "person of interest" to "suspect" in the disappearance of her daughter.

One week later on the 8th it is reported that Casey could soon face new charges in the disappearance of Caylee.

According to reports, a grand jury is set to convene to consider homicide charges for Casey. That grand jury could convene as early as next Tuesday.

Jose Baez stood next to Casey when word came out about the Grand Jury convening on the case and told the media, "Should an indictment come down Casey will surrender herself. She's not running from this, she has never attempted to run away from the situation."

According to most legal experts, proving a homicide case without a body is difficult, but they say that it is not impossible.

The detectives said that they just started to put things together starting with the hair in the back in the trunk. And they had reason to believe that Caylee was dead. The fact that the hair showed death banding made them confident that they had enough evidence moving forward. And even if they never discovered the remains of Caylee they felt that they had enough evidence to prosecute Casey criminally and obtain a conviction.

Meanwhile, the State Attorney's Office released more documents and surveillance videos. One of the videos that were released was the video of Casey withdrawing money at a Bank of America on July 15th, the day Caylee was reported missing.

Investigators said the documents give more insight into the check fraud charges revealed after Caylee was reported missing.

Along with the documents, surveillance video shows Casey walking into the Winter Garden Target just before 10 a.m. on July 10th wearing a black dress. In the video, you can see her purchase clothes, including the blue No. 82 hoodie she was wearing during her initial arrest on child neglect charges.

The video also showed Casey leaving the Winter Garden Target around 10:36 a.m. and she was next seen on surveillance video entering the Waterford Lakes Target at 11:10 a.m. wearing different clothes. In another video, Casey is seen buying food.

Investigators said that in both cases, Casey paid for the items with the stolen checks written out of Amy Huizenga's account.

That same day deputies said they've installed a surveillance camera outside of the Anthony family home on Hopespring Drive.

The camera will monitor any possible clashes at the house, and comes in addition to increased patrols.

Casey is due back in court on Friday when a judge will be considering a slew of motions from her attorney, including one to allow her to visit "places of interest" in her daughter's disappearance without the public knowing where she goes. Texas EquuSearch said they will be back in Central Florida on Friday to continue their search for Caylee.

On October 10th Cindy registers the Caylee Marie Anthony Foundation.

This foundation is widely believed to have been used to fund an "inmate commissary account" for Casey, an account from which an incarcerated person (as Casey was during her trial) can purchase clothing, soaps and shampoos, food stuffs and candy from the commissary provider in the jail. Caylee's Fund doesn't appear as a 501(c)(3) in Publication 78, which is the authoritative list of IRS-approved charities.

When we went to the listed website for nonprofit organizations in the State of Florida we saw two banners that read:

This organization has not appeared on the IRS Business Master File in a number of months. It may have merged with another organization or ceased operations.

This organization's exempt status was automatically revoked by the IRS for failure to file a Form 990, 990-EZ, 990-N, or 990-PF for 3 consecutive years. Further investigation and due diligence are warranted.

Casey Officially Charged With Murder

On October 14th, Casey was arraigned on the newest check fraud charges, to which she has pleaded not guilty through her attorney. She was not required to appear at that arraignment.

While the check fraud case against Casey was being heard in one court room, a nineteen member grand jury was hearing the facts in the first-degree murder accusations against Casey.

The first person to testify that morning was a familiar face: Casey's father, George.

Before entering the courtroom, George said he loves his daughter, and that testifying at Tuesday's hearing was the hardest thing he has ever had to do. He also asked for prayers for his missing granddaughter.

Mark NeJame, George's lawyer, would not specify as to what exactly was said inside before the grand jury.

"George answered all questions directly and honestly," NeJame said. "He just did, I think, what no human being could ever be prepared to do."

Several Orange County investigators and forensic experts also testified in the case.

Baez asked that everybody reserve judgment until they know all of the facts.

"I would just simply ask that, from this point on, everyone try their best to engage in fair and neutral balanced reporting that asks the tough questions, because, I sincerely believe that when we have finally spoken, everyone, and I mean everyone, will sit back and say, 'Now I understand,'" Baez said.

By that afternoon the grand jury handed up a seven count indictment against Casey, including first-degree murder and aggravated child abuse in the disappearance of her daughter, Caylee.

State Attorney Lawson Lamar read the charges at an afternoon news conference.

The first-degree murder charge specified that between June 15th and July 16th, 2008, Casey did "from premeditated design, effect the death of Caylee Marie Anthony," according to Lamar. Because the count is a capital offense, Casey will not be allowed to be released on bail.

The indictment also included counts of aggravated manslaughter and providing false information.

Casey was booked into Orange County Jail. Her first appearance in court will be on Wednesday morning.

The first-degree murder charge carries a possible death penalty if she is convicted.

During Lamar's news conference, Orange County Sheriff Kevin Beary said that, despite the indictment, his primary objective is still finding Caylee.

"Despite the charges filed against Ms. Anthony today, I want to remind everyone we have not achieved our primary objective in this investigation. We have not recovered little Caylee Anthony. ... We will continue to do everything we possibly can to recover little Caylee," Beary said. "The grand jury has concluded that little Caylee is deceased."

Casey's lawyer, Jose Baez, said he's upset after word of the grand jury proceedings was leaked.

With Casey by his side, Baez said it's just the latest attempt by the sheriff's office and media to try and smear his client.

He said all of the leaks in the case would have any panel believing Casey is guilty without hearing all the facts, and he believes it's all politically motivated.

"I understand there is an election going on, and I understand that those days are numbered, and I understand that Casey Anthony is public enemy number one and that the State Attorney's Office and the sheriff's department are under a great deal of pressure to close this case. I don't think Lawson Lamar would, and I certainly hope Lawson Lamar would not, utilize a missing child to keep his job," Baez said.

Baez insists the truth about the case and his client's innocence will come out with time.

The Orange County Sheriff's Office said Casey did not turn herself into Orange County deputies.

Capt. Angelo Nieves said while deputies were following her after she was indicted, her mother Cindy reportedly pulled her vehicle over at Narcoossee Road and State Road 417, and Casey got out.

Casey then got into a full-size gray sport utility vehicle, which drove off.

Undercover detectives stopped the SUV a short time later, and arrested Casey on seven charges, including murder, child neglect, and lying to the police.

The following day Casey made her initial court appearance on charges that she murdered Caylee.

Casey at her arraignment with attorney Jose Baez

Dressed in a blue jail jumpsuit, Casey only said one word during the appearance, by acknowledging Judge John Jordan with a "yes" when he called her name.

After that, he read all of the charges on the seven count indictment a grand jury handed up the previous day and then ordered her held without bond.

Casey's lawyer Jose Baez was by his client's side for her court appearance.

However, Baez did not make any comment on the case when leaving.

There was only one issue... little Caylee was still missing.

On Tuesday, he said in a press conference we haven't heard the full story on the case, and accused State Attorney Lawson Lamar of possibly bringing the case to a grand jury in order to help him win re-election.

Casey's mother and father are also standing by their daughter. On Wednesday, George said that he still believes that Caylee is alive.

Meanwhile, since Casey's murder indictment, questions have been raised as to whether Baez will remain her attorney in the case. According to Todd Black, Baez's representative, Baez will remain on the case to represent Casey on the murder charge.

Black said right now the case has not been declared a capital murder trial, and said Baez has been preparing for this possible scenario, and has a team of attorneys, including one that can handle a capital murder case.

Casey is being held under level one protective custody at the Orange County Jail's Female Detention Center.

Under the protective custody umbrella, Casey will spend her days in a cell by herself without any inmate contact. Protective custody is normally used in high-profile cases.

While in jail, Casey will be allowed out of her cell for one hour per day to take a shower, sit in the dayroom and make phone calls.

Additional time out of the cell can be granted at the discretion of the officers and attorney visits are allowed anytime.

On the 17th Casey entered a plea of not guilty to charges that she killed her missing daughter.

Having entered the plea, Casey will not have to show up for her arraignment, scheduled for October 28th.

On the day of Casey's arrest she was interviewed by the FBI.

She told the agent, "I still have that feeling, and that presence. I know that she is still alive. Whether you have a bucket load of evidence downstairs that contradicts that says otherwise or all you have is speculation or nothing at all. I mean whatever it is there's still that chance.

The FBI agent replied, "We have more than speculation. We have a lot."

On October 21st, the charges of child neglect are dropped against Casey on assumption that Caylee is dead. On October 28th Casey is arraigned and pleads not guilty to all charges through her lawyer.

A second court date is set for November 5th for the check fraud charges. And her Murder trial is scheduled for January 5th, 2009. Pretrial date set for December 11th.

The plea came as investigators announced they are testing and reviewing a small dress found in the woods last weekend that they described as "very, very similar" to a dress belonging to Caylee.

The search by EquuSearch for Caylee has been called off again.

Texas EquuSearch was searching areas near Orlando International Airport for the 3-year-old a few weeks ago, but had to call off the search because they said conditions were too wet following Tropical Storm Fay.

However, after returning, the group said conditions have not improved enough to continue.

They may try again in about a month. The group said when they return, they also plan on searching for Jennifer Kesse. The 24-year-old vanished in January 24th, 2006 near her Orlando apartment.

On October 24th, the Orange County Sheriff's office report says that the forensic tests on the trunk of Casey's car showed evidence of human decomposition, and a hair found in the trunk was "microscopically similar" to one in Caylee's hairbrush. The report also confirmed the presence of chloroform.

On October 31st, officials at the jail had to warn Jose Baez about hugging Casey during visits.

Many people close to the case felt as though there was a little too much closeness between Casey and her lawyer.

November & December

At Casey's November 5th court date the Judge agreed to continue Casey's check fraud hearing to December 11th.

At the end of the first week in November, Texas EquuSearch led a group of volunteers in a search of a 25-acre area around Orlando International Airport for Caylee, but when nothing is found they suspend their search. They remain in the Orlando area and focus their search on Jennifer Kesse.

On Thursday November 13th, officials thought they finally got a break in the case when divers searched a lake in Blanchard Park for Caylee. A plastic bag was recovered containing what appeared to be bones and toys, and weighed down with bricks. Authorities, however, said the find was not significant to the investigation.

At this point the searchers are getting aggravated with the dead ends and the fact that Casey refuses to help authorities find her daughter.

But law enforcement has a slight glimmer of hope when forensic scientist Henry Lee examined Casey's car on the 14th. Many believe that it will be just a matter of time before the case is finally solved.

The next day the Anthony family's private investigator, Dominic Casey, searches the area where Caylee's remains later are found. The search is videotaped. The family's attorney denies asking Dominic Casey to search there. The defense later questioned who sent him to the area; he said that a psychic gave him the tip. His search did not turn up anything because most of the area was under several inches of water at the time.

Just two and a half months after hiring him, George and Cindy have parted ways with high-profile attorney Mark NeJame on November 20th. Both sides announced the resignation Thursday.

Mark NeJame, quit the job, saying only Caylee's imprisoned mother knows the truth about what happened. He also indicated that he was off the case because of disagreements with the Anthonys.

NeJame said there was little more he could do to help them in the search for the child.

The Anthonys issued a statement saying they respect NeJame's decision.

Caylee's grandparents continue to insist that their granddaughter is still alive. And they also believe that little Caylee was in Orlando this week.

The family released a photo that was taken Sunday at the Florida Mall by two women with a cell phone camera.

The photo shows a girl playing; who they feel looks a lot like Caylee. It has been e-mailed to both the Orange County Sheriff's Office and FBI.

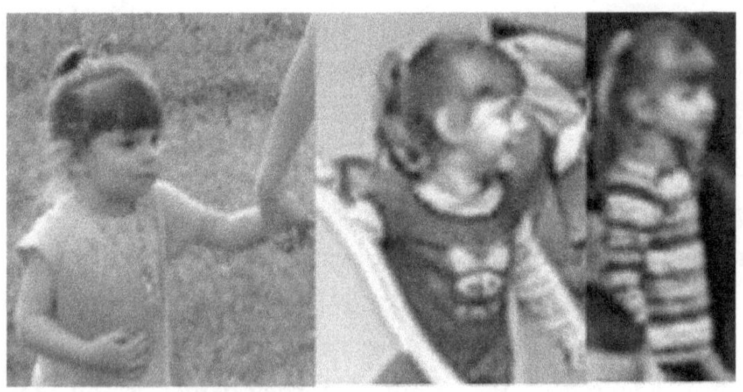

Caylee on the left, girl from mall on right

"There are just too many characteristics that stood out that it could be her," said Michelle Bart, the family's new spokesperson. "We're not saying that it is her. We're saying it's another tip that somebody in the community believed it was her."

George said at this point, he's going to start skipping the chain of command and aggressively align himself with anyone who can help the search effort for a live Caylee, whether it's law enforcement or the media.

"Is the system broken? Yes. That's evident every single day. Not only with my granddaughter but all these other children," said George.

During the search for Caylee the Sheriff's Department received over 6,200 tips. There were sightings of Caylee everywhere. Literally every state had some sighting of what is believed to be Caylee. One sighting was during the Macey's Thanksgiving Day parade. Many called offering advice and tips and even psychics called to give their thoughts on Caylee's whereabouts.

On the 25th the judge ordered prosecutors to turn over all evidence to the defense. He also ruled the defense could not test the hair found in Casey's trunk, because there was too little of a sample left. Forensic tests released last month confirmed that hair linked to Caylee and found in the trunk of Anthony's Pontiac Sunfire came from a decomposing body. Other DNA evidence also suggests that a corpse was in the trunk.

Both the prosecution and the defense released witness lists of those whose testimony they'll ask for at trial. The prosecution named more than 80 people, including George and Cindy and lead defense attorney Jose Baez. The defense listed only three witnesses, including a forensics expert and a criminal justice professor.

Judge Strickland also denied the prosecutors' request to impose a gag order in Casey's case, saying he could not state that continued publicity would pose a threat to her trial or even that a gag order would stem the flood of media attention.

On December 4th, the audio and video of jailhouse visits between Casey and her family are released by the Sheriff's Department. The state initially said it will not seek the death penalty.

Wednesday night December 10th, George and Cindy appear on an episode of CNN's "Larry king Live" which was filmed in California.

"There isn't a motive, and they haven't found a motive," Cindy said on CNN's "Larry King Live."

She added, "They told us they thought it was an accident, and she's scared and tried to cover it up. They don't feel there's a motive."

Cindy stressed that five searches for the girl's body have "come up with nothing. There's nothing that they have found that, you know, has given them any evidence that Caylee is no longer with us."

The Anthonys said they believe that the girl is still alive and that someone has her, noting several reports of sightings.

Larry King asked if Cindy believed that they would find Caylee.

She replied, "Oh I believe we are going to find Caylee if the investigation goes the right way."

Larry King also asked George, "Why wouldn't your daughter have called you and say, 'Caylee's gone.'

George replied, "That's really a good question."

Cindy added, "From what we understand there have been threats.to not only Caylee's wellbeing but to our family's wellbeing."

Larry King asked, "By?"

Cindy replied, "By the people who have Caylee."

Larry King, "So you think Caylee was taken, your daughter obviously knew her daughter was taken; for what purpose?"

Cindy, "I'm still trying to sort that out."

Larry King, "What does your daughter think George?"

George, "Well our daughter thinks that Caylee needs to be found."

Part four

Caylee's Remains Are Found

Casey had her pretrial court date today December 11th. But 9th Circuit Judge Stan Strickland postponed Casey's trial at the request of her defense attorney Jose Baez. The attorney said he had not received all the evidence due him from the prosecutors and was not ready to proceed with the January 5th trial.

Baez asked Strickland whether the trial could be delayed until March and also asked for a change of venue.

The judge scheduled a hearing for January 15th to consider a new trial date as well as a possible change of venue.

Also this week, Baez said he was seeking a court order for surveillance video from a local mall taken the day of the reported sighting of Caylee.

He is asking the Florida Mall be ordered to turn over the footage captured in November in a play area of the Orlando shopping center, where an employee says she snapped a photo of a Caylee look-alike on November 16th.

"I took my last cell phone picture as the woman (accompanying the little girl) tried to cover her head with her arm to hide from me taking her picture," mall employee Halima Solomita said.

Meanwhile the skeletal remains of a small child were found this same day less than half a mile from the home of Caylee's grandparents.

There was no immediate word on whether the bones, reportedly discovered wrapped in a plastic bag and bound with duct tape, were those of a boy or a girl.

A police spokeswoman said, "All we know is that remains of a child have been found."

Orange County sheriffs and forensics teams were working at the scene at the intersection of Hopespring Drive and Suburban Drive, on the edge of the Anthonys' neighborhood.

Sheriff's Office spokesman Jim Solomons said that a utility worker found the body at 9:32 a.m. in a wooded area less than a half-mile from the house Caylee lived in with her grandparents and mother.

The water meter reader reportedly picked up the bag and a small skull rolled out that sources say strongly resembled that of a little girl.

There were some unconfirmed reports of duct tape around the mouth area of the child's skull.

Police said that the Anthony family has been notified of the discovery and no one is being allowed inside of their house. Sheriffs were preparing a search warrant for the Anthony home.

Orange County Sheriff's Captain Angelo Nieves

Orange County Sheriff's Captain Angelo Nieves wouldn't say whether the bones seemed to be those of the missing little girl.

"At this point, it would be reckless to conclude that. We do have skeletal remains consistent with a small child. We will work with the medical examiner to make a proper identification." He said.

Orange County Sheriff Kevin Beary said his deputies were investigating at the scene with the FBI.

"We're all working on this case together," he told reporters at an afternoon press briefing. "We've got a lot of lab work to do, a lot of DNA work to do, a lot of crime scene work to do. We may be here all night."

Todd Black, the spokesman for Casey's defense attorney, said that he hoped the discovery was not related to their case.

"If it is, it is a sad day," he said.

The medical examiner declined to offer details about its involvement. "We have been advised to do a recovery, but until our investigator comes back with the information we have no comment," said Sheri Blanton, senior program manager for the Orange County Medical Examiner's office.

It is more difficult to identify a child's body than an adult's, experts say.

Dr. Lee Jantz, coordinator of the forensic anthropology center at the University of Tennessee, said the first thing medical examiners will do is compare photos of the child with the skull, in hopes of making a bone structure comparison. In high-profile cases the DNA of the bones will also be tested.

Mandy Albritton, a member of EquuSearch said their volunteers did not check the location in early September because it was submerged in water. And when they returned in November, the site had been fenced off.

One of EquuSearch's volunteers, Deborah Smith, searched the area three times and said "she had a bad feeling" because Casey had said her daughter was nearby.

"It's really wet and steep and there's lots of snakes back there," she said.

"I do believe its Caylee Marie," Smith said.

Minute-To-Minute timeline of

Thursday, December 11th, 2008

9:32 a.m.: A utility meter reader stumbled across a plastic trash bag that contained a small human skull with duct tape wrapped around it and hair still attached.

The remains were found in a very low wooded area about twenty feet off of the road. They were under some vines, behind a rotten log with leaves settled on top and silt settled on top of that.

It was very difficult to see.

The medical examiner's office determined that it was not in consistence with that body being placed there in the early stages of decomposition. (Soon after she died)

The skull was on a mat of hair that had separated from the skull during the decomposition stages. And clearly had duct tape still attached to it. But not attached to any tissue as there was no more tissue on the skull by this time. But there was hair and the duct tape appeared to be in the front of the skull.

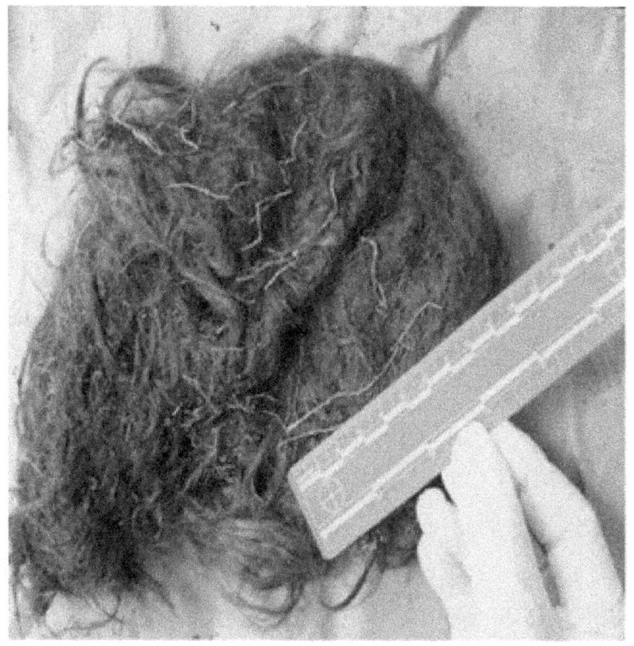

The mat of Caylee's hair

The duct tape is in three layers and it goes all the way around the skull and is stuck in the hair.

Besides the duct tape there were some other items also found along with the skull.

There was a trash bag, a Winnie the Pooh blanket and there was a laundry bag.

And all of these items have a link to the Anthony's home.

11:07 a.m.: FBI headed to the scene.

11:10 a.m.: Anthony family spokesperson Michelle Bart said Cindy and George do not believe that the discovery is that of their granddaughter. The Anthonys are returning from California where they were on "Larry King Live."

All that the authorities will say is that the remains of a small child were found. They would not tell them if it was a boy or a girl.

Cindy later said that by not knowing if it was Caylee or not made it the longest flight that they have ever taken.

George and Cindy are scheduled to arrive at Orlando International Airport around 4:25 p.m.

11:17 a.m.: The Sheriff's Department confirms the discovery is a small child. Utilities worker said a skull rolled out of the bag when he picked it up.

11:18 a.m.: Anthony's spokesperson said they have not been notified by sheriff's office.

11:30: a.m.: Sheriff's Office: We don't know if the body is Caylee Anthony.

11:35 a.m.: Sheriff's office establish media center at a church near intersection of crime scene.

11:40 a.m.: Anthony spokesperson Michelle Bart says she is flying to Orlando this afternoon.

11:46 a.m.: FBI lab will examine the remains.

11:48 a.m.: Orange County Sheriff's department Captain Angelo Nieves says the Anthonys have been notified.

11:49 a.m.: George and Cindy Anthony say Caylee is still alive.

The first thing that the detectives felt was that they needed to tell Casey to see what her reaction to the news would be.

They set it up so that she sees it on her own to see how she reacts.

So they bring her into a room inside the jail where she can sit down and the television is on and it is covering the news of the child's remains being found.

You can't hear what is going on in the closed circuit video but you can see her sit down and as she watches the news of the discovery she starts crying.

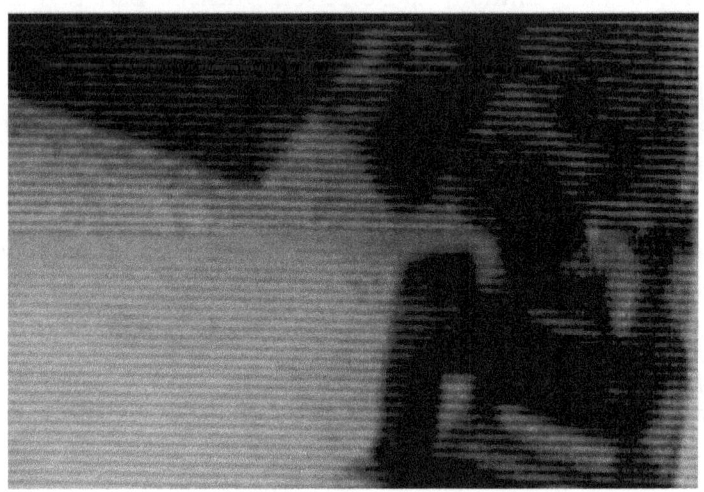

Her being upset could be interpreted in two ways.

#1 She's upset because, "oh no my daughter's really dead."

Or #2 "Oh no they found out where I threw her body."

11:55 a.m.: Baez arrived at the jail just before noon to inform Casey of the discovery and stayed about an hour and a half, officials said.

"She has been seen by a Corrections Health Services psychologist and her status was reviewed," officials said in a statement, adding that Casey was under psychological observation, which is not the same as suicide watch.

12:05 p.m.: News reports say that about 12:05 p.m., a woman drove up to the Anthony home and rushed inside. She was followed shortly by a sheriff's deputy who knocked on the door and asked the woman to leave.

12:06 p.m.: The Anthonys said through a representative that the area where the remains were found had already been searched. Texas EquuSearch says that when they tried to search this area in September, it was under water. When they returned in November, the area had been roped off.

12:10 p.m.: The Medical examiner arrives on the scene where the remains were found.

12:37 p.m.: Mobile command unit arrives on the scene of the discovery.

12:47 p.m.: Cold rain is making the search for evidence difficult. The remains have not yet been removed. One man said he had been searching a very short distance away from where the remains were found. He also said, while they were looking for the girl, there was a feeling among the group that there was something eerie about the area they were searching.

1:05 p.m.: Investigators say they will be on the scene for an extensive period of time.

1:10 p.m.: Sheriff Kevin Beary arrives. It is learned that the utility worker who found the remains works for the Orange County Water Department.

Sheriff Kevin Beary

1:25 p.m.: Sheriff Kevin Beary says, "Bottom line, it's real simple, folks, we've recovered this human skull, it appears to be that of a small child, and now the investigation continues. We've got a lot of lab work to do, a lot of DNA work to do, a lot of crime scene work to do. We could be here all night."

1:38 p.m.: Beary told the media that the FBI at Quantico is awaiting any remains that Orange County forensics wants examined. He said the discovery has been made a priority and they would work through the weekend if necessary.

1:44 p.m.: The sheriff's office closes the intersection of Suburban and Hopespring Drive, preventing parents from picking up their children at Hidden Oaks Elementary School.

2:07 p.m.: According to the sheriff's office, the body was found approximately 50 to 60 feet into the woods. Sheriff Beary said the State Attorney's Office has asked them not to release any information about any of the evidence that was found.

3:30 p.m.: Beary says that the sheriff's office is seeking a search warrant for the Anthony's home. Beary said the Anthonys are being cooperative and warns he does not want "craziness" at the Anthony home. He said the home has been secured "pending more investigation." The house has the "possibility of being more of a crime scene later," he added.

3:50 p.m.: Sheriff is trying to get a warrant to search the Anthony home. The remains have been removed from the discovery scene.

4:05 p.m.: Mark NeJame, the former attorney for George and Cindy Anthony, says that he has spoken with lead detective John Allen and with the FBI. He said that Allen told him that the Anthonys were called about the remains before they left California so they would not find out from the media.

NeJame also said that part of the reason he resigned as the Anthonys lawyer was because they were in denial about their daughter's involvement in Caylee's disappearance and that he could not endorse them saying Casey is innocent. "I resigned a few weeks ago because I could not support, in any way, shape or form, Casey."

"I've been expecting this day for a while and although it is a very, very sad day, I think in many ways we can now really pass on our full blessings to this child and allow her to go in the peace that she deserves and allowing her mother to be prosecuted as she deserves," NeJame said.

4:10 p.m.: Beary told the media again, "I want no craziness at the Anthony house."

4:20 p.m.: The Anthonys arrive at Orlando International Airport from a trip to California.

4:25 p.m.: Casey's attorney Jose Baez files a motion to preserve and inspect evidence and forensics found in the discovery. It will be heard Friday morning at 11:30 a.m.

4:58 p.m.: Beary says that they are going to let the ground around the alleged crime scene dry overnight and start searching for evidence again on Friday morning.

5:01 p.m.: Texas EquuSearch arrives on the scene where the remains were found. Also, Todd Black, Jose Baez' spokesman, said Baez would not be making a statement until the medical examiner releases her findings.

5:46 p.m.: Tim Miller, founder of Texas EquuSearch, says that the area where the child's remains were found was under water when they tried to search in September. They suspended the search because they were afraid they would push any possible remains down into the mud or destroy them. "The smartest move I ever made was to stop the search the first time," Miller said.

6:03 p.m.: Deputies called off the search at the scene for the evening. The sheriff's office will remain out at the site overnight. They also said the utility worker went into the woods to relieve himself when he found the bag. He opened the bag, noticed the bones and called police. The sheriff's office clarified the bag was found only 20 to 30 feet into the woods. Sheriff Beary told reporters earlier in the afternoon it was found 50 to 60 feet.

6:08 p.m.: A search warrant has been signed for investigators to go into the Anthony home. They could be at the house between 8 p.m. and 9 p.m. to serve the warrant.

8:31 p.m.: Sheriff's investigators have shown up at the Anthony home to serve the search warrant. They brought in brown bags and boxes.

Sheriff's spokesman Carlos Padilla said that authorities believe the remains are Caylee's for three reasons:

1. No other children have been reported missing in the area.

2. The remains are consistent with those of a child of Caylee's age.

3. The remains were found near the home of the grandparents, where the 2-year-old and her mother were living just before Caylee disappeared.

Authorities cordoned off the home of George and Cindy as they continued to search for evidence in the case of missing Caylee Anthony (now presumed to be the child found near the Anthony's home.)

George and Cindy returned to their home late Friday afternoon for the first time after the discovery of a child's remains was found.

George and Cindy were escorted into their home by two men who appeared to be guards. A short time later they left the home and were taken away by the same men. With a tense expression on her face and carrying a dog, Cindy had nothing to say to the media as she left the home.

Around 10 p.m., a group of people pulled up to the Anthony home and planted a memorial to Caylee made up of a white cross covered with a T-shirt adorned by a photo of Caylee and the letters R.I.P.

The duct tape reportedly found with the remains of the child's body could help tie the unidentified skeleton to Caylee, a forensic pathologist says.

Pathologists should be able to identify the body quickly from dental records, Baden said, and the plastic and duct tape could provide additional vital clues, including fingerprints. They could also provide clues to how the child died, and to who dumped the body.

"The beauty of duct tape — no matter rain, snow, sleet — that fingerprint will stay there," Baden said, adding that if someone used their teeth to rip it, it could yield DNA evidence too.

"Right now, they would be looking at all the contents of the plastic bag and they would be looking at the plastic bag itself," Baden said. "The fingerprints on the outside often get dissolved away by weather, but the inside of the plastic bag, the fingerprints would be there."

"One important thing that I've hoped they've done already is take an air sample from the bag because they found chloroform in the vehicle and the cause of death still has to be determined," Baden said.

Finding chloroform could poke holes in the prosecution's first-degree murder case, if this is Caylee's body, he said.

"If it is chloroform as the cause of death, then it could be an accidental overdose and would not be capital, first-degree murder, because sometimes chloroform is used as a babysitter, to put a baby to sleep while mom goes out partying," Baden said.

If dental records cannot be used to identify the body, DNA evidence will be used to identify the skeletal remains. The remains will also be examined for signs of trauma.

"If there are fractures to the skeleton, then that goes again to first degree—intentional suffering on the part of the baby," Baden said. "They can tell if the baby suffered."

On Tuesday December 16th, Judge Stan Strickland ruled that Cindy will not have access to the site where investigators believe they have found Caylee's remains,

The judge called the latest defense motions which asked for a second autopsy and access to crime scene photos, video and sketches from the site, "pure folly."

"I can't assist you in interfering with a murder investigation," Judge Stan Strickland told defense attorneys for Casey.

Some of the remains have been sent to the FBI lab in Quantico, Virginia, in an effort to identify them. Authorities have said the remains are believed to be Caylee's, but a positive identification is pending.

Meanwhile, the Kid Finders Network called off their active search for Caylee.

This week's motions came after Casey's attorneys were denied their request last week to observe the autopsy on the remains and conduct their own forensic tests. A judge said the motion was premature because the body had not yet been identified.

Because the judge wouldn't allow the defense team to get their own hands on evidence dug up from the site, lawyers asked this week if they could appoint someone else to oversee the examination of the remains.

Strickland shot down the request, saying that Casey's defense team had no right to interfere with an ongoing investigation.

"There's no time clock on an investigation, and if law enforcement doesn't do an exhaustive job, defense will argue it was shoddy and inadequate," Strickland said, in explaining why he rejected the motion.

"Law enforcement has the obligation to get out there and do whatever they need to do, disrupt whatever they need to disrupt," the judge said. "... I can't stand in their way."

Defense attorneys have asked to be allowed to examine the remains after they are identified and autopsied. Strickland has reserved a ruling on that request until a positive identification is made.

The second request by the defense team involves the site where the remains were found. Defense attorneys were asking that Strickland order police to turn over photographs, schematic drawings and video from the site.

Authorities initially told the defense their experts would be allowed to examine the scene after they finished processing it. However, work at the site continued after what Orange County sheriff's Captain Angelo Nieves called "significant finds." A source said that additional bones were found at the site.

Defense attorneys told Strickland they had flown in a host of experts last week, but have had to allow them to return home without a chance to examine the crime scene.

"It is imperative to the defense to have its own experts process the crime scene in as close to its original condition as possible," the motion said. "Due to the large amount of time and anticipated destruction of the crime scene (the defense has witnessed video of law enforcement sifting through numerous buckets of dirt) it may be impossible for the defense to have an accurate representation of what the crime scene looked like when the remains were found, much less the location.

"Photographs, video and schematic drawings are required, so that the defense will at the bare minimum have an idea of what the crime scene might have looked like before it was processed and possibly contaminated."

Ann Marie Delahunty, attorney for the Sheriff's Department, told Strickland, "It's not an excavation site; it's an active crime scene. We are preserving what needs to be preserved. We are doing the job we're supposed to do."

She noted that the remains have yet to be identified as those of Caylee, and said authorities are unwilling to release photos of the skull of "this little girl ... to be broadcast all over the news."

Authorities can release selected photographs to defense attorneys, much like they would in a public records request, she said. But "we are not in a position to release every photograph that's been taken out there," Delahunty said. "That would be completely inappropriate at this time."

The parties agreed on that, although defense attorney Jose Baez said he wanted a timeline on when the photos would be available and pledged not to distribute them to any third party.

Delahunty noted that those taking the photographs "are on their hands and knees sifting through dirt right now," but agreed to turn them over as soon as possible.

The 9-1-1 call from the Orange County Utility Company and 9-1-1 was released shortly after the discovery of the child's body.

On December 18th, Captain Angelo Nieves said more bones have been found, and the search has expanded. By the time the search was completed only a portion of the skeletal remains were recovered. It is believed that wild animals may have carried some of the remains away from the dump site.

Also on this day Judge Strickland denies another defense motion, and rules Casey can face the death penalty if she is convicted of murdering Caylee.

Finally, on December 19th, the authorities said that the remains that were found in a wooded area have been positively identified as belonging to Caylee Anthony.

The cause of the Caylee's death will be listed as homicide by undetermined means, said Jan Garavaglia, medical examiner for Orange County, Florida. (She is also known as Dr. G: Medical Examiner from the television show with the same name) Dr. Jan Garavaglia was the Chief Medical Examiner with Florida's District Nine Medical Examiner's office in Orlando, Florida.

She said she does not expect enough additional evidence to surface for that finding to be revised.

The remains were identified through DNA testing, comparing a sample from the remains to a sample known to be from Caylee. Some of the remains had been sent to the FBI lab in Quantico, Virginia, for testing.

A "large percentage" of Caylee's skeleton has been recovered, Garavaglia said. The bones showed no sign of trauma before death.

A child's skeleton has many more bones than an adult's, she said, and not all are fully developed. "Some of the bones recovered are no larger than a pebble." she said.

Garavaglia said the manner of Caylee's death, an opinion based on factors including an examination of the body and circumstantial evidence, was determined to be homicide.

Cindy was notified of the test results by the medical examiner's office, Garavaglia said.

Officials at the Orange County Corrections Department said Casey was notified of the results by a chaplain about 1:45 p.m., per jail policy. One of Casey's defense attorneys, Jose Garcia, entered the jail earlier, corrections officials said in a written statement.

"Due to happenstance, not policy, attorney Garcia was not in the presence of the inmate when the notification was made," the statement said. "We will not be commenting on the demeanor of inmate Anthony or her reaction to the news."

The Anthony family's pastor, Thomas Shane Stutzman of Eastside Baptist Church, arrived at the jail about 2 p.m. but left 19 minutes later because Casey had refused his visit, as she was meeting with Garcia at the time, jail officials said.

Garavaglia would not disclose specific information regarding the remains other than to say they were completely "skeletonized." Toxicology tests on the remains are pending, she said.

"Our number one priority from day one was to locate little Caylee Anthony," Orange County Sheriff Kevin Beary said. "We have stayed the course, and we will continue to do so until we have thoroughly completed our investigation into this tragedy."

The sheriff grew emotional while responding to a reporter's question about the effect of the case on him personally.

"Having a kid ... I've raised two girls, goodness gracious," Beary said, his voice breaking. "The bottom line is, no child should have to go through this."

The case has left an "open wound" in the community, he said, but he thinks closure will not come until after the trial.

George and Cindy did not give up hope that Caylee was still alive until they were notified of the test results, their attorney, Brad Conway said. He took no questions but read from a statement.

"They now know that their precious granddaughter is safe and hope that she will serve as the angel that protects thousands of missing children and their families," he said, adding that the Anthonys want "the same answers as everyone who has been assigned to investigate and prosecute this case" and will be available to authorities.

"As you can imagine, the Anthonys are grieving deeply over this loss," he said. "Please respect their privacy and understand they will stand together as a family in order to get through this. ... This is a tragic moment in the lives of good and honorable people. Please treat them respectfully so they can grieve with dignity over the loss of this precious child, Caylee Marie Anthony."

The sheriff's office said that the utility worker who found the skull December 11th had called police three times, August 11th, 12th and 13th regarding the site where the remains were found.

That utility worker, Roy Kronk, came forward Friday. Reading from a statement, he said that "back in August of this year, I previously reported to Crimeline and to the sheriff's communications center that I had spotted something suspicious, a bag in the same area."

"I have been and will continue to cooperate fully with the ongoing investigation by the sheriff's office and the FBI," Kronk said.

He refused to provide details of what he saw at the site where the remains were found.

His attorney, David Evans, said Kronk "has no connection whatsoever to this case, has no connection whatsoever to the Anthony family or any of the proceedings that have gone on before. He is here as a concerned citizen and no more. Those who have specified to the contrary could not be more wrong."

Evans said Kronk was asking for privacy for his co-workers, who have been the subject of "intrusive news-gathering activities." Some of those colleagues, he said, "protected his privacy and sacrificed their own in doing so."

Kronk will not be granting interviews at this time, Evans said.

Police said that in his first call on August 11th, the worker reported seeing a gray bag on the side of the road. A deputy responded, Nieves said, but the worker was no longer at the scene, and the deputy did not see the bag.

On August 12th, the worker called a police crime line. The call was sent to a detective, who told the meter reader that the area had been searched and cleared by cadaver dogs, police said.

On August 13th, the worker reported finding a bag in a swampy area, and a deputy was dispatched. The deputy looked at the area but found nothing, thinking the "bag" may have just been trash, Nieves said.

The meter reader revisited the site last week, apparently while working in the area, authorities said, and found the skull.

The site was searched earlier, Beary said, but was flooded at the time.

Nieves said that police were conducting a thorough review of the tips and their response but emphasized that the meter reader has been cooperative and is not a suspect. Roy Kronk could be eligible for the reward offered for information leading to Caylee's return.

Beary acknowledged that there were questions surrounding those tips but said the only way to find the answers was to conduct an investigation.

Jose Baez filed a motion on December 23rd, requesting pictures, X-rays and other documentation of the remains of Caylee when they were originally found and during the autopsy. Judge Strickland agreed and ruled that the documents must be turned over within two weeks.

On Christmas Eve an anonymous donor dropped 125 gift-wrapped toys from Bloomingdale's off at Caylee memorial site. The Orlando Union Rescue Mission were called in to retrieve the toys and said the toys would be given to the 84 children in the organization's custody.

On December 29th Casey's brother Lee hired criminal defense attorney, Thomas Luka.

Part Five

The Questions Continue

On January 8th, Judge Strickland made his ruling concerning Baez having the crime scene photos from the location where Caylee's body was discovered. He said Jose Baez can set up a secure database for images of Caylee's remains, but photos cannot leave Baez's office until he can prove that he has a secure Web site. He also cannot make copies of the photos.

Meanwhile, Judge Jose Rodriguez denied a request by Zenaida Gonzalez's lawyers to depose Casey before her criminal trial.

On the 13th, utility worker, Roy Kronk appeared on "Good Morning America," saying he first saw a suspicious bag in August in the area where he eventually found Caylee's remains. He claimed the deputy he reported the bag to did not want to investigate any further, because the area was under water and infested by snakes at the time.

George's suicide attempt

George's suicide attempt occurred on January 22, 2009. On that day, former Anthony family lawyer Brad Conway contacted law enforcement and reported George missing.

In his 911 call, Conway said that George "has taken several bottles of medication from the house as well as some pictures."

When the police who showed up at the Hawaii Motel in a seedy section of Daytona Beach on January 22nd,they didn't know what to expect. All they knew was that they were looking for George.

During the day George had been sending text messages to his family suggesting that he was about to harm himself, telling them he wanted to be with Caylee. Tracking George's cell phone, authorities traced him to the motel. When George let officers in the room, they discovered family photos, two empty pill bottles and a rambling eight-page letter, in which George claimed to have swallowed some pills.

When he was brought to the hospital he told a nurse, "I haven't taken anything," according to one police source. He could be hospitalized under the Baker Act for up to 72 hours.

But George's attorney Brad Conway insists it was a suicide attempt—that George took sleeping pills and blood pressure medication and mixed them with alcohol. Whatever the case, it was a bizarre episode, one that took place amid startling new disclosures about Casey and her family that as far as prosecutors are concerned, significantly tighten the case against her.

What's more, based on a review of a trove of recently released documents from the state attorney's office—along with the media's interviews with family and friends—it becomes clear that the family has been seriously dysfunctional for years. George and Cindy were frequently at odds and, though almost everyone agrees that Cindy was an exceedingly devoted grandmother, she and Casey had an intense rivalry.

The evidence laid out in the documents, much of which comes from clues gathered from Caylee's body also adds heartbreaking new details about the way Caylee may have died.

Investigators discovered Caylee's mouth had been sealed with duct tape and a small heart-shaped sticker had been placed over her mouth.

"You have to think about a person who would duct tape a child," says Pat Brown, a Washington-based criminal profiler who is familiar with the case. "Nobody is going to duct tape a child after she is dead."

A source close to the investigation said that the duct tape is "of considerable value."

When pressed on whether that means fingerprints have been found on the tape, the source would only say, "Read between the lines." It may also turn out that the items found with Caylee that can be linked to the Anthony home, such as a blanket and a toy horse, undercut Casey's contention that she dropped her daughter off with a babysitter then went a month while the child was supposedly missing before authorities were notified.

"We've got a really solid case against Casey," says the law enforcement source. "We know that the killer had to have access to the house and also had to know what Caylee liked and what her favorite toys were."

It is an open question how much the disclosures helped put George over the edge. There is little doubt that he was in genuine anguish the day he went missing. According to Daytona Beach police chief Mike Chitwood, who was at the motel, George appeared "melancholy."

Later, on the ride to the hospital, says Chitwood, he said, "You just don't understand. You'll never understand what this is like."

Authorities were able to have George committed for observation. A few days later his lawyer said that, "George had regained the will to live."

Many of the family's friends have given their own observations of the Anthony family. Their interviews make it clear that recent years—even before Caylee's murder—have been tough on the family. Casey and Cindy quarreled constantly, according to one source who knows the family well. "They were always at each other's throats about something," says the source. "Cindy would tell Casey she was immature, and Casey would tell Cindy she was ruining her life. They couldn't communicate if it wasn't for their fighting and bickering."

Things were scarcely better between Cindy and George. In an interview with the FBI, George said that he and his wife had separated for more than six months starting at the end of 2005. He said that they had reconciled, but there was no mistaking the rift between them.

"I've watched Cindy berate George over the littlest thing, just nasty, mean stuff," says one family friend. "She'll say, 'George, you're so stupid,' in front of his friends."

According to the FBI interview, at one point Cindy wanted to divorce George but changed her mind because she feared losing the house and her savings in a settlement.

The main problem in their marriage seemed to be their vastly different personalities. The friend who knows them describes Cindy, who works as a nurse, as the domineering type. "Cindy is very type A, and she really runs that house." She goes on to say, "She's the one who earns the money. George sort of defers to her, does whatever she wants and treats her like royalty."

As George, a former police officer, explained to authorities, his own work record has been spotty—including short-lived business ventures with his father and on his own after he left the police force.

During one period when he was unemployed, he sheepishly told investigators, he fell prey to an Internet scam. He provided few details of the swindle, except that it involved e-mail come-ons and $2.2 million purportedly in a United Kingdom bank.

"I should've known better; it was stupid," he said. He admitted he lost about $30,000 of the family's money—and then lied about it to Cindy, telling her that he had blown the money on gambling. At the time of the interview with authorities he said he still hadn't come clean with his wife. "She doesn't know I did this scam thing," he said.

Not only were there issues between Cindy and George, but also between Cindy and her own brother Rick Plesea.

Mainly the suspicious circumstances under which Caylee went missing created strain between Cindy and her brother Rick.

A slew of e-mails between the two that were released by investigators show that Plesea quickly concluded that Caylee was almost certainly dead and that Casey was somehow responsible.

He said that he couldn't understand why Cindy, who staunchly defends her daughter, didn't draw the obvious conclusions. "No parent would be at a nightclub every Friday after their daughter is kidnapped," he wrote. "She has no remorse and doesn't care about anyone except herself. You are so far out in left field on this, you have lost touch with reality."

There is also reason to believe that at other times Cindy had little regard for her daughter. Grund, who has been interviewed by investigators and is considered a witness, recalls a dispute between Cindy and Casey, "All of a sudden, Cindy starts railing on Casey," says Grund. "Cindy tells Casey what a loser she is and starts saying really awful stuff right in front of me. Then she asks me things like, 'How could you be with her?'"

Many people feel that George's suicide attempt was more than just the strain between him and his wife.

Numerous people have stated that they believe that George decided to commit suicide as he knew that the DNA test that was done to prove or disprove that he was Caylee's biological father, was due to be released. And many say that he feared that it would reveal that he was in fact Caylee's father. And that he had been having sex with his daughter just as she said. The following is George's suicide note to his wife, Cindy.

Cynthia Marie,

As you get this letter, this should be no surprise that I have decided to leave the earth, because I need to be with Caylee Marie.

I cannot keep going because it should be me that is gone from this earth, not her. I have lived many years, I am satisfied with my decision because I have never been the man you, Lee, Casey & especially Caylee Marie deserved.

I have never been the man any of you could count on. I have always let each of you down in more ways than I can remember. I do not feel sorry for myself, I am just sorry I burden all of you the way I have.

My loss of life is meaningless.

Cynthia Marie, you have always worked the hardest, given the most to me, and I have never Thanked you. 28+ years ago, you corrected me, a man who has now found his identity in life. What I mean is, you always challenged me the right way and I always could never live up to your expectations. You have always been smarter, more knowledgeable & thought things through & I love you for that.

I cannot be strong anymore. Caylee Marie, our grand-daughter, I miss her. I miss her so much. I know you do too.

You were always the one that provided for her. What did I provide?

I blame myself for her being gone! You know for months, as a matter of fact for a year or so I brought stuff up, only to be told not to be negative.

Caylee Marie, I miss her. I miss her. I want my family back.

I sit here, falling apart, because I should have done more.

She was so close to home, why was she there? Who placed here there? Why is she gone? Why?

For months, you & I, especially you always questioned, why?

I want this to go away for Casey. What happened? Why could she not come to us? Especially you, why not Lee?

Who is involved with this stuff Caylee?

I am going Krazy because I want to

Go after these people Casey hung with prior to Caylee being gone.

That is why I got that gun. I wanted to scare these people. You know, they know more than they have stated, you cannot sugar coat, kid glove these people. They need hard knocks to get info from.

Sure that will not bring Caylee Marie back, but was Casey threatened? You know, Casey does not deserve to be where she is.

I miss her, I miss her so much. I am worried for her. Her personal safety is always on my mind.

I try to deal with so-so much, as I do you also.

I have never wanted to my family for sorrow in any way. I realize families have ups & downs but we have suffered our share & then some.

Cynthia Marie, you have always deserved more, and with me being gone, you will. I have always brought you down. You know that. You are better off. Lee will be there for you. Mallory is such a great woman. I see how you are with her. She is a keeper. Future daughter-in-law. I smile when I say her name. Mallory, please take care of yourself, Lee & Cindy. Someday you will be a great wife to Lee, and a fantastic mom. Cindy is a great Grammy and will love you forever.

Getting back to why I cannot live anymore: I cannot function knowing our granddaughter is gone. Caylee Marie never had a chance to grow. I wanted to walk her to school (the 1st day). I wanted to help her in so many ways....I could go on & on.

I sit here empty inside for her. For you, for us. Jose keeps calling.

Yes, you deserve more & you will have freedom to enjoy what you deserve.

I have taken what meds was given to me with alcohol & I am ready to give up. As I can tell by my writing and thinking, I am getting very stupid. Wow, what a word STUPID. Yes, I am. Again, I do not feel sorry for myself(...unintelligible) I am STUPID. I cannot deal with stuff anymore.

The loss of Caylee Marie. The loss of Casey. The loss of us, Cynthia Marie, the meds, I am ready.

Saying good bye, please understand it is for the best. I do not deserve life anymore. Anymore us.

You are the best, you always have been. I am sorry for all that I have done to us.

You know I never got to say goodbye. I am at this place and all is getting foggy & my writing is all over the place.

I love you, I love you, I hope you get to see Casey soon. All the people we met, wow, the writing is getting weird, I love you, I am sorry – I will take care of Caylee – once I get to God hopefully

I want to hold her again, I miss her, I will always love us, I am sorry Cynthia Marie, I called my mom today, ...(unintelligible) I am so tired, at least I shaved today, wow – I'm tripping out, I am sorry,

I love you – Cynthia Marie

Caylee Here I come

Lee, I am sorry

Casey

George ended his letter with no final message for Casey.

Cindy arrived at the hospital Friday afternoon to visit her husband.

She told investigators George was upset and depressed about the death of their granddaughter.

She said she asked her husband the day before to pick out some jewelry for Caylee for her funeral, and that may have made him even more depressed.

Meanwhile, it was a mainly quiet day at the family's Orange County home.

Casey's attorney Jose Baez said he won't be commenting on the events surrounding George.

Baez showed up at the Orange County Jail late Friday morning, but said the visit was not in reaction to what happened to Casey's father.

Baez himself has come under fire this week when he denied allegations he's taking money for entertainment deals surrounding the case.

However, published reports have also come out about complaints about Baez to the Florida bar.

Baez filed new motions in the case Thursday, including a request to get records from the search group Texas EquuSearch.

Those motions were heard in court on January 30th.

Motion #1 to kick prosecutors off the case: Denied.

Motion #2 requesting to inspect remains site: Granted.

Motion #3 requesting EquuSearch records: Denied.

Motion #4 regarding defense's witness list: Moot, already resolved.

Judge Strickland also ruled that Casey won't be able to skip any more of her upcoming court hearings.

The judge ruled that Casey must attend all court proceedings.

A judge ordered her to appear in court the last time, even though her lawyer had said Casey waived her right.

The judge said her waiving her rights could create future problems. Especially if she lost trial, she would then be entitled to an appeal based on the mere fact that she did not attend all of her court proceedings.

February 10th, 2009
The Memorial for Caylee

George and Cindy prepare to speak during the memorial for Caylee Caylee's remains have been released but won't be at the public memorial service, an attorney for the family said.

The remains are at the Bryant Funeral and Cremation Chapel in Orlando. Caylee's grandparents, George and Cindy, have not yet decided when Caylee's private funeral and burial will take place, according to family attorney Brad Conway.

The public memorial service was held at the First Baptist Church of Orlando, the city's largest mega-church.

Casey will not attend. She is still being held at the Orange County jail, where she might watch the service on television.

The memorial, which drew a large crowd, was under tight security. Officers were provided by private firms and the Orange

County Sheriff's office, and private donors paid for them, officials said.

Mourners were required to pass through metal detectors, and were not permitted to carry bags into the church. Conway said the family had blocked some people from attending the service. Prior to the service he said, "They know who they are, they will be respectively turned away."

Many people believe that this also included Cindy's estranged brother Rick.

The morning service at First Baptist Church in Orlando was every bit a call for people to give their lives to Jesus Christ as the only way to heaven as it was a celebration of the short life of the little girl whose tragic death has made worldwide headlines.

The memorial service was called, simply, "Remembering the Life of Caylee Marie Anthony" - began with piano medley of Caylee's favorite songs such as, "Twinkle, Twinkle Little Star," followed by other kids favorites "This Little Light of Mine," "Jesus Loves the Little Children," "This is the Day That the Lord Has Made" and "If You're Happy and You Know It Clap Your Hands." Accompanying the classics on an overhead screen were pictures of Caylee.

During the medley George and Cindy along with their son Lee, entered the spacious First Baptist Orlando worship center accompanied by a large contingent of friends and family.

First Baptist Orlando's Pastor David Uth set the tone for the one hour 45-minute service.

"We are here to celebrate the gift of Caylee Anthony. Though short, her life made a huge impact on many people," he said.

Uth asked the 1,000 or so in attendance as well as those watching on television and viewing by live Internet stream to pray - not only for George, Cindy and Lee Anthony - but also for Caylee's mother. "Please pray for Casey," he urged, "and pray for the Lord to speak peace into her life."

Uth also touched upon another theme throughout the passionate and hopeful, service.

"Lord," he prayed, "we look forward to seeing Caylee when there is no more night and we no longer have to say good-bye. We look forward to that day when you wipe away every tear."

The emotional messages were punctuated by 12 live songs performed by a team of vocalists, including First Baptist Orlando's Kyle Thomas as well as singers from the Anthony's home church, Eastside Baptist - Katie Cox, Nancy Rodriguez, Glen Cox, Pastor Herkie Walls, and the trio "Broken Vessels."

The list of songs varied in theme from lamentation - missing those who are now gone - to future glory - being reunited with our loved ones in heaven. Those themes were reflected in the songs' titles, including "Child of Mine," "No More Night," "One More Day," "Because Jesus Lives," "I Can Only Imagine," Homesick" and "To Where You Are." One other number, "Caylee's Song," was written specifically for Caylee and performed by Jon Whynock.

Uth told the gathering though they grieve, there is always cause for hope because of He who died on the cross for mankind. Assuring Christians that God has His eye on them, he quoted from Isaiah 43:1-2: "Fear not, for I have redeemed you; I have called you by name, you are mine. When you pass through the waters, I will be with you; and through the rivers, they shall not overwhelm you; when you walk through fire you shall not be burned, and the flame shall not consume you."

Uth also continued the theme of heaven by quoting from John 14:1-3: "Let not your hearts be troubled. Believe in God; believe also in me. In my Father's house are many rooms. If it were not so, would I have told you that I go to prepare a place for you? And if I go and prepare a place for you, I will come again and will take you to myself, that where I am you may be also."

Following Uth was Shane Stutzman, who addressed the reason why such tragedies occur. Stutzman, the former senior pastor of Eastside Baptist Church in Orlando (where the Anthonys are members), is now senior pastor of Northside Baptist Church in Orangeburg, S.C.

"It's difficult to say good-bye to someone as precious as Caylee or to understand why this happened," he said. "We all have many questions, but too many questions can often leave you empty."

Stutzman pointed to what he said is the only source for answers.

"Jesus is the one who has all those answers," Stutzman said. "He knows what everyone in this room is going through. The Bible tells us that if we would but call upon His name, He will answer us."

Stutzman also touched upon the theme of eternity. "If we know Jesus Christ, then we never have to say good-bye to Caylee. We just need to say, 'See you later.' Believe me, the Anthony's are going to be a family forever."

In a stirring moment George, Cindy and Lee took the stage to share their thoughts and reflections of Caylee.

Lee spoke first. Fighting back tears, he addressed those who "are frightened, angry, mournful and don't understand." He urged them to "fill your heart with patience and grace." Referring to "those of us who will never be the same," he urged those listening to "fill your heart hearts with forgiveness" for those who are suffering most. He also called the Memorial Service "a day for the family to unite."

Lee concluded his remarks by speaking directly to Caylee, referring to her as "CMA": "Each day you teach me how to live," he said through tears. "I love you. I am so proud of you. I hope you are proud of me too." He then ended by saying, "I will never forget the promise I made to you," though he did not elaborate.

Lee was followed to the microphone by his father George who strained to keep his composure. George recalled how little Caylee used to refer to him by the nickname she gave him. "Though I was

Grandpa George, she used to call me Jo Jo," he said. "She knew how to push my emotional buttons just by smiling at me or giving me a hug."

On a more somber note, George said Caylee's memorial is a reminder there are other families out there whose "children are missing and need to be brought back." To those whose families still intact, George reminded the parents to "hug your children, because they can be gone in a second."

Returning to the theme of heaven, George noted that though he knows Caylee is there and that he will one day see her again, "her presence is still in our home today. I can still see her coming through the door and lighting up the room."

On a more personal note, George talked about Caylee's love of vegetables - especially green beans - how the two of them used to share a bowl of popcorn just about every night, how he taught her to sing the song, "You Are My Sunshine," and the locket he wears that says, "You are my Caylee, my little sunshine."

He also mentioned the most conspicuous absent party of the morning, Caylee's mother, Casey.

"I miss my daughter," he said. "She deserves prayer and understanding. Please take the time to write a letter to her and let her know that you are thinking of her."

George concluded his remarks by talking about the difficulty of the long ordeal.

"Nothing is what it used to be," he said. "There is a new 'normal' every day. One thing I've learned is that we need to be positive in order to get through the difficult things of life."

Cindy followed him to the mike. She recalled the day when she first heard the news that she would have a granddaughter.

"I remember when Casey told me I would be a grandmother," she said. "I had total peace and joy about it. And when I held Caylee for the first time, she completely stole my heart. I knew she was a special child. She was the perfect baby."

To support that claim, she told of how Caylee, who, along with Casey, lived with her and George, "would never wake up crying, but would always wake up laughing."

Like her husband, Cindy also shared some of her favorite memories of Caylee such as the way she loved coloring, having grandma - whom she referred to as "Cece" - read stories to her, throwing tea parties for imaginary friends and playing dress-up while decking herself out in multiple strands of beads. She also spoke of Caylee's love of Spiderman, saying good-night to the stars and how she over and over again watched her favorite movies, among them "101 Dalmatians," "Sleeping Beauty," "Lady and the Tramp" and "Bambi."

And also like her husband, Cindy mentioned her daughter.

"It breaks my heart that Casey is not here to honor the child she so loves," Cindy said. "Thank you for giving me the greatest gift I have ever received - Caylee Marie, Stay strong, my child."

Cindy noted the importance of her granddaughter's life and said her faith has sustained her during this traumatic time.

"I believe Caylee's purpose was to give us hope," Cindy said. "As for me, faith is the reason why I stand here today with a smile. I couldn't have endured the past seven months without faith."

Stutzman concluded the service with a prayer of gratitude.

"Thank you, Father, for giving us the opportunity to be here for such a time of this. Help us to truly share Jesus Christ with all those with whom we come into contact," Stutzman said.

The official service was followed by a releasing of about a dozen doves, attended only by the Anthony party and the pastors of First Orlando.

On February 18th, new documents and photos were released in accordance with the Sunshine Law of Florida.

***Keep in mind that all items found at the crime scene may or may not be related to this crime, but certain evidence found seems to be.**

The local news station is also reporting that **another thousand pages of evidence** will be released next week.

HERE IS SOME OF THE INFORMATION IN THE DOCUMENTS:

Evidence on the body suggests that the child's death was not accidental but an intentional act.

CASEY ANTHONY'S REACTION TO FINDING OF CHILD'S REMAINS:

Casey's reaction to the breaking news that a child's remains had been found close to her house was videotaped by jail officials. She was closely observed and was purposefully taken to a jail nurse's station (in December) and seated where she could see breaking news coverage on TV about the child's remains.

THIS IS DAYS BEFORE THE CHILD'S REMAINS WERE IDENTIFIED AS CAYLEE ANTHONY.

"Casey Anthony doubled over twice, appeared to begin hyperventilating, began rocking back and forth and was visibly upset, and asked for medication."

DEBUNKING A THEORY OF THE CHILD'S PARENTAGE (FAVORED BY SOME ON TRUE CRIME BOARDS)

Based on the STR typing results, the DNA obtained from specimen Q18-1 (CAYLEE ANTHONY) **could not have** originated from a biological offspring of the individual represented by specimen K9 - LEE ANTHONY.

LEE ANTHONY IS NOT THE BIOLOGICAL FATHER OF CAYLEE ANTHONY.

CASEY ANTHONY DIARY EXCERPT DATED JUNE 21st

I have no regrets, just a bit worried. I just want for everything to work out okay. I completely trust my own judgment and know that I made the right decision. I just hope that the end justifies the means. I just want to know what the future will hold for me. I guess I will soon see.

- This is the happiest that I have been in a very long time. I hope that my happiness will continue to grow.

- I am finally happy, let's just hope that it doesn't change.

Facing page (left side of book)

Everyday is a brand new beginning

CARPE-DIEM-SEIZE THE DAY-

THE DUCT TAPE & GAS CAN

Forensic reports show the duct tape found wrapped around the skull of Caylee Marie Anthony matched the Henkel brand duct tape stuck on a gas canister at the Anthonys' home.

FBI Forensics reports show that investigators did not find George, Cindy or Lee's fingerprints on the duct tape found on Caylee's skull.

FBI Lab: Based on examinations, "the pieces of duct tape found on the body and on the gas can are "comparable to one another in all physical attributes and in the chemical composition of their backing and adhesive components." Therefore," they originated from the same source roll of tape or from rolls of tape manufactured in the same manner."

"During a search of the southernmost outside shed at the Anthony home, crime scene investigators located a red metal gas can with a piece of duct tape on it. On the tape within a black oval was written the work "HENKEL". This tape appears to be of the same make and brand as the tape found on the body. This gas can was photographed and collected."

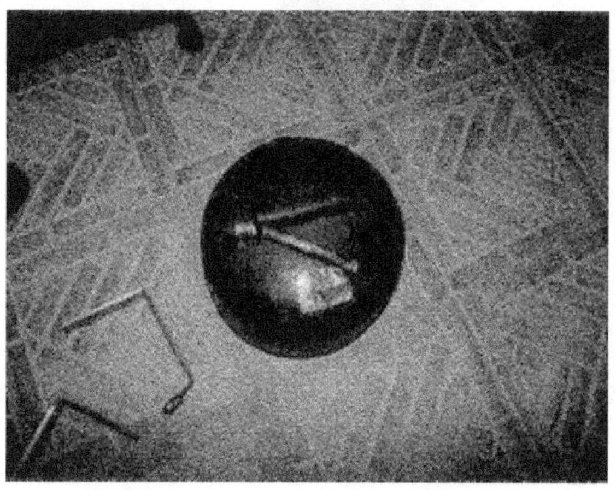

THE GAS CAN WITH DUCT TAPE

THE HEART STICKER

While processing the duct tape, the FBI lab found a perfect shape of a heart that was consistent with the adhesive side of a heart shaped sticker. In the search area, investigators found a small heart shaped sticker similar in size. The sheet from which the sticker came was not found on scene.

HEART STICKERS FOUND IN CASEY ANTHONY'S BEDROOM

CASEY ANTHONY'S CAR

Reports show Caylee's body was stored in her mother's white Pontiac for some time before her remains were removed and relocated.

CUSTODY OF CAYLEE

The legal and forensic documents show that Casey considered herself a bad mother and that her parents, George and Cindy, had considered taking custody of their granddaughter Caylee on more than one occasion.

SOME OF THE DEBRIS & OTHER ITEMS FOUND AT CRIME SCENE

This is a partial list of what was found:

Human teeth

Bones

Animal bones

A pregnancy test

Numerous pieces of plastic bags

Several discarded soda cans

A broken Winnie the Pooh helium balloon

Barbie doll legs

A disposable camera

A piece of "Henkel Consumer Adhesives" duct tape, the same kind found wrapped around the skull and attached to a gas can at the house.

DUCT TAPE FOUND ON SCENE

A World of Disney bag near Caylee's remains

WORLD OF DISNEY BAG FOUND ON SCENE

Inside the bag investigators discovered a Gatorade Cool Blue bottle with unknown liquid and white sediment. A syringe in a wrapper was found inside a toilet paper roll that was in the bottle. It would later test positive for the drug Chloroform.

DISPOSITION OF REMAINS & CLOTHING FOUND

Caylee's remains were found inside of two black plastic bags and a canvas laundry bag.

A similar Whitney Design canvas laundry bag wrapped in a black plastic bag was located on the top shelf above the laundry machine in the Anthony home.

Detectives found:

A stained Winnie the Pooh blanket

A pair of size 24 month pink and white stripe shorts,

A pink size 3T shirt with the words "BIG TROUBLE comes small" written on the front

Pieces of a child's pull up

The sheriff's office asked the FBI to compare the black plastic bag found with Caylee's remains to the garbage bags collected from the Anthonys' house; to compare the duct tape found on the remains to the duct tape on the gas can from the Anthonys' residence; and to examine multiple garbage bags, a Bissel steam cleaner, Dirt Devil vacuum cleaner, and a Bissel spot cleaner for possible decomposition materials or other related items.

EVIDENTIARY ITEMS FROM THE ANTHONY HOUSE

Several shirts from Caylee's room with the same brand name of Circo.

1 (One) pink shirt in particular had iron letters saying "get my good looks from my mom."

The tag of this shirt had RN 74299 stamped on it - this is the same number off of the tag found on the shirt collar that was found with the child's remains. This shirt was photographed and collected.

Child pullup diapers - which had characteristics similar to the one found with the body.

These were also similar to the pullup diapers from Caylee's child's backpack found in

Casey's vehicle: The backpack had been removed from Casey's car by Cynthia Anthony after the car was recovered from Johnson's Towing.

The pullup diapers were photographed and collected.

After the crime scene had been discovered and was being processed, a search warrant was served at the Anthony home:

"Cynthia (Cindy) Anthony read the copy of the warrant I gave her. In the presence of us all, she made a statement that "one of Caylee's "Winnie the Pooh" blankets was missing."

"Cynthia stated that she had people walk "that area" meaning where the body was discovered, a month ago and there was nothing in the area then."

EVIDENCE TURNED OVER TO LAW ENFORCEMENT BY GEORGE & CINDY ANTHONY

When Casey was first arrested in July of 2008 Cynthia (Cindy) Anthony voluntarily turned over to LE the following:

(All of these items were sent to the FBI Lab)

A diaper bag in which there were 3 child's size pull up diapers - with a princess pattern.

The characteristics of these diapers were similar to the ones found with the body.

Items inside a black plastic bag with yellow draw string. This bag style/type is similar to the ones found with the body.

A dinner knife found in a black purse.

ROY KRONK - MAINTENANCE WORKER WHO FOUND CAYLEE'S REMAINS

Roy Kronk was not sure if the skull dropped or if it was simply uncovered.

According to the position in which the skull was found, the skull could not have fallen out of a bag or dropped as Roy Kronk mentioned.

The skull had been in its found position for some time.

In the middle of April the defense received yet another blow in the case when The State of Florida announces that it reversed its earlier decision and is going to seek the death penalty if Casey is found guilty.

Many experts say that the State's decision to do this was a tipping point in the juror's final verdict. The States requirement for the death penalty is that the person would have had to plan out the murder in advance or kill the victim in the process of committing another felony.

Here is the state's definition in Florida, "If a person committing a predicate felony directly contributed to the death of the victim then the person will be charged with murder in the first degree - felony murder which is a capital felony. The only two sentences available for that statute are life in prison and the death penalty."

This opened up the door for the defense to offer up an explanation as to Caylee's death as an accident.

During the final week of May, Andrea D. Lyon, a professor at DePaul University College of Law, in Chicago, joins Casey's defense team. Jose Baez hopes that her expertise in law will give them an edge in Casey's defense.

On June 17th, Judge Strickland seals the jailhouse video that was made of Casey the day she is informed that her daughter's remains were found near her parent's home. He rules that the tape is highly prejudicial.

Two days later on Friday, June 19th, 2009, Caylee's autopsy information is released to the public. But not before a court battle with George and Cindy where they asked that the autopsy report be sealed.

George testified before Judge Stan Strickland Friday. In a tearful plea, George asked that the autopsy report be sealed.

"Although the public has the right to know, we as family are asking the court to hold off until it becomes necessary at the time of our daughter's trial, George said. "We believe that allowing the medical report to be released will allow others to dissect, misinterpret and sensationalize the information that will ultimately tarnish Caylee's memory and cause severe harm to our family."

Brad Conway, the attorney for the Anthonys, said the release of 2-year-old Caylee's autopsy would cause great anguish to the family if it was released at this time.

The Anthonys claim since Caylee's remains were turned over to them after being found last December, they should have control over the information.

The autopsy results show that by the time Caylee's remains were found, they were skeletonized, which prevented medical examiners from determining an exact cause of death.

The fact that the State could not provide an exact cause of death the defense knew that the chances of Casey being convicted of murder were almost impossible. Mainly because they could not come right out and say that Casey murdered Caylee and how she did it.

The results also said there was a piece of duct tape placed over Caylee's mouth.

In total three pieces of Henkel brand duct tape were found loosely attached or near the skull, which was the primary deposition area. Another piece was found 6.27 feet southwest of the skull. The State said the duct tape was on the face of the child prior to death; however, there were a problem with that theory.

The pieces of duct tape are of odd size. The lengths of duct tape were not long enough to wrap around the head. If you were going to wrap tape around the head, you would use one long piece – not three (or four) separate pieces attached end on end. And if you were going to cover only the nose and mouth area of a child, you wouldn't need to use 8-10″ pieces of tape. Also, there were no indications that any other parts of the body were bound (hands, feet).

The skull was found upright, with the jaw or lower jawbone still attached, buried up to the eye sockets. Instead of the tape being found against the frontal area and embedded in the soil, it was found loose with some of it above the leaves.

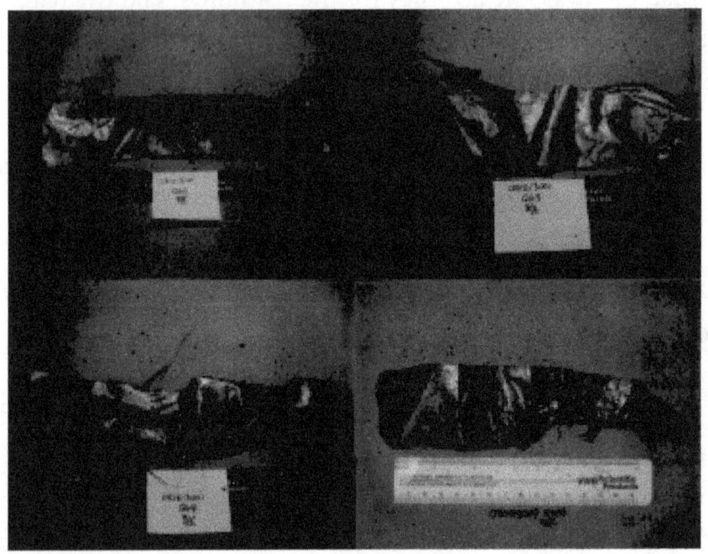

Roy Kronk said that he saw behind one of the trees was a gray, vinyl-like bag... and there was something round and white...

He recalled the events to detectives when he found the skull in December, *"I saw something white that was protruding up out of the water. It appeared to me, it just looked like the top of a human skull."*

At that time of the sighting in August, the bag was submerged in water. Just the top of this was sticking out.

Kronk did not investigate the scene further in August because he said that the area was wet and he found a snake. From a distance, gray duct tape on a partially-submerged bag can look just like vinyl because of the pattern. In this case, that was what Roy Kronk saw. No gray, vinyl-like bags were found *near* the skull from the recovery scene, only duct tape, black bags, and a white laundry bag.

Also cloth letters spelling out the words "big trouble comes small" were found near the remains.

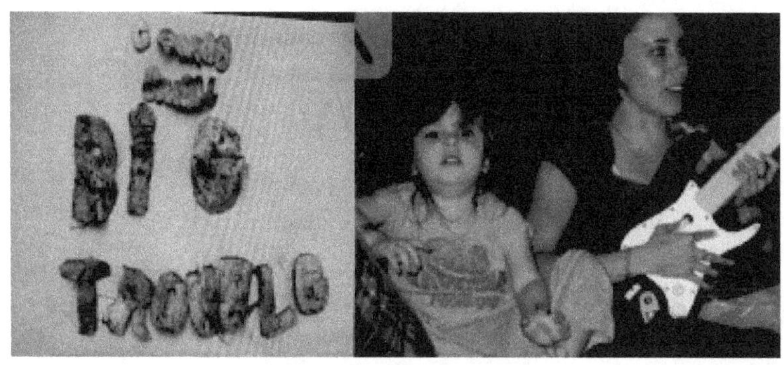

The letters from the shirt she was wearing at the time of her death and to the right a picture of Caylee wearing the shirt while she was still alive.

"There was very little to work with. It was very thorough but it doesn't answer any question. What it does do is leave speculation open," Conway said.

The judge ruled that the autopsy would be made public and George and Cindy were visibly upset when leaving the courthouse.

Casey's lawyer, Jose Baez, was also concerned. While Casey sits in jail, more and more information about her daughter's disappearance is coming out.

Baez is worried that all the newly released information may be hurting his chances to properly defend Casey.

"We believe that the results of any documents to the potential jury pool could be damaging," Baez said.

On August 5th, George gives his deposition to the state as the prosecutors prepare for the upcoming murder trial.

As he was walking into the courthouse, George told the media that it would be another hard day, one of many since Caylee died and Casey was arrested for her murder.

He also shared his frustration about not being able to get a job.

George said, "I'm just nervous. A year ago, I never would have thought I'd be doing something like this. I was just, the old George. I was just some guy who lived on Hopespring Drive. I've been on interviews and stuff like that, (but) as soon as they see me, it's, like, 'You're this guy.' They really don't want to bring me on, thinking that something negative will come out of it. I just want to work."

Ten weeks later on October 17th, new testimony released from George's deposition revealed inconsistencies as detectives tried to find out what happened to Caylee. During the deposition, George kept changing his story and the timeline of events, especially when it came to crucial information about evidence.

The previous week, both Lee and Cindy spent hours answering questions about Casey and Caylee. The family's depositions won't become public until someone files them with the court.

In the meantime Casey remains locked up in the Orange County Jail. As of August 2009, her trial date has not been set.

Two days later on August 7th, the state attorney's office released more documents, including photographs, maps, e-mails and a 3-D animated movie.

The newly released information includes a three-dimensional animated movie of the area where Caylee's remains were located and an 1,100-page report from the Metropolitan Bureau of Investigation.

According to the documents, an investigator confirmed that there was no blood in the trunk of Casey's car. It was confirmed that only a mysterious stain was located in the trunk, which reeked of human decomposition.

The photos released on the 7th include images of trash collected as evidence and a T-shirt similar to one worn by Caylee that says "Big Trouble Comes in Small Packages" on it.

The documents also include a report on Casey's cell phone use.

On September 3rd, Casey learned she would be tried for check fraud before her murder trial.

Casey's lawyers tried to delay the check fraud charges until after the murder trial, but the judge denied that request.

The August document release was not the only major release of documents in the case. Almost one month later, on September 4th, the State released new documents include three hours of audio and video recordings, as well as some additional photos.

One of the documents talks about Casey's demeanor when she was released on bail in August 2008.

Tracy McLaughlin, an associate of Leonard Padilla's, recalled in an interview with authorities the first time she met Casey, which was on the day she was released from jail on bond. McLaughlin said that her job was to observe Casey.

"I'm a little bit nervous to meet her because I'm thinking that poor gal," McLaughlin said. "She's gotta be upset. She comes in happy as can be. 'Hey!" 'Hi' gives me a big hug and just, 'oh I want to take a shower' and not a word about Caylee."

In an audio recording, Leonard Padilla recounted to Orange County investigators the original story Casey told him about how Caylee first disappeared.

Padilla said Casey told him Zenaida Gonzalez, Caylee's "mystery babysitter, kidnapped the toddler, then held Casey down and handed her a list of things to tell police for the next 30 days.

According to Padilla, Casey said Zenaida told her it was "payback.

Padilla told investigators that he didn't believe Casey's story from the beginning.

Also in one of the audio files released was a conversation, apparently recorded in August 2008, between Cindy and Commander Matt Irwin of the Orange County Sheriff's Office. The two met and talked over lunch.

Right at the start of the recording Cindy made it clear she was upset with the way Detective Yuri Melich questioned Casey and her family, and that she was not going to take a polygraph test.

"I'm going to cooperate as much as I can, but I don't have to take that polygraph and I'm not going to—not the way I was treated last night (by Yuri)," Cindy was recorded saying.

Cindy said she became upset with Melich after reading the transcript of his questioning of her daughter.

"I don't trust Yuri. I read through his line of questioning through the discovery. ... I was appalled. ... He's not asking her questions, he's telling her stories. He's telling her a scenario and wants her to respond to it. ... She's told us from day one he never listened to her. Now, granted, she did tell some lies, but again, a couple times he actually cut her off when she tried to tell him things."

When Irwin said Caylee's disappearance could have been the result of an accident, Cindy said she didn't believe that for a second because Casey would come to them even when Caylee skinned her knee.

"I realize Casey lied, but bottom line is it still doesn't change my beliefs that Caylee is not dead, that Caylee is still alive and is out there and I'm not changing those beliefs until someone brings me proof beyond a reasonable doubt otherwise," Cindy said.

Irwin reassured Cindy that authorities never considered her, her husband George or her son Lee, of having a role in Caylee's disappearance.

"Knowing what I know today, I still would have called 911," Cindy said.

During the conversation, Cindy told Irwin that she had to be strong for the family because the rest were so emotional. She said it was hard for George to come to the realization that he would not be Casey's knight in shining armor and save the day, and that they would have to depend on someone else to do that.

The state attorney's office also released a video of various scenes shot by private investigator Jim Hoover. The clip jumps back and forth between items pertaining to Casey's case and Hoover's own home movies of his family.

In one scene related to the case, the Anthony family's private investigator Dominic Casey is searching the wooded area where Caylee's remains were found with a metal rod.

Another scene shows a television tuned to the Nancy Grace show on the day the remains were discovered. The person behind the camera zooms in on the TV to show George and Cindy leaving their house, escorted by Hoover.

The released materials also included dozens of photos of Caylee, as well as several photos of the Amscot parking lot where Casey left her car after Caylee first disappeared in June 2008.

On September 17th, 2009 – Casey's defense team files a motion to dismiss the murder charges against her because the state allegedly failed to preserve evidence in the case. The motion is denied.

In preparation for the upcoming trial the state had Casey sign a document on October 7th, swearing she did not report Caylee missing until July 15th, when Cindy called 911, and that she told deputies she dropped Caylee off with a woman named Zenaida Gonzalez.

The television show "*48 Hours*" on CBS profiled the case against Casey on October 18th, featuring interviews with Casey's family and attorneys. Casey's defense team said that deputies and the FBI botched the case and arrested Casey too soon. They added that they believe a stranger killed Caylee.

One week after the show aired, Tampa radio host Bubba the Love Sponge offered the Anthonys $25,000 to appear on his show after George and Cindy were reportedly given $20,000 for the interview with "48 Hours."

Casey's legal team has been trying to get the civil suit brought against her by the real Zenaida Garcia dismissed. But on October 21st Circuit Court Judge Jose Rodriguez ruled Casey's civil case will not be dismissed.

On late November, Jose Baez, in an effort to focus the blame away from Casey, suggests Caylee could have been murdered by Roy Kronk, the meter reader who found her body. The defense alleged Roy Kronk may have killed Caylee.

In a motion filed with the court, Jose Baez claimed there is evidence of a possible history of inappropriate behavior with young girls. Kronk has also allegedly used duct tape to restrain women.

Many feel that this is just a ploy to distract the public but the next day Roy Kronk's ex-wife, Jill Kerley, appears on a TV program where she says that she also believes he, "probably was the one who murdered Caylee Anthony, or had something to do with it."

On November 22nd, The Casey Anthony document page count tops 12,300, making the case against Casey one of the biggest in Orange County history.

Then on November 24th, Jose Baez accused Texas EquuSearch's Tim Miller of lying to the court. The defense disputed EquuSearch's claim that only 32 people searched in the area where Caylee's remains were eventually found. Casey's defense team said that they found more people in the course of their own investigation, and want the judge to order EquuSearch to turn over all records relating to their search for Caylee.

Judge Stan Strickland ruled on several motions on December 9th.

One of the motions filed by Casey's defense team was to destroy all of the jailhouse recordings.

Casey's lawyer also urged the judge to prohibit jail officials from videotaping sessions between her and her client, as well as visits from Casey's friends and family.

She said that she has been told that the videos are for security and that the sound is disabled, but said that she and Casey both have the "feeling that perhaps we're being listened to." The motion was denied.

A motion to dismiss nine charges in Casey's check fraud case was also denied.

The only motion that the judge did grant was a motion to keep audio an interview with a former EquuSearch volunteer private.

On December 11th, 2009, almost a full year after the remains of little Caylee were discovered, Casey's lawyer Andrea Lyon asked Orange County Circuit Court Judge Stan Strickland to stop the prosecutors from seeking the death penalty against Casey.

Lawyer Andrea Lyon said that the "real reason" prosecutors are seeking the death penalty against Casey is because they want to "get as biased a jury as they possibly can."

Lyon said a jury that is qualified to serve in a death penalty case is more likely to convict defendants.

But prosecutor Jeff Ashton told the court that the state is not seeking the death penalty; rather, the jury and judge will decide whether or not it is appropriate.

Ashton said the death penalty question is not for the prosecution to answer. "Everyone who is indicted by a grand jury in the state of Florida for the crime of first-degree murder is eligible for the death penalty," he said.

"The decision by the prosecutor is simply, should a jury, and ultimately, a judge, be allowed to make this decision?"

Further explaining why he believed the case was eligible for the death penalty, Ashton speculated what jurors might infer from the facts presented to them. He suggested that Caylee's killer may have either given the toddler a substance to knock her unconscious before applying duct tape to her mouth and nose, or had physically restrained her before doing so.

"As the killer looked into her face, maybe her killer even saw her eyes, as the tape was applied," he said.

As he spoke, Casey sobbed, as her lawyer comforted her.

Lyon noted that there is "no evidence ... that this tape had anything to do with the death of this child."

In her argument, the defense attorney noted Caylee's undetermined manner of death, saying that the death penalty infringes on Casey's constitutional rights.

"They cannot be seeking the death penalty in good faith because there is insufficient evidence ... to establish first-degree murder," she argued.

The judge said he would make his rulings as soon as possible.

Casey's parents also appeared in the courtroom for Friday's hearing.

One week later on December 18th, Judge Stan Strickland denies the request to take the death penalty off of the table.

2010

Casey pleaded guilty Monday January 25th, to check fraud and was sentenced to time served.

Casey admitted stealing a checkbook from Amy Huizenga, and writing four checks worth nearly $650. She wiped tears from her eyes as she spoke briefly in court.

"I just wanted to let everyone know that I'm sorry for what I did," she said. "I take complete and full responsibility for my actions, and I'd like to apologize to Amy. I wish I'd been a better friend.

Attorney Jose Baez asked the court to give Casey credit for time served and place her on probation in the check case. The judge agreed that Casey already has spent more time in jail than any sentence she could receive in the check case.

Baez said that Casey has made full restitution. And that before her arrest, she had no prior criminal record, he added.

The guilty plea means Casey now has six felony convictions on her record.

Casey's parents were present in court for the plea. George waved to his daughter as she was led from the courtroom.

One month later on February 26th, the State Prosecutors requested a private hearing with the judge, without Casey or her defense team present, and without the public involved. In a new motion, prosecutors said they have received certain materials and information, and they have "good cause" to delay their release.

On March 8th, Judge Strickland set the trial date for May 9th, 2011. (62 days later)

By mid-March more than $25,000 was paid to a forensic entomologist. Another $5,000 was paid to a University of Florida Soil and Water professor. The State Attorney's Office tab for the case is already at $35,651.

These amounts will be covered by taxpayer money.

Then on March 18th, the distinguished advocate J. Cheney Mason joins the defense team at an indigence hearing on the invitation of Jose Baez. When asked why he had accepted the invitation, Mason replies "Because it's fun."

At this hearing Casey is declared indigent which means that taxpayer money will now be used to pay for both the prosecution and the defense costs.

New documents came to light on April 8th, when the State revealed letters between Casey and a pen pal, fellow inmate Robyn Adams, who is currently in a federal prison.

Casey knew details about Caylee's remains before they were made public knowledge, according to a police interview with a fellow inmate of Casey's.

After a chaplain informed Casey of the recovery, Casey told fellow inmate in the Orange County jail, Robyn Adams, that law enforcement had found the body of a small child. She went on to say that the child was found "with a baby blanket inside a black garbage bag," police said in the witness report, which was included in hundreds of pages of documents released by prosecutors.

"As a note, the information regarding the baby blanket and black garbage bag was not made known to the jail chaplain so Casey had knowledge of items only the suspect, certain law enforcement personnel and the certain medical examiner's personnel knew," the report said.

Anthony's conversation with Adams allegedly took place soon after December 11th, 2008, the day media outlets had reported a child's skull had been found by a utility worker less than a mile from the Anthony home.

The detail about the baby blanket did not come to light until the next month, when the state attorney's office released a report on items discovered with the remains.

Adams also told police that once when searchers previously thought they had found Caylee's remains but were mistaken, Casey giggled "not like in an evil way ... like ... it's not my daughter," the witness report said.

Adams said, "But once the set of remains were found near her home, Casey became terrified."

Also included in the documents are allegations from Adams and another inmate that Casey told them that she used to "knock out" her daughter so that she could go out at night without hiring a babysitter.

Adams, with whom Anthony exchanged 50 letters while incarcerated, told investigators that Casey told her that she sometimes used "stuff" to put her daughter to sleep. Another inmate, Maya Derkovic, said Anthony told her a similar story, but never said how she "knocked out" the toddler, according to the documents released Tuesday.

Investigators suspect chloroform, a powerful sedative, could have played a role in the death of Caylee after police say traces of the drug were found in the trunk of a car driven by Casey and in a syringe that was found near the toddler's remains inside of a Gatorade bottle.

In addition to the inmate interviews, more than 250 pages of letters written between Casey and Adams in the early months of Casey's incarceration were released by prosecutors.

The defense team for Casey emphasized in a statement that the letters written by their client "do not contain a single reference to chloroform or any admissions of guilt."

"The letters released today reflect the natural desire for companionship when isolated for 23 hours a day, and clearly demonstrate Casey's unconditional love for her daughter Caylee," the statement said. "Casey Anthony maintains her innocence and looks forward to her day in court."

In the letters, Casey says she thinks about Caylee daily.

"I miss my Caylee so much," she wrote in one of the letters.

"Not a day goes by that I don't think about Caylee and wish that I could have protected her better," another reads.

Adams told investigators that Casey told her that there was no Zenaida Gonzalez, the babysitter Casey originally claimed had abducted Caylee. Adams said that Casey told her that Zenaida was the first name of a childhood friend, according to the court documents.

Casey's defense team said Adams' sole purpose in corresponding with Casey was "to create leverage to get out of prison early."

In another revelation, in the letters released Casey writes she was sexually abused by her brother when she was younger.

"The worst part is, when I tried to confide in someone before... they turned on me. I was to blame for my own brother walking into my room at night and feeling my breasts while I slept," she wrote.

The Anthony family categorically denied such allegations.

"The Anthony family denies that there was any improper sexual behavior in their family nor was there ever a time when Casey told them of sexually inappropriate conduct by her brother or father," the family's attorney, Brad Conway, said in a statement.

Also among the pile of flowery, hand-written notes, Casey repeatedly complains about what she called her "family's betrayal".

Casey said she learned that after jail house visits, her brother and father were reporting on her to the police early on in the investigation.

"I find out that my brother was acting according to scripts, via law enforcement, when he came to visit me back in July and August and he was reporting back to them with whatever I told them," she wrote.

After Anthony found out her mother had applied for a trademark for Caylee's name, she wrote in one letter, "B-E-T-R-A-Y-A-L!!! I'm so sick to my stomach even thinking about this".

"I've done everything possible to hold my family together and I continue to get stomped on, thrown under the bus, and it doesn't surprise me anymore when it happens," she wrote.

Beyond the complaints and more personal revelations, Casey discusses boys and letters she received from admirers repeatedly asking to marry her. She talks about what's on television, often punctuating with exclamation points and smiley or frowny faces.

"I need a vacation!" she wrote. "I am thinking of Costa Rica... want to come with? (Unfortunately we have to wait until we are released. Someday!)"

Anthony's defense team reportedly did not object to the letters' release, telling the media that they are not concerned with the content of the letters.

Then just over a week later the case would take a turn that would make all sides take notice.

On the 20th of April the original judge assigned to the case, Stan Strickland, recuses himself and is replaced by Judge Belvin Perry Jr. after the defense contended he was biased against her.

In a motion filed 12 minutes before the court closed on Friday, April 16th, defense attorney Jose Baez accused Strickland of forming a "personal relationship" with blogger Dave Knechel, who writes under the pseudonym "Marinade Dave."

Knechel's blog includes made-up legal motions with titles such as "Casey Anthony must die!" "Caylee's murder: Premeditated and pretty stupid too" and "Guilty as charged."

Baez alleged that the judge called the blogger to inquire about his health and did not disclose the relationship with the defense. He also contends in court papers that the judge recognized Knechel at a court hearing and summoned him to the bench.

Strickland denies there was any personal relationship, saying in his order that he made only "infrequent sojourns into the blogosphere." He added that the blogger had criticized "those who came onto the blog for the sole purpose of bashing the defendant and her family." He said he thanked the blogger in open court for being "both fair and civilized."

Video of an October 19th hearing shows a bailiff pointing at Knechel. Off-camera audio reveals snippets of a conversation with the judge in which Knechel says people are reading his blog because he does a "good job, very simple."

Although Strickland denied wrongdoing, he acknowledged that repeated accusations of bias would be disruptive at a trial.

"Since the undersigned has now been accused of bias and wrongdoing, potentially each denial of a defense motion will generate renewed allegations of bias," Strickland wrote.

Here is the statement that Judge Strickland made on the situation.

"Over the past 20-plus months, in between media interviews, guest appearances on television shows and press conferences, defense counsel has filed a litany of motions."

"At its core," the judge continued, "defense counsel's motion accuses the undersigned of being a 'self-aggrandizing media hound.' Indeed. The irony is rich."

Attorney for Casey's parents, Brad Conway, told the media. "Judge Perry is a good judge; he knows the law," "Stan Strickland is just as good and knowledgeable. He's also extremely patient. He lets you say what you have to say, then he rules."

Conway recalled that when he first appeared before Perry years ago, the judge invited him into chambers and gave him two rules: "One, the train leaves at 8:30 a.m. be on it. Two, be prepared."

Conway said that Perry assured him, "If you follow those two rules, you'll be fine."

On May 11th, Judge Belvin Perry said he will still allow the state to seek the death penalty. Casey broke down in tears in court when Caylee's name was mentioned by the defense during the court hearing.

On June 15th, 2010, the second anniversary of Caylee's disappearance, George and Cindy appear on *Good Morning America*.

"The last two years have been just unbearable," an emotional George told "Good Morning America" in an exclusive interview as he sat alongside his wife, Cindy. "To think about the last time we saw Caylee and Casey together, hear her voice, to see her little eyes and get a hug and kiss from her. It's not easy."

"We've been dealing with this almost as long as Caylee was alive, because Caylee wasn't quite 3 when this started," Cindy said. "So it seems like this nightmare has lasted longer than the moments than we had with her. That makes it very, very difficult.

"And I miss the last three years that I could have had with her, or the last two years. And then thinking about her starting school..," Cindy said before breaking into tears.

Though she maintains her daughter Casey is innocent and has "faith in the system," Cindy said that she did initially consider that Casey could have played a part in Caylee's disappearance. Acknowledging that a jury might feel the same way, Cindy said, "Anything can happen" when Casey goes to trial in the spring.

"I mean the thought did cross our mind in the very beginning. There may have been an accident," Cindy said. But Cindy said she dismissed the thought, even though Casey refused to tell her where Caylee was.

"I'm not angry about it so much as I am frustrated because I might be able to better understand why she's where she's at now. Because, I still truly believe that she is innocent," Cindy said. "There's got to be a motive there that's much greater than this whole picture."

Cindy acknowledged that her daughter lied to investigators early on, but said nothing proves she did anything more than that.

"A liar doesn't make you a murderer," she said.

"People drive from New Jersey or Wisconsin or whatever to come out and we're kind of like on the Disney route," Cindy said. "They come in and they want to see, you know, take a picture of our house or come in and say they've met us or whatever."

Cindy also backed off statements she made in a panicked 911 call in 2008 at the beginning of the case in which she said the car Casey drove smelled like "there's been a dead body in there," saying that she was only trying to get police to respond quickly.

"You can't take back anything that you say or feel at the time and I don't take it back," Cindy said. "All I know is I was desperate to get someone out to my house, desperate... When you're desperately needing something, especially when it comes to your children, you pretty much do or say whatever it takes to get help."

"I don't know where Casey was pulling stuff from, the stuff she's talking about. I have no clue," Cindy said. "It was very hurtful to George because I think for her to say that she had a dream, for her to even say that I think it was very hurtful for him."

While Caylee may be gone forever, the Anthonys described how difficult it has been for them to be away from Casey while she spends a reported 23 hours of every day in her cell.

"I miss her. I miss her too much. And I think about where she's at. She shouldn't be there," Cindy said.

The Anthonys said they rarely see their daughter for fear of the media onslaught that's sure to follow any meeting.

"We'd love to, but we've been advised by her attorneys because they will play our videos over and over again and someone will sit there and critique," Cindy said. "If she cracks a smile, if she doesn't crack a smile. If she has a tear, if she doesn't have a tear."

Even in court the Anthonys said their daughter can't look at them while under the watchful eye of television cameras and reporters.

"I just want her to stay strong, know how much I love her," she said. "I've had dreams that Casey's home. I have faith that Casey will be home."

In a rare spontaneous meeting during a court recess in March, Cindy said she was able to give Casey a Mother's Day card.

Though Caylee will not be coming home, George said he found a way to carry the toddler with him in a tattoo of the girl printed above his heart.

"Caylee's always in my mind. She's always in my heart. When I put her on my skin, she's really inside of me," George said.

He said it was desperation to see his late granddaughter that caused him to attempt suicide on Jan. 23rd, 2009.

"People thought when I tried to take my own life that that was some kind of publicity stunt or something like that. No, it wasn't," he said.

"It was because I wanted to be with Caylee... I'm still her grandfather... I'm going to experience that grandparenting again one day. I will. I will," he said.

Two weeks later on June 30th, Casey's defense attorney Andrea Lyon steps down from the case.

Jose Baez confirmed that Lyon has left the defense because of financial issues. He filed paperwork with the Orange County Clerk of Court's office reflecting Lyon's departure.

"We're sad to see her leave, but we completely understand that it's a fiscal reason," Baez said.

He said Lyon will remain "fully accessible to us if we need her at any time."

Attorney Cheney Mason, a veteran of high-profile murder cases, remains on the team, and Baez said, "You're really not going to notice any difference in the way the team operates."

Casey's defense will not be jeopardized by the departure, he said.

"She would not have left if she felt it would affect Casey. I know that," Baez said.

Casey is aware of Lyon's departure from the team and was grateful for her work, Baez said.

As for adding new members to the team as the trial approaches, Baez said, "I can't say at this time. If the need arises, yes, if it does not, no."

July & August

Casey's defense team filed a last-minute memorandum with the court late Wednesday night, July 14th, arguing the 911 calls Cindy made after learning Casey's 2-year-old daughter, Caylee, had been missing for weeks, should not be admissible during trial.

Prosecutors have claimed the calls show a progression of fabrication by Casey, but the defense argued the statements Cindy made—specifically in the final of three calls, when she reported Caylee missing were just her attempt to get law enforcement to respond faster.

In one of the 911 calls, Cindy told the dispatcher:

I found my daughter's car today, and it smells like there's been a dead body in the damn car.

The following day, July 15th, Cindy, along with Casey's brother, Lee, and Casey herself, are in an Orange County courtroom for a hearing on the memorandum. The hearing began at 2 p.m.

Cindy looks very tired and stressed in the courtroom. She seems worried. She has on no makeup...probably expects to be an emotional hearing. George is with her.

Lee's girlfriend, Mallory, is there with lee. Lee hugged his parents before sitting next to his mother. Attorney Thomas Luka is representing Lee.

Defense withdraws motion regarding Texas EquuSearch volunteer information. Judge appointed special magistrate to go with the defense during inspection of evidence. The special master will take notes, tag documents and bring any questions and copies for the judge to inspect.

Cindy is the first to be questioned on the stand. Lee is asked to step out of the courtroom as he can't be in the courtroom while Cindy is testifying.

During questioning Cindy constantly says, that she does not remember. It has been two years since she made these calls.

In cross examination, Cindy is asked if whether she would know the smell of a dead body. In previous statements, she said as a nurse, she experienced smell of dead body, rotting flesh and smell of dead tissue.

Cindy said that Casey started crying when she admitted she hadn't seen Caylee for 31 days. Cindy said that she then panicked. Cindy says she still believes Caylee is alive.

Casey is crying while Lee is on stand testifying. Lee mouthed, "I love you", which caused Casey to burst into tears. Lee was being questioned about how his mother reacted when Casey told them she hasn't seen Caylee for 31 days.

Judge Perry ruled that the frantic 911 calls Casey's mother made in 2008 will be heard by the jury.

On July 18th, Robin Lunceford, an inmate at a Florida state prison, claimed Robyn Adams and Maya Derkovic, another pen pal of Casey's, conspired to lie in court to get their own sentences reduced.

The next day, state corrections officials said Robin Lunceford is under investigation for operating a scam that involves the prison phone system.

Upon the judge's request, prosecutors provided recordings of conversations between Jose Baez and Robin Lunceford.

By the end of July the defense team filed court papers, saying Roy Kronk should have been investigated more thoroughly.

Casey's attorneys said the former Orange County meter reader has a history of "inappropriate behavior with young girls, abusing, restraining and holding women against their will.

Lawyers did not immediately reveal what they will ask Kronk, but they are expected to question him about accusations from his ex-wife, Jill Kerley, who claimed he was abusive.

Casey's attorneys claimed there is just as much circumstantial evidence against Kronk as there is against Casey.

Kronk's attorney, David Evans, said he is anxious for his client to get it done.

Evans said Kronk is still living in Orange County, but he has not been working, and has stopped volunteering with dishonorably discharged veterans.

He also added that his client has been following the case against Casey closely.

The month of August 2010 held numerous twists and turns for the entire Anthony family.

In the very first week Judge Perry denied a motion from the defense to take the death penalty off the table as they said that it was unconstitutional.

Then on August 14th, Cindy, appearing with George on the "Today" Show, called Casey a victim, and claimed there was still no connection between Caylee's remains and Casey.

At this point it seemed as though Cindy had put blinders on as to what was going around her. She seemed to totally disregard the 31 days that Casey lied to her about the whereabouts of Caylee. The fact that she lied about being out of town during that time or the fact that she had been lying all along about working at Universal and having a nanny name Zanny that took care of Caylee while Casey worked.

Many would say that is a major connection between Caylee's remains and Casey.

Then two days after they went on the "Today" show, their attorney Brad Conway announced that he will no longer be their attorney, but added it's not their fault.

"I've been in this 19 months. I've got thousands of hours of time into it. George and Cindy Anthony are good people. They deserve good counsel, Conway said. I would have stuck this out to the end if that was possible."

Instead, Conway blamed Casey's lawyer, Jose Baez.

In a statement, Conway claimed Baez provided wrong information in a court motion filed in the last week.

Conway says because he may be called as a witness, he can't represent anyone involved in the case. That includes George and Cindy.

Sources close to the case told the media Conway's resignation centers around a defense motion which says Mark NeJame, attorney for Texas EquuSearch, allowed Conway to view documents.

Apparently this would only happen if the Anthony's signed a waiver allowing NeJame to represent Texas EquuSearch.

NeJame said no such deal ever existed.

"They never even bothered calling him. They never even bothered checking in with him. If they did and they had done their homework properly and they'd done their due diligence, which they should have done, they would know there's absolutely no truth in the fact that any consideration was giving whatsoever for Mr. Conway coming in on behalf of his clients coming in to look at those documents." NeJame said.

NeJame said he allowed Conway to view the documents because it was the right thing to do.

Conway also said "George and Cindy Anthony have done nothing improper." He puts the blame on the defense not verifying facts alleged in the motion.

He added he still planned to attend court hearings in the case, and said he will continue to search for the full truth regarding the murder of Caylee.

The same week Judge Perry made a ruling that allowed Casey's defense team to examine all of the EquuSearch records.

September & October

The first 10 days of September the defense questioned a number of law enforcement officers to see if they had any information that may be helpful during Casey's trial. This questioning also included Detective Yuri Melich.

With Casey's trial coming soon the defense team added three new lawyers: Ann Finell, of Jacksonville; Dorothy Clay Sims, of Ocala; and Charles Greene, of Orlando. Attorney Jose Baez says that he is very confident that he will prevail when the case goes to trial but did ask the judge for more time to review some of the evidence.

Judge Perry announced that the trial will go for six days a week and only allow one day for the weekly break. This means that jurors in Casey's upcoming trial will be expected to listen to testimony six days a week. Some say that this is a smart move on the part of the judge so that the case can conclude that much quicker. While others say that the longer week could cause juror fatigue and affect the overall outcome of the case.

To better understand the effects of the human body decomposing in the outdoors, the case against Casey heads to Tennessee during the last week of September.

The reason for the trip is because four scientists at a so-called "Body Farm in Knoxville claimed there could have been a decomposed body in Casey's car in 2008, shortly after her daughter, Caylee, went missing.

Casey's attorneys hope to find ways to prevent the Body Farm's 41-page report from entering the court room during her trial.

The body farm has corpses left strewn across isolated woodland in the hills of Tennessee and are put there on purpose to help forensics experts better understand human decomposition. The researchers then let nature take its course, gathering vital clues from insects, the decaying bones and odors.

Nicknamed the 'body farm', the research laboratory in Knoxville provides a unique opportunity for CSI teams to replicate murder scenes in the most realistic setting possible.

The site has bodies being studied in various situations, and various stages of decomposition.

Investigators in Central Florida sent the team in Tennessee carpet and odor samples from the trunk of Casey's car.

The scientists said they believe a portion of the total odor could be human decomposition.

The "Body Farm science is fairly new, and air samples from a car trunk have never before been introduced as evidence in a murder case.

On the 28th Judge Perry ruled that the defense may conduct DNA tests on a pair of Caylee's shorts, as well as a canvas bag found at the site where the 2-year-old's body was recovered.

However, he denied the defense's request to have that testing conducted by a foreign laboratory.

Casey's lawyers had a Dutch scientist lined up to do the testing for free, but the judge ruled the evidence cannot be taken out of the country, and must be done by a scientist accredited in the United States.

Both sides did agree on another lab, National Medical Services, in Pennsylvania to conduct the DNA tests.

Casey's lawyers also spent Tuesday questioning Dr. Jan Garavaglia, the Orange-Osceola County medical examiner who performed Caylee's autopsy in 2008.

"Dr. G." as she is known from her reality TV series, ruled the death a homicide of "unknown origin".

No cause of death has since been specified in the case.

Meanwhile, Judge Perry also ruled on several other motions Tuesday, September 28th, including one granting the defense's request for more time to finish depositions of the remaining expert witnesses called by the state.

The judge has now set that deadline for seven more weeks at November 19th.

As September came to a close and October was just starting Casey's defense team said that after sorting through thousands of pages of documents belonging to the search group Texas EquuSearch, new witnesses could prove someone else killed Caylee.

While poring over thousands of documents from Texas EquuSearch, the defense is cold calling volunteers and asking where did they search and when.

"In about two-and-a-half hours, we discovered over 50 new witnesses who all the records said had not been on Suburban Drive. And they have just told us over the phone that they were," said Cheney Mason, one of Anthony's attorneys.

One of those witnesses could be key to proving the defense's theory that Caylee's body was dumped a quarter of a mile from her home "after" Casey was arrested. This would give the defense team proof that they need that someone else killed the toddler and not Casey.

The search group has long said the area where Caylee's remains were eventually found were underwater when they were in town. However, the defense is hoping to prove otherwise.

Texas EquuSearch founder Tim Miller said it's a waste of time.

"We've got some other missing person cases I need to be on," Miller said. "Of course, this is expensive again and I feel as though this is all in vain if you want to know the truth. I don't believe anything positive's going to come out of it for the defense at all.

But Casey's defense team says it has dozens of new witnesses who could help create doubt when the case goes to trial.

For the second day, Casey's defense attorneys called volunteers with Texas EquuSearch. They are looking for anyone who may have been in the area where Caylee's remains were eventually found. Jose Baez added that it's likely it wasn't the exact spot where Caylee's remains were found, but that'll be determined later when investigators follow up.

By the 5th, of October, the defense said they've made hundreds of calls and have found more than 100 people who said they searched Suburban Drive with Texas EquuSearch or on their own.

But, for the first time, the defense and the search group responded to accusations a volunteer may have made false accusations about where they searched.

"Many calls coming in people say it was underwater. We've got one person out there that says it wasn't. Well they're either lying or they have to convince more people." said Texas EquuSearch founder Tim Miller.

He said he's confident the area where Caylee was eventually found was underwater when thousands of volunteers with Texas EquuSearch combed through the east Orange County neighborhood in 2008.

But only one volunteer, however, has told the defense otherwise.

Miller wouldn't comment specifically about what the volunteer stated, but he said, "I don't think her story is over with."

The volunteer said, in a sworn statement, she searched the spot where the body was found.

Another searcher told investigators that the volunteer who made the claim tried to get him to go along with her story.

The sheriff's investigation is looking into the possibility of falsified records.

"The original form that was filled out is not in our file. Where this other one came from? I don't know. That's the investigators' job, Miller said.

"It is my understanding that she has testified under oath that she was there. Is there any evidence to contradict that yet? I haven't come across any yet, said Jose Baez.

Baez admits he hasn't looked through all the documents as of yet.

The defense called volunteers on Monday and Tuesday, looking for anyone who might have been in the area months prior to when Caylee's remains were eventually found.

The process is being done behind closed doors at the watchful eye of an appointed magistrate.

The defense called hundreds of volunteers and said they found about 150 people who said they were in the Suburban Drive area.

But, Texas EquuSearch has thousands of volunteers and the defense doesn't believe they will be able to finish calling all the volunteers by the end of the work day and has asked the judge to give them more time to review the EquuSearch documents and look for potential witnesses.

Casey's defense once again tried to get a judge to block the public from seeing who is visiting and calling her in jail, and what she's eating.

The defense wants all of Casey's jail records sealed.

A Court of Appeals in South Florida came out with a new ruling saying releasing an inmate's personal calls doesn't further the purpose of the Public Records Act.

Casey's attorneys said the release of her commissary log and phone calls served to only embarrass and invade her privacy.

Meanwhile, the Florida agency funding Anthony's defense is objecting to a number of costs her attorneys are requesting the state pay for.

The Justice Administration Commission is the agency in charge now that Casey has been declared broke.

Her attorneys are putting together a budget if the case reaches a penalty phase.

They're asking the agency to pay for a private investigator, psychiatrist and travel expenses among other things.

Next, officials from the Justice Administration Commission will ask Judge Perry to hold a hearing to discuss the other costs in more detail.

Once the issue of Casey's defense costs came to light a member of Casey's defense team stepped down from the high-profile case.

The defense filed a motion in Orange County Court, notifying the court that Linda Kenney-Baden will be withdrawing from the case.

Court documents said Kenney-Baden is stepping down not because of any issues with the case, but because the work she's been brought on board to do is done.

"As out of state counsel I have been traveling to Florida and elsewhere to properly represent Ms. Anthony," she wrote in her motion.

She added that it is her "understanding that the Justice Administration Commission prohibits payment of such costs to out of state attorneys even though they have rendered and are rendering their services free of charge."

Kenney-Baden will remain as a consultant and appear periodically throughout the trial.

A deposition was scheduled Monday October 25th, in the case against Casey; this time from lawyers representing the woman who claims Anthony ruined her life.

Attorneys for Zenaida Gonzalez are expected to question Robyn Adams, who claimed to be one of Casey's jailhouse pen pals.

Adams said Casey confided in her about several facts in the death of Caylee, including a claim that the woman she called "Zanny the Nanny" never existed.

Zenaida Gonzalez is suing for defamation, but Casey and her parents have repeatedly insisted that this Zenaida Gonzalez is not the same woman Casey said took her daughter.

The following week the prosecution released another 1,000 pages of documents pertaining to Casey's case.

2011

January & February

On January 4th, 2011, Judge Belvin Perry, Jr. postpones ruling on over two dozen defense motions to exclude evidence from the trial. Over the next several months Judge Perry rules for or against these various motions to exclude evidence.

Just two days later Jose Baez is fined $583.73 in prosecutor's attorney's fees for a "willful violation" of an earlier court order for failing to turn over expert witness discovery information to prosecutors before a certain deadline. One week later Baez pays the fine.

In the second week of February, Judge Perry ruled on several motions regarding testimony allowed in trial.

He denied a motion to ban testimony about Casey's "history of lying or stealing" and a motion to ban Casey's MySpace entries and messages from Cindy while Caylee was missing.

He partially granted a motion to ban testimony related to Casey's sexual history.

By February 21st, Jose Baez has missed yet another court deadline. This time Prosecutors said they want Jose Baez held in contempt of court over the missed deadline.

The State later dropped the motion to find Jose Baez in contempt after during a March 4th, hearing after he apologized for missing the deadline.

March & April

With the trial of Casey in the near future both the defense and the State were working hard to prepare for the trial.

In the first week of March the pretrial hearings on what evidence will be allowed in trial lasted three days, included emotional testimony from George, Cindy and Lee Anthony. Casey was visibly upset during Cindy's first testimony. Orange County Sheriff's detectives John Allen and Yuri Melich also testified during these hearings.

On March 15th, in an effort to get the Judge to throw out Casey's murder charge, Defense expert Dr. Werner Spitz said there is no scientific information indicating that Caylee was murdered, despite Dr. G ruling her cause of death as homicide.

The effort was not successful and the charge of murder remained in place.

The defense also asked that all of Casey's statements that she made to detectives before she hired an attorney be excluded from the trial. The State knew that these inconsistencies would play a major role in their case and they asked Judge Perry to allow them into evidence.

Judge Perry sided with the prosecution and allowed all of her statements to be allowed during the trial phase.

Finances for the trial were a big topic during the second week of March when court documents revealed that the cost to move Robyn Adams from a prison in Tallahassee to Orlando for the trial will be covered by Orange County taxpayers.

This revelation was followed by the Orange County court administrators revealing that they have concerns that state cuts made to county clerks of court could actually put the trial in jeopardy.

But even with the financial concerns the trial was still scheduled to proceed in less than two months.

During the final week of March the defense argued that the use of cadaver dogs was not an accurate enough science to use in trial.

Judge Perry denied the defenses argument regarding the use of a cadaver dog and in return the defense filed a motion telling the judge he got his facts wrong and were requesting a rehearing on the matter.

The judge denied the defenses motion for a rehearing.

On the 28th, the State deposed private investigator Dominic Casey on his search in November 2008, of the location where Caylee remains were discovered just one month later.

As the hearings continued on into April the defense team and the prosecutors had numerous outbursts in court over what is and is not scientific evidence, Judge Perry ruled that anymore such behavior would result in a fine of $100 per outburst, with the proceeds to go to the United Way.

With all of the antics happening inside and outside of the Orlando courtroom the case has drawn its share of media coverage that was played out all across the country.

The Orange County Clerk of Courts received a handwritten false motion from an inmate at a Michigan prison, calling for the removal of Jose Baez. The inmate claimed to be acting on Casey's behalf because she was "not competent" to file it, herself. Judge Perry denied the inmate's motion.

The final weeks of April brought forth numerous rulings on the scientific evidence in the case.

On April 21st, Judge Perry ruled that the analysis from "the body farm" of a stain in the trunk of Casey's car will be allowed in as evidence.

The following week the Judge ruled evidence of residue from a heart-shaped sticker found on duct tape near Caylee's remains, cadaver dog alerts and strands of hair from Casey's car trunk will also be allowed to be presented during the trial.

The next day Judge Perry denied a defense motion to exclude evidence of chloroform in Casey's trunk, as well as the Google searches for “chloroform” and ”how to make chloroform” on the Anthony family's home computer, from trial.

May

One of the biggest obstacles of this case was trying to find an impartial jury pool to choose from.

The decision was made to seek out the jury from outside of the Orlando area hoping to draw from a jury pool that was less likely to have seen and been influenced by the intense media coverage surrounding the case. And on May 2nd, Judge Perry told one attorney on each side in private where the jury selection will be held.

The judge said he will reveal the location to the news outlets who have signed a formal agreement on May 8th, the day before, but it cannot be publicly reported until 8 a.m. on the morning of jury selection.

Judge Perry gave the lawyers two days to object to the jury location. An appeal to the fact that the news outlets had to sign an agreement was filed with an appeals court in Daytona.

Meanwhile, George and Cindy request one last private meeting with Casey before the trial, but they do not want that meeting to be recorded and released to the public.

On May 6th, an appeals court in Daytona Beach ruled that Judge Perry is allowed to keep the site of jury selection a secret until the morning of May 9th, but he could not force members of the media to sign a confidentiality agreement to learn the location early.

The Jury selection proceedings were going to occur in a Clearwater, Florida, courthouse, about 100 miles southwest of Orlando.

They kept the site in Pinellas County location secret until Monday morning, hoping to minimize the media rush in the area from which citizens will decide Casey's fate.

Casey was privately booked into the Pinellas County Jail, in Clearwater the previous day.

Once jury selection is complete, the jurors will be transported back to Orlando for the trial, which is now scheduled to start on May 17th.

Part Six

The Trial

May 9th, 2011

JURY SELECTION

Day 1 of Casey Anthony's trial

If O.J. Simpson was the trial of the last century then Casey Anthony is the trial of this century.

Casey broke into tears as the judge read potential jurors the indictment accusing her of killing her 2-year-old daughter and then lying to law enforcement.

The major question posed by Orange County Superior Court Chief Judge Belvin Perry Jr. to the 66 jurors who came before him was whether they'd be able to remain sequestered in Orlando for up to eight weeks for the trial. More citizens will be called into court Tuesday and perhaps beyond.

"Our system of justice depends on people like you willing to serve," the judge said. "You are being asked to perform one of the highest duties of citizenship."

Perry allowed the dozens of men and women to go home for various reasons. Many cited financial hardship saying they or their family would suffer if they couldn't work for two months. Others said they had to take care of loved ones. One man said he was active-duty military, about to ship out to Alaska for his U.S. Coast Guard responsibility.

This was the first phase in the jury selection process. The other phases include asking jurors, one by one, for their take on the death penalty, which Casey would be eligible for if convicted on the murder charge.

Lastly, the jurors will be quizzed on their knowledge of the case and other positions including if they have an opinion, prior to the trial, on Casey's guilt or innocence. Throughout the selection process, Perry can weigh arguments from members of Casey's legal team and state prosecutors and decide to exclude certain men and women from the jury pool.

On May 10th Judge Perry dismissed an entire pool of 50 jurors after a former Texas EquuSearch volunteer who helped search for Caylee was summoned for jury duty and discussed the case with other jurors.

The next day the first round of jury questioning finished, with a 3-day total of 69 jurors retained.

Judge Perry held juror Jonathan Green in contempt of court for talking to a reporter about the case during a court recess. Casey was briefly escorted out of the courtroom after complaining of dizziness while the judge read the charges against her to a new jury pool.

Besides winnowing down the jury pool, Perry also issued several decisions that were all setbacks for the defense.

That included denying Casey's lawyers motion for more time to prepare for the trial, as well as questioning whether there was enough racial and ethnic diversity in the potential jury pool gathered in Clearwater.

Perhaps the most significant ruling came when, in a written order, Perry determined the jury can consider evidence about an alleged "decompositional" odor coming from Casey's trunk, and hear from certain expert witnesses. The defense had stated that the analysis was unreliable and too closely tied to the FBI, suggesting it could be prejudiced against their client.

The judge conceded that Casey's trial could be the first time the "chemical signature of the odor of human decomposition or the identity of the volatile chemical components of human decomposition" might be considered during a trial in Florida.

Still, he wrote, "The expert's testimony will assist the jury in understanding the evidence and in determining facts in the case."

On Wednesday, May 18th, after half a day in the courtroom, all has been stopped for the day and the trial is put on hold for what is being called a "private matter."

What initially was speculated as possibly being a "plea deal" accepted by Casey or a motion possibly being filed by the defense re: Judge Perry's push to get a jury sworn in on this case, it turns out to be a "private matter, nothing to do with this case" says lead defense attorney, Jose Baez.

Earlier in the day, Casey's defense team had objected to the judge's current rulings and procedures, mainly that they don't like the feeling that they are being pressured to move along with jurors.

Many think that the delay is because of Casey possibly agreeing to take a plea deal. This theory is being considered because when Casey came back into the courtroom after lunch, she was looking down as she went to the defense table. She smiled, but she was seen wiping her eyes at one point...maybe she was crying. Is that a possible sign of her accepted a plea deal? On the other hand, the feeling is that the defense, so far, was doing pretty good with the jurors that they've been getting.

Many people could not imagine that Casey, after all this time of being stoic and insisting that she was innocent, would all of a sudden accept a murder conviction deal.

And many can't see the prosecution offering a plea deal of manslaughter. They have too much evidence; it may be circumstantial evidence, but there's a lot of it.

And everyone is asking... why wasn't Jose Baez in the courtroom when they left for the day today?

The court is in recess until tomorrow morning at 8:30 a.m.

The following day glimpses of the real Casey Anthony showed up in court. As Casey was walking out of the court, for a break, she passed Jose Baez and started arguing with him, throwing her hands up as she walked by. She was moved along by the police officer (who has responsibility of watching over her in court) on out to the holding cell.

On the final day of jury selection, as Judge Perry was questioning a prospective juror about her feelings about the death penalty, a woman named Elizabeth Anne Rogers, who was sitting as a spectator in the courtroom, yelled "She killed somebody anyway!"

As the courtroom cameras panned over to see who had made this outburst, Judge Perry said something along the lines of "Escort this person out of the courtroom and hold her for me." As the cameras found the person in question, we saw this woman being quickly escorted out by Sheriff's deputies. As she was being led out, she apologized "I'm so sorry."

After the woman was out of the courtroom, and after the juror who was being questioned was also out of the courtroom, Defense attorney, Cheney Mason, stood up and objected to the juror being allowed to move forward in the questioning, since she had witnessed this woman's outburst. Judge Perry called a brief recess, saying that he wanted to research "something".

When the court came back from recess, Judge Perry asked Court Deputies to bring the woman, who had made the outburst, back into the courtroom. As the cameras were focused on the door to the holding cell, in came the 30 year old woman, who was visibly shaken. She looked pitiful and was sobbing.

When Judge Perry asked her what her defense was, and why he shouldn't automatically sentence her for "Criminal Contempt of Court", she apologized, saying "I'm so sorry", continuing, in between sobs, that she was diagnosed as being bi-polar, suffers from post-traumatic stress disorder, takes a number of medications and was also on methadone.

She continued that she was in the courthouse (at Courtroom (R)) for her fiancée's trial for domestic abuse. After answering Judge Perry asked her when she last took her medication, she stated that she last took medication this morning at 6 a.m. Continuing to sob in between her statements, she begged Judge Perry to not punish her, saying that she was a sick woman, she's "not a bad person".

He asked her if she worked. She answered yes, that she volunteered at the SPCA. However, her sole income was state disability benefits for her mental illness.

Taking all that in, but still being quite mad, Judge Perry stated that her outburst was a grave action during a serious criminal case, and that after two long weeks they were in the final stages of selecting a jury.

He continued by saying that because of her outburst, the defense was now requesting that the juror being questioned at the time of her outburst, be dismissed for cause. He found her guilty of "Contempt of Court". He continued by saying that the sentence should be 179 days in jail. However, he would take into consideration her condition, but also considering the gravity of the situation and that he was probably going to lose a juror, he then reduced her sentence to two days in jail.

She asked if she could turn herself in later on in the evening. The judge denied her request; Judge Perry informed her that a public defender would be assigned to her case, since she qualifies for one due to the fact that she stated to him that she doesn't have at least $2,500 in any assets. Then the juror who was being questioned was excused, due to the woman's outburst.

Jury selection took longer than expected and ended on Thursday May 20th, with twelve jurors and five alternates being sworn in. The panel consisted of nine women and eight men.

May 24th, 2011

Finally after nearly three years of legal twists, turns and delays the trial of Casey Anthony finally began on May 24th, 2011 the case of the State of Florida v Casey Marie Anthony opens in Court 23A at the Orange County Courthouse, Orlando, Florida.

Prospective spectators waited in a line outside the courthouse, some since 5 a.m., hoping to get a seat ticket inside the courtroom. When everyone finally got into the courtroom, they saw Cindy and George seated in the back of the courtroom.

George sat down and held an open bible on his lap; Cindy held a brown teddy bear on her lap. Concerned about possibly tainting the jury, court deputies spoke to Cindy about the teddy bear, but they let her keep the bear when she agreed to keep it down so that jurors would not see it.

The lead prosecutor in the case was Assistant State Attorney Linda Drane Burdick. Assistant State Attorneys Frank George and Jeff Ashton completed the prosecution team. Lead counsel for the defense was Jose Baez, a Florida criminal defense attorney who was yet unproven as a defense lawyer. Attorneys J. Cheney Mason, Dorothy Clay Sims, and Ann Finnell served as co-counsel.During the trial, attorney Mark Lippman represented George and Cindy Anthony.

Typically the trial has a defense table and on the opposite side is the prosecutors table. And normally they both face the judge.

But in Casey's trial, Attorney Mason told the court administrator that he wanted the jury to be able to see Casey and he wanted her to be able to see them rather than being at an angle.

This turned out to be a brilliant move by the defense because the jurors were facing Casey the whole time.

While the jurors were in the courtroom she portrayed herself as innocent and rather naive. She would sit there nice and proper.

They also made the decision to sit her in a lower chair so she looked smaller and came across as a petit innocent woman. They also dressed her in clothes that she would never normally wear. She wore little dowdy blouses and her hair was pulled back. She looked more like an innocent soccer mom rather than a child killer that the state wanted to paint her as.

But the one thing that no one ever thought was that she was nervous or scared. Many people say that she never looked as though she was in fear of a conviction.

PROSECUTION OPENING STATEMENTS

Immediately after the jury entered the courtroom, prosecution attorney, Linda Drane Burdick got up and began her opening statements. She started by telling the jury that the focus of this trial, although it is against Casey Anthony, still needs to remember that there is a victim in this case, two year old Caylee Anthony. She continued by telling how Caylee, up until her death, had led a seemingly idyllic life. Caylee was a happy little girl who lived at her grandparents' home, "in Orlando on a street called Hopespring Drive". Then Linda began talking about how Casey lied and lied and lied, for 31 days, to her parents, her friends and the police, about where little Caylee was. She lied about working at Universal Studios. Linda then told of how Cindy frantically called the police, saying that "it smells like there's been a dead body in the damn car".

Linda then talked about what happened during the 31 days that Caylee was missing. How Casey entered a "hot body" contest at a nightclub called Fusion. She then spoke about the forensics in this case, the hair found in Casey's car trunk that had banding on it that can only come from a decomposing body.

How cadaver dogs "hit" on Casey's car trunk and in her parents' backyard. And then came in the computer searches found on the desktop computer that was in the home of Casey, that included "Chloroform, neck breaking, acetone, shovel, self-defense, how to make chloroform". She stressed that only Casey was home at the time of all the searches.

During the prosecution's opening statements, Casey shook her head several times. She cried a little bit at the beginning, but most of the time, as Linda explained the prosecution's theory of how only Casey could be the one responsible for the death of Caylee. Since Casey and the defense team are seated directly across from the jury box, the jurors could see her shake her head, with a sad look on her face, seemingly saying that what the prosecution was saying was incorrect.

At the end of her opening statement, photos of Caylee alive, and the last picture taken of Caylee, her skull, were shown to the jury, side by side.

DEFENSE OPENING STATEMENTS

When it came time for Jose Baez to give his opening statement he just yanked the rug right out from under them.

He started by saying that everyone wants to know what happened. How in the world can a mother wait 30 days before ever reporting her child missing?

He said that the answer was relatively simple, she never was missing.

He told the jury that Caylee died on June 16th, 2008 when she drowned in her family's swimming pool.

He said that Caylee loved to swim and she could get out of the house and into the backyard where the pool was located.

He said that she was found by George. She immediately grabbed Caylee and held her in her arms and immediately began to "cry and cry and cry."

He said that shortly after that George began to yell at Casey screaming, "Look what you done! Your mother will never forgive you! And you will go to jail for child neglect for the rest of your frigging life!"

He told Casey that she would spend the rest of her life in jail for child neglect. Then he told the jury that it was George who proceeded to cover up Caylee's death.

He was basically telling the jury that Caylee was never murdered. It was just an accident.

He totally changed the manner of death from homicide to accident.

This revelation totally shocked the media. It however did not shock the prosecution or the Anthonys as he already informed them that this was where he planned on going with his defense strategy.

Baez says that this is why Casey went on with her life and failed to report the death for 31 days. He also told the jury that it was the habit of a lifetime for Casey to hide her pain and pretend that nothing was wrong.

It was his next statement that turned the entire trial into a new direction.

He told the jury that this habit of a lifetime for Casey to hide her pain and pretend that nothing was wrong was because she had been sexually abused by her father since she was eight years old.

He said, "At 13 years old she could have her father's penis in her mouth and then go to school and play with the other kids and act as if nothing had ever happened."

The defense wanted to shift the blame from Casey to George. They wanted him to become the bad guy, and get the attention off of Casey.

And George was an easy fall guy because he admitted that he was one of the last people to see Caylee alive. And all of the evidence that they found at the dump site was tied to the Anthony's home so that played into the defense strategy of focusing the blame on George.

He also said that her brother Lee also had made advances toward her.

Prior to the trial, Baez said he and Co-counsel Cheney Mason had George come to their office and told George that Casey claimed he abused her. Baez said George "sat for perhaps 40 seconds with his head bowed. He didn't say a word. We certainly noted that he didn't deny it. Cheney and I looked at each other in wonderment."

Baez recalled that George finally said "Oh my God."

If this wasn't enough to get the jury's attention, Baez also questioned whether Roy Kronk, the meter reader who found Caylee's bones, had actually removed them from another location and placed them in the area where they were ultimately found.

He also claims that the police department's investigation was compromised by their desire to feed a media frenzy about a child's murder, rather than a more mundane drowning. That somehow the police wanted this to be a major crime of murder rather than a mere accident.

He also admitted to the jury that Casey had lied about there being a nanny who kidnapped Caylee named Zenaida Fernandez-Gonzales.

Prosecutors called George as their first witness, and, in a response to their question, he denied having sexually abused his daughter and he said that he had nothing to do with disposing of Caylee's remains.

The defense questioned George about a family pet dog that they had when they lived on Ohio. They asked George how the dog was buried after it had passed away.

He said that they buried the dog in their yard where they used to live at. He said that they would place their dead pets in bags and wrap them with duct tape. The defense was trying to show that the family pets were disposed of in the same manner that Caylee was disposed of in that swamp.

He also testified that he did not smell anything resembling human decomposition in Casey's car when she visited him on June 24th,but he did smell something similar to human decomposition when he picked the car up on July 15th.

They also discussed the suicide attempt by George after Caylee was found. The defense tried to say that George couldn't take the heat and that the guilt had gotten to him.

The next day, May 25th, the prosecution calls various friends of Casey who testify about her fabricated stories during June and July 2008 of having a job and employing a nanny for Caylee. The Anthony's neighbor testifies that in mid-June 2008 Casey borrowed a shovel from him to dig up a bamboo root.

After the opening statement of Jose Baez, Roy Kronk issues a statement through his attorney denying any involvement in the disappearance of Caylee.

STATEMENT ON BEHALF OF ROY KRONK

Yesterday the Casey Anthony defense team, in its opening statement, suggested that Roy Kronk was somehow involved in the placement and disposition of the remains of Caylee Anthony. This defense theory regarding Mr. Kronk is completely false. The suggestion that Mr. Kronk took possession of Caylee's remains is totally lacking in logic or explanation. It did not happen.

Roy Kronk is and remains a private citizen whose sole connection to the Anthony case is that he, among all those searching, located the remains of Caylee Anthony and immediately, and repeatedly, reported his find to local law enforcement. He has provided sworn statements to law enforcement, a sworn deposition to the defense, and will provide sworn testimony at trial. He has been truthful throughout.

In their unrelenting search to conjure up villains to deflect attention from Casey Anthony, the defense team has tried repeatedly to cast Roy Kronk in the role of bad guy, even to the extent of making statements about him on national television that they knew to be false.

As he has done from the outset, Mr. Kronk will hold his head high and continue to speak the truth about what he found and will trust in the judicial system to reach a just result in this case.

David L. Evans

Attorney for Roy Kronk

Week 1

George was the first witness called after Baez's opening argument. He denied the molestation and any knowledge of the alleged drowning.

He said it was an accident to which Casey's father, George, was familiar with. Baez said George tried to cover up the drowning at Casey's expense.

As week one of the trial comes to a close, capped off Saturday by the compelling testimony of Casey's mother, Cindy, an outsider to the case can only speculate if the jurors feel the truth is coming into focus.

The prosecution team has brought in witnesses ranging from ex-boyfriends to women who partied with Casey. But even those who knew her best seemed to be describing two very different people.

When asked by prosecutors if Casey's behavior changed after June 16, 2008, the date on which Caylee was last seen, witnesses including Lazzaro and his roommates, who spent time with her during the 31 days, said Casey was her usual self. They said she was friendly and upbeat, never mentioning that her daughter was missing and making excuses for the toddler's whereabouts.

When pressed by Baez, the same witnesses affirmed Casey was a good mom with a strong bond with her daughter. In fact, during Friday's testimony, Mallory Parker, the fiancée of Casey's brother Lee, broke down on the stand as she described the relationship between Casey and Caylee as "amazing."

All this was topped off with the compelling testimony of George and Cindy.

George has been brought to the witness stand on three days, on Friday recounting the day he retrieved Casey's abandoned car from an Orlando tow yard. When pressed by Assistant State Attorney Jeff

Ashton, the former police officer said the odor that came from his daughter's car smelled like a human corpse.

The odor was so powerful, George said he could not drive it home from the impound lot where it had been towed two weeks before without rolling down the windows, he said.

"I did worry for my daughter and granddaughter," George testified, noting that he had not seen Casey or Caylee since June 24th. "I didn't want to believe what I was smelling."

The defense pointed out—and George admitted—that he did not call police after noticing the smell, nor did he tell authorities about his concerns.

"Looking back, sir, there's a lot of things I wish I would have done," George said, after being pressed by defense attorney Jose Baez as to why he didn't contact police immediately.

Casey's white Pontiac Sunfire took center stage in the fourth day of trial.

It was towed by a wrecker service to an impound lot on June 30th and remained there for about two weeks, the wrecker service's operations manager, Simon Birch, told jurors.

Closed up, the car gave off the faint smell of human decomposition, Birch testified.

"It's a very, very unique and distinctive smell," Birch said, noting that he has had the misfortune of coming into contact with decomposition in cars numerous times.

Birch said the smell became more noticeable after George and his wife arrived to pick up the car and they opened first the door and then the trunk.

George recalled his mind racing with concern for his daughter, whom he had believed was in Jacksonville, Florida, with the car, and his granddaughter, whom he had not seen in nearly a month.

"Please God," he recalled thinking as he prepared to open the trunk, "don't let this be Casey or Caylee."

The smell did not seem to dissipate after they removed a lightly-filed garbage bag from the trunk, Birch said.

But after being called back to the stand later Friday, George said he did not notice the stench was stronger after he opened the trunk and removed garbage from the trunk.

In response to a question from Baez implying he was somehow trying to distance himself from evidence in a potential crime, George said, "I would not have walked away ... from something. That's not in my make-up. ... I believe I'm a pretty good guy."

Before challenging George, Baez questioned why Birch never called police, even after learning the car had been towed by authorities for forensic analysis.

"I had no idea why it was towed to forensics," Birch said.

William Waters, a friend of Casey's who testified that he went shopping with her on July 5th, testified that she had a friend's car at the time. He said she explained that she did not have her own because it needed an alignment or a tune-up.

The car also figured in testimony Thursday, when George testified about an argument he had with his daughter over two missing gas cans from the storage shed at his house.

On June 24th, George called police to report the break-in and report the gas cans missing. He testified that he saw his daughter later in the day and argued with her about the missing cans. He had a hunch she had them, he testified, as she had taken them before.

George said that when he went to get them out of his daughter's car, she bristled, brushed past him, quickly opened the trunk and retrieved the gas cans. Then she threw them down and told him, "Here's your fucking gas cans."

The cans are significant because duct tape on them appears to be the same as that found on the mouth of Caylee's skeletal remains, which were found six months after the child went missing. The type of tape, prosecutor Linda Drane Burdick told jurors in her opening statement this week, is relatively rare.

George said that when his daughter returned the gas cans to him, there was no tape on them. He said he had put the tape on to replace a missing vent cap.

In earlier testimony, prosecutors displayed evidence and questioned witnesses suggesting that Casey seemed unburdened in the days after her daughter disappeared—attending a party and going shopping for furniture, clothes and beer.

Jurors saw silent surveillance videos of Casey shopping at Target, Ikea and other stores in the days following her daughter's disappearance.

The videos were shown over the objection of defense attorneys, who said they were irrelevant to the charges against her and could improperly impeach her character and state of mind in the eyes of the jury.

They also heard Waters testify that Casey attended an Independence Day party at his house on July 4th, 2008, about two weeks after Caylee was last seen and that the two also went shopping the next day. She gave no indication that anything was wrong either time and only briefly mentioned her daughter, Waters testified.

Waters' testimony was similar to statements Thursday from numerous witnesses who said Casey did not mention her daughter's disappearance until her mother, Cindy, reported the girl's absence to police on July 15th.

Among the witnesses was a former boyfriend, Ricardo Morales, who said Casey was "happy, smiling" during his encounters with her in July.

Another friend, Matthew Crisp, testified that he met Casey for lunch on July 7th and asked about Caylee. Casey told him that

Caylee was "on a play date with one of her girlfriends who also had a child."

Another former boyfriend, Anthony Lazzaro, and his roommates said that when they asked where Caylee was, Casey told them she was with her nanny, mentioning that the nanny was taking her to Universal Studios and to the beach.

In cross-examination by lead defense attorney Jose Baez, those who saw Casey and her daughter together testified that Caylee was well taken care of and that Casey, at least to their knowledge, appeared to be a good mother.

In a dramatic moment Friday morning, Mallory Parker, the fiancée of Casey's brother broke down when asked to describe Casey's relationship with her daughter.

She described the relationship as "amazing."

"Casey and Caylee had a very special bond," Mallory said with a quivering voice while under cross-examination by Casey's lead attorney, Jose Baez.

Casey appeared to cry as Mallory spoke.

On Saturday, May 28th, Cindy gave jurors in her daughter's capital murder trial a detailed glimpse of her efforts to connect with the 2-year-old girl in the weeks following her disappearance, recounting reason after reason her daughter gave for keeping the toddler away from home for nearly a month.

The reasons included work meetings, a car accident and sudden plans to hang out at a hotel with a wealthy suitor Cindy said she had long heard about, but had never met.

Testimony from Cindy dominated the Saturday court session, which ended just before 1 p.m.

After describing her last day with Caylee, spent visiting the girl's ailing great-grandfather in a nursing home, swimming at home and then looking at pictures and videos, Cindy testified about her efforts to talk to Caylee between June 16th, the next day, and July 15th, when she was finally reported missing to police.

"There was always a reason I missed her," Cindy said.

At first, Cindy said, she believed Caylee was staying with her nanny, Zanny, while her daughter attended work meetings. Then, Casey told her mother that she was taking the girl to Tampa, Florida, for an outing with a co-worker and her child.

Cindy testified that when they didn't return as expected her daughter told her a serious car accident had left Zanny injured, and that she felt obligated to stay and care for her.

When her father, George, ran into her at home on June 24th, when she was supposed to be nearly 80 miles away in Tampa, Casey explained she had returned to get insurance information for Zanny and get some things from home, Cindy testified.

When asked why she didn't bring her daughter home, Casey said she "didn't think about it," her mother testified.

After that, Casey told her mother that she, Caylee and Zanny were staying at an Orlando hotel with a wealthy suitor, according to Cindy's testimony. When she failed to return home as expected, Casey then explained the delay by saying she was working on a closed Make-A-Wish event that Caylee could attend, but Cindy could not.

Cindy testified she went to Universal Studios where she believed her daughter worked to confront her over a money issue. That's when Casey told her she wasn't in Orlando, but rather in Jacksonville, Florida at the suitor's condo.

Cindy broke down on the stand early in her testimony, while looking at pictures of Caylee's Winnie the Pooh-themed bed, depictions of her backyard playhouse and an image of her visiting the nursing home. At one point, she interrupted prosecutor Linda Drane Burdick's questioning to ask that Caylee's image be taken off a computer screen in front of her.

"I'm trying not to cry," she said.

During a break following testimony in which Cindy was discussing how she and her husband, George, bought and installed an outside playhouse for Caylee, Casey could be seen crying and gesturing angrily as she spoke with her attorneys.

If the jurors are looking for answers in Casey's face, they may come away empty-handed. While Casey has broken down in court on several occasions, particularly when the subject turns to her relationship with Caylee, she is often not showing any feelings as she hears the recollections of the men and women who once made up her life.

On Saturday, Casey was essentially stone-faced until a court recess in the middle of her mother's testimony. Then Casey was seen sobbing and speaking passionately to her attorneys. The defendant regained composure when her mother retook the stand.

While many questions remain, weeks lie ahead in the trial, so there is hope for a clearer picture of Casey and those 31 days. Court will resume on Tuesday with the continuation of Cindy's testimony.

Week 2

When court resumed on Tuesday, May 31st, the jurors had a front-row seat this week to the vivid yet imaginary world that Casey created in the weeks after Caylee disappeared in 2008.

The jury heard detailed stories from her mother, her brother and finally, Casey herself, of her business trips to Tampa and visits to an old flame that later proved to be false. Through recordings of Casey's police interviews, jailhouse visits and a 9-1-1 call, the silent woman at the defense table finally spoke.

Throughout the conversations, one sentiment is conveyed to Casey again and again: *Stop lying, or face the worst of consequences.*

In a July 16th, 2008, police interview, which the jury heard Thursday, Orange County Sheriff's Sgt. John Allen told Casey, "the time had come to reveal the truth."

"By burying this ... you are not going to get yourself to a better place, OK," Allen said. "What you're going to do is you're going to cause everybody else around you to suffer. And at some point this is going to come out; it always does."

In jail visits with her brother and parents following her arrest, Casey alternately cries, giggles, expresses love to her family and insists her sole focus is finding Caylee, according to tapes of those visits played for jurors

"If you can speak to the media directly, my concern for me is Caylee," a tearful Casey tells her brother, Lee, on July 25th, 2008, from an Orange County, Florida, jail. "No one has said for me that I love my daughter, that I want her safety and that she and the rest of my family is my only concern. All I want is to see her again, to hear her laugh, to see her smile and to just be with our family. Nothing else matters to me at this point."

The same day, Casey's mother, Cindy, asks her during a visit, "Are you protecting Caylee? Are you protecting me?"

"I'm protecting our family, yes," Casey replies. "Not from anything I've done."

"Is someone threatening us?" Cindy asks, she then asks again after receiving no answer.

"Just leave it at that, please." her crying daughter replies, adding that she will write her and elaborate in more detail.

Asked during the visit what Casey wants her mother to give the media as a message to Caylee, Casey breaks down as she says to tell her daughter, "that Mommy loves her very much, and she's the most important thing in this entire world to me, and to be brave. I truly, truly love that little girl, and miss her so much."

"I know in my heart, I know in my gut, I know with every ounce of my being that we will be with (Caylee) again," she tells Lee during a July 28th visit.

Casey gives her family information on places to look for Caylee and shares information in an effort to track down a person named Zenaida Fernandez-Gonzalez, saying she was a nanny who kidnapped the little girl.

After the playing of the first taped conversation between Casey and Lee, Baez moved for a mistrial, saying it had damaged his credibility in the eyes of the jury. In the conversation, Lee tells his sister that Baez might not pass along messages or information to her if he deemed it not in her best interest.

Judge Perry denied that motion, saying Baez should have risen the issue months ago.

Earlier, jurors heard a tape of a police interview in which, under intense questioning, Casey admits she had purposely misled investigators attempting to find Caylee, but maintains the little girl was kidnapped by Gonzalez.

The interview with an Orange County sheriff's sergeant and two detectives was conducted July 16th, 2008, in a conference room at Universal Studios. It came after the officers had accompanied Casey there, only to have her confess that, despite her previous claims to the contrary, she no longer worked there.

In the interview, investigators pleaded with Casey to tell the truth about what happened to Caylee.

"None of us are sitting here believing what you're saying because everything that's coming out of your mouth is a lie," Detective Yuri Melich told Casey during the interview. "Everything. And unless we start getting the truth, we're going to announce two possibilities with Caylee: Either you gave Caylee to someone that you don't want anyone to find out because you think you're a bad mom. Or something happened to Caylee and Caylee's buried somewhere or in a trash can somewhere, and you had something to do with it. Either way, right now it's not a very pretty picture to be painting."

Asked later whether Gonzalez accepted money, Casey said, "I would not have sold my daughter. If I wanted to really just get rid of her, I would have left her with my parents and I would've left. I would've moved out. I would've given my mom custody."

"Did you ever locate the Zenaida Fernandez-Gonzalez that Ms. Anthony described to you?" prosecutor Linda Drane Burdick asked Melich, who took the stand Wednesday. "No, I did not," Melich answered.

On cross-examination, Baez expressed skepticism that Melich did not suspect Casey at that point of foul play in Caylee's disappearance. Melich said he did not, although he knew that Casey had lied, and "I couldn't understand why the mother of a missing child would go to (this) extent if we're just trying to find her child."

But, he said, Casey was "adamant" that she was telling the truth about Gonzalez the nanny kidnapping her daughter.

Earlier, prosecutors set about debunking Casey's previous statements to her friends and family, presenting testimony that she never had a wealthy suitor named Jeffrey Michael Hopkins and she had not worked at Universal Studios since 2006, despite years of claims to the contrary.

A man named Jeff Hopkins testified that while he knew Casey from middle school, her claims of dating him and him introducing her to Gonzalez were fabrications. Hopkins said his name wasn't even Jeffrey Michael Hopkins, the name Anthony had given as a wealthy suitor living in Jacksonville, Florida, with a son named Zachary.

Hopkins testified that he had no children and described Casey as an acquaintance. He said he has never lived in Jacksonville and that while he once worked at Universal Studios, he was not there at the same time as Casey.

Asked by Baez whether all of Casey's stories were "one great fiction," Hopkins said, "Yeah, that's correct."

Following Hopkins to the stand was Leonard Turtora, assistant manager of loss prevention at Universal Studios. Turtora testified that after he was contacted by authorities investigating Caylee's disappearance, he searched the Universal Studios database and found Casey had not worked there since 2006 and even then worked for a third party, Colorvision, that operated on Universal property.

According to testimony, Casey claimed to work as an event planner at Universal Studios until after Caylee was reported missing.

She was forced to own up to the lie after detectives brought her to Universal Studios and met Turtora there. She directed them to a building Turtora said he knew was not an events building.

"Melich began to look around and asked if we were in the events building," Turtora said. "Ms. Anthony looked at me, put her hands in her back pocket and stated, 'I don't work here.'"

The name Juliette Lewis, given by Casey as another co-worker, also was not found in the database, nor was a Zenaida Gonzalez. Casey had told authorities after Caylee went missing that Gonzalez had a seasonal ID for Universal but was working only as a nanny.

Melich was called back to the stand to testify. He had testified about a written statement from Casey and an interview he conducted with her in the early morning hours of July 16th, just after Caylee was reported missing. A recording of that interview was played for jurors Wednesday.

Asked whom she had told about the kidnapping, which supposedly had occurred 31 days earlier, Casey said in the interview she had told no one besides Hopkins and Lewis. Asked for their phone numbers, Casey told Melich she didn't have them at present but could find them.

Asked by Melich during the interview why she hadn't notified authorities for the 31 days Caylee had been missing, Casey said, "I think part of me was naive enough to think that I could handle this myself, which obviously I couldn't. And I was scared that something would happen to her if I did notify the authorities or got the media involved, or my parents, which I know would have done the same thing. Just the fear of the unknown. Fear of the potential of Caylee getting hurt, of not seeing my daughter again."

After the jury left for the day, prosecutors told Perry that defense attorneys had just notified them of a new expert witness. Perry said the potential witness, Dr. Sally Karioth, should prepare a report, as all expert witnesses must, and outline what she will testify about. He said he would rule later on whether to allow the witness to testify.

In the following days, Gonzalez's alleged role would expand from an occasionally mentioned nanny to a central character in Caylee's disappearance. When initially questioned by Orange County Detective Yuri Melich on July 16th, 2008, about Gonzalez,

Casey provided a description of her without hesitation. That interview was played to the jury on Wednesday.

Casey said she'd known Zanny for four years after they met working together at Universal Studios. She provided a physical description of Gonzalez, her address, even her mother's name.

Other characters were also fleshed out. Hopkins, a former Universal Studios co-worker, according to Casey, lived in Jacksonville and had a son named Zachary who played with Caylee.

And then there was Juliette Lewis, another co-worker at Universal, who now lived in New York, Casey said. She also had a daughter Caylee's age.

Casey claimed she called Lewis and Hopkins when she realized Caylee was missing. But prosecutors claim Casey was not looking for her daughter in the month she was missing.

Casey frustration level with her parents, particularly her mother, was rising around the time her 2-year-old daughter disappeared, for reasons including that her mother was increasingly unable to watch the child so Casey could hang out with her friends, one of those friends testified.

Amy Huizenga told jurors in Casey's trial that the two previously were close friends and that Casey complained frequently about her parents, particularly her mother. Casey's relationship with her mother was "strained. It was hard. Her mom was continually agitated with her," Huizenga said. "I remember she told me her mom had told her she was an unfit mother. She was extremely upset about that."

But Casey was agitated at her mother as well, as she had to cancel plans "fairly frequently" because she had no one to watch her daughter, Huizenga testified. It was happening more frequently during the spring of 2008, Huizenga said, and the "frustration was greater."

In late June, Casey told her that she was keeping Caylee away from her parents, as they were having marital problems and were considering divorce, and "she wanted to keep Caylee out of the drama."

But actually, by late June, Caylee was missing.

Earlier, jurors heard an obscenity-strewn phone conversation Casey made from jail just after her arrest, in which she lamented that no one was listening to her, denied knowing what had happened to Caylee and said authorities weren't trying hard enough to find the nanny she claimed had kidnapped the child.

Also Tuesday, jurors heard a recording of the call made to her parents' home on July 16, 2008; the day after Caylee was reported missing.

In the call, Casey speaks to her mother, her brother and her friend Kristina Chester. She asks her brother to give her the phone number of her then-boyfriend, Tony Lazzaro.

A tearful Chester tries to get answers out of Casey regarding Caylee's whereabouts. The child had last been seen June 16, a month earlier.

"I got arrested on a fucking whim today," Casey tells Chester on the call, "because they're blaming me for stuff that I would never do, that I didn't do.

"They're twisting stuff," Casey says. "They've already said they're going to pin this on me if they don't find Caylee. They've already said that."

"Casey," Chester says later in the call. "Your daughter, your flesh and blood, your baby." But Casey cuts her off, saying, "Put my brother back on the phone. I don't want to get into this with you. ... I haven't slept in four days."

Asked by Chester during the call why she isn't crying and upset, Casey said on the recording, "I have to stay composed to talk to detectives. ... I can't sit here and be crying every two seconds like I want to."

Jurors also heard a call to the Orange County, Florida, Sheriff's Office made July 15th by a hysterical Cindy, reporting her granddaughter missing. The call was made, Cindy testified, after her daughter told her she had not seen Caylee for weeks.

She testified that she made her 9-1-1 call, her third to police that day, after she and her son, Lee, had confronted Casey, who admitted that Caylee had been missing for a month and that she believed the nanny, who she identified as Zenaida Fernandez-Gonzalez, had kidnapped her.

"My daughter's been missing for 31 days," Casey tells the dispatcher on the recording after her mother put her on the phone. "I know who has her. I've tried to contact her. I actually received a phone call today. I got to speak to my daughter for about a minute."

"Why didn't you call 31 days ago?" the Orange County sheriff's dispatcher asks on the recording.

"I've been looking for her," Casey replied, "and have gone through other resources to find her, which was stupid."

As the call to 9-1-1 call was played, Cindy put her head down on the witness stand and sobbed.

Told by Chester in the phone call that authorities can't find Gonzalez, Casey says, "Nobody's fucking listening to anything I'm saying. ... They can't find her in the Florida database (of driver's licenses). She's not just from Florida."

Under cross-examination, Cindy testified that her daughter was a good mother to Caylee.

"Casey was a very loving, very caring mother," she said. "She had a very easy, very quick maternal instinct that was very evident as soon as Caylee was born. She reminded me of myself when my kids were born, and just how natural she was with Caylee."

The little girl adored her mother, she testified, and followed her nearly everywhere. As Cindy testified, Casey smiled and wiped her eyes.

Cindy also testified that her daughter had been telling her about Gonzalez along with numerous other people, a boyfriend, a co-worker and a man named Eric Baker, whom she believed to be Caylee's father for years before Caylee went missing. At the time, she said, she never had a reason to believe those people were fictitious. "I just found out they were imaginary people," she testified.

She said her and her husband's efforts to find Gonzalez had continued up to six weeks before the trial started, taking them to places including New York and California.

Earlier, Cindy testified that on July 15th, George picked up a certified letter from a tow yard, which said that Casey's Pontiac Sunfire, registered to her parents, had been there for a couple of weeks.

Cindy testified that her daughter had told her that the car was with her in Jacksonville, Florida, and she called her and told her "she had a lot of explaining to do." She asked her to come home.

After George drove the car home from the wrecker yard, Cindy, a nurse, said she smelled the car and asked, "What died?" She testified that she knows what human decomposition smells like but said it was just an expression and that she didn't really believe someone had died or a body had decomposed in the car. She said that at the time, she was satisfied that the smell was some garbage her husband said he found in the trunk.

But "the smell in the car was like something I had never, it was pretty strong," she said.

After her husband left for work, Cindy said, she retrieved her daughter's purse from the car, along with a doll. She broke into tears as she described finding the doll in Caylee's car seat, "like it was sitting where Caylee would have sat."

She tearfully recalled putting the doll on an ice chest in the garage and wiping its face and hands with a disinfecting wipe, then spraying its body and the interior of the car with Febreze, a commercial substance that helps eliminate odor. She said she also put a dryer sheet in the car.

She acknowledged telling authorities in her frantic 9-1-1 call that her daughter's car smelled "like there's been a body" but told Baez she said that in an effort to get deputies to arrive faster.

Cindy also testified that her description of Casey's car smelling "like someone died" was just a "figure of speech."

Cindy testified that her daughter was not answering her phone after the car was picked up July 15th, so she contacted Huizenga, picking her up at a mall and asking her to take her to her daughter. She was directed to Lazzaro's apartment.

On the stand, Amy Huizenga recalled the tense confrontation that followed. Cindy was demanding to see Caylee, she recalled, and Casey said she was with her nanny.

It was "a massive explosion of mother and daughter," Huizenga said.

Under cross-examination, Cindy testified that she and her granddaughter swam together on June 15th, the day before Caylee was last seen. Asked whether she was certain she had removed the ladder from the above-ground pool, she said, "as certain as I can be. I do recall taking the ladder down."

But she acknowledged mentioning to a co-worker the next day that she thought someone had been swimming in her pool, as she had found the ladder up and the gate open.

The case has drawn attention across the nation and beyond. On Tuesday morning, about 250 people were standing in line for a seat in the courtroom, a record so far. Sixty of them were seated, more than the usual 48, as fewer media were attending.

As week two concludes, it now appears Allen was right in his prediction that Casey's stories ultimately would lead to suffering for others. However, it is yet to be seen whether the second part of his prophecy will be realized: that the truth will come out.

Week 3

Potential jurors in Casey's first-degree murder trial were asked during jury selection in May if they could look at the remains of a victim as simply evidence and not let their emotions sway them one way or the other.

This week, jurors were put to the test.

Week 3 of the trial began with forensic testimony about how someone searched for "chloroform" and "neck-breaking" on the computer in the home Casey shared with her parents in Orange County. By Thursday, panelists were fully immersed in the physical reality of the 2-year-old's death: bones, decomposition, odor and all.

The prosecution called key forensic witnesses, who described in graphic detail, the state of Caylee's remains when she was found in a wooded area on Dec. 11th, 2008, six months after she went missing.

"This is the skull with the hair and tape along with some leaf litter and other debris that was received at the same time as the other specimens," Orange County Chief Deputy Medical Examiner Dr. Gary Utz said as he described a photo of Caylee's remains.

Jurors saw images of the tiny, decaying shorts and Winnie the Pooh blanket found with Caylee's remains. Animals had chewed up Caylee's bones by the time law enforcement discovered them, according to testimony.

At times, the typically stone-faced defendant bowed her head and tried to avoid looking at graphic images of her daughter's remains.

The trial ended an hour and a half early Thursday, with Orange County Chief Judge Belvin Perry Jr. telling members of the media in the courtroom that Casey was ill.

Jurors were not told why the trial ended early Thursday, and Perry asked them not to speculate. He said court would be in recess until Friday.

After the jurors left, Perry spoke to members of the media in the courtroom, saying that Casey was ill and that neither the prosecution nor the defense had any comment on the matter. The judge asked reporters not to question either side about it. The details of Casey 's illness were not given.

During a short break before the announcement, Casey drank a bottle of water quietly as attorneys spoke together and went back to Perry's chambers. She was escorted out of the courtroom during the break, and then brought back in, but lay her head down on her arms at the defense table. She did not stand as the jurors left the courtroom.

In a statement released Thursday evening, Orange County Jail spokesman, Allen Moore said Casey had been returned to jail and was receiving medical attention from the facility's health services provider.

"No information can be released regarding her treatment or medical condition due to HIPPA and Florida Medical and Mental Health Confidentiality Laws," Moore said.

For security reasons, Moore also declined to state whether Casey would return to court Friday.

"Orange County Corrections will never reveal the transport of any inmate in our custody due to the security risks posed by such knowledge being made public," Moore said.

Earlier on Thursday, testimony centered on the recovery of the skeletal remains of Caylee from a wooded area in December 2008. Casey cried as photographs of the remains were displayed in the courtroom and avoided looking at the screen where they were displayed.

As the photographs were displayed Thursday, jurors heard testimony from Orange County Sheriff's Office crime scene technician Jennifer Welch, along with Steve Hanson, chief investigator for the medical examiner's office, and Gary Utz, Orange County chief deputy

Welch detailed items found with the little girl's remains, including a black plastic bag, an off-white canvas bag, a red plastic Disney bag, a pair of shorts, a blanket and "clothing remnants." Duct tape could be seen on the facial region of the skull, she testified.

Casey's parents were not in the courtroom while the photos were shown Thursday.

Jurors also heard a recording of a 9-1-1 call in which a utility worker reported that meter reader Roy Kronk claimed to have found a skull at the site where the remains were found.

Questioned by Baez, Welch agreed that it was paramount that a crime scene or remains not be tampered with, saying it could affect an investigation.

Numerous photographs were introduced into evidence of the skull, along with the duct tape on it and other items found at the scene, such as the canvas laundry bag.

Utz testified the skull had its jawbone, or mandible, still attached, which was relatively rare given the stage of decomposition. The duct tape, he testified, was helping keep the jawbone attached, along with hair on the skull.

Thursday morning, jurors heard testimony from Casey's brother Leer, who testified that while his sister was out of jail on bail the month after Caylee was reported missing told him an alternate version of how the little girl was kidnapped by her nanny.

He said his sister told him in August 2008 that she had met the nanny, Zenaida Fernandez-Gonzalez, at an Orlando park along with Gonzalez's sister. Casey told him that Gonzalez held her down and told her that she was taking Caylee from her because she wasn't a good mother, "to teach her a lesson," Lee said.

Gonzalez also warned her not to go to the police, according to Casey.

Lee recalled his sister saying, "She couldn't believe it was happening, and it felt kind of surreal to her," he testified.

She said she did nothing to stop her child from being taken, he recounted, because "she was scared and she didn't know what to do."

His sister told him that, from time to time, Gonzalez would contact her through Casey's MySpace page and directs her as to what to do and where to go. She went to the locations, she said, in hopes of seeing or retrieving her daughter but was never successful in finding her.

Casey's account, as related by Lee, differed from the one she gave authorities after Caylee was reported missing. She maintained to police she dropped the child off at the nanny's apartment that morning and never saw her again.

"Zanny never materialized?" Baez asked Lee Thursday. "To this day, no," he replied.

Neither side asked Lee about the sexual abuse allegations during his testimony.

Lee also testified Thursday that he was the one searching the Internet on the Anthony family computer July 15th and 16th, 2008. A computer examiner testified Wednesday that no searches for Zenaida Fernandez-Gonzalez were found on the computer until July 16th, dealing a potential blow to Casey's claims to authorities that she was frantically searching for her daughter in the month before her disappearance was reported.

Computer experts testified that in March, someone using the desktop computer, located in the home Casey shared with her parents, searched for terms including "chloroform," "inhalation," "how to make chloroform" and "head injury."

The searches were found in a portion of the computer's hard drive that indicated they had been deleted, Detective Sandra Osborne of the Orange County Sheriff's Office testified.

However, she told jurors, deleted material remains on a computer's hard drive and can be retrieved until it is overwritten by new data. It had not been overwritten on the Anthonys' computer, she said, and "a complete Internet history" was obtained.

It appears the computer user first searched for "chloraform" on Google and received results for "chloroform," said John Bradley, owner of the software development company that created the software used to retrieve the data. One of the search results was from Wikipedia, which was accessed, he testified.

On the other terms, he said the user either typed those terms in to search, or in some instances may have clicked on hyperlinks on the Wikipedia site.

Bradley agreed with Baez's assertion that the links do not tell jurors what was on the websites accessed, and that some sites could have been jokes or information on self-defense. He also agreed he could not say how closely the user was examining the websites or whether a user was looking at multiple browsers.

There were two user-created profiles on the computer, but Osborne told Baez she could not tell who performed the searches.

Earlier in the week, jurors heard testimony regarding a foul odor emanating from Casey's trunk. A scientist testified that compounds associated with human decomposition were found there, and a cadaver dog handler testified that his dog "alerted" to the trunk.

Despite objections from the defense, jurors saw a video in which images of Caylee's skull and the duct tape found across the front of it at the scene were superimposed over a photo of a Caylee alive, smiling, with her mother.

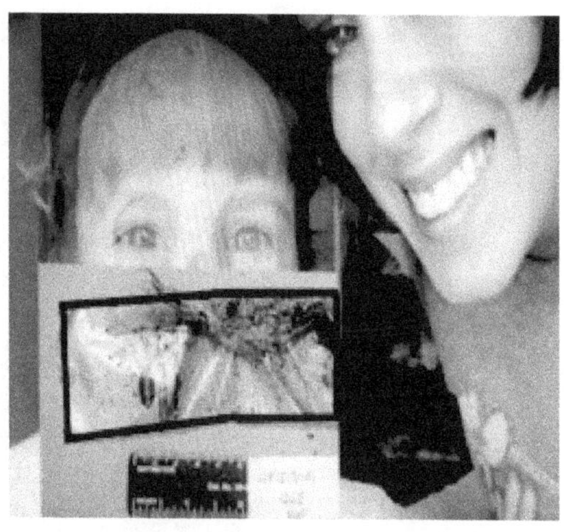

The duct tape found on Caylee's skull could have been sufficient to kill the little girl, prosecutors said Friday.

"I believe that the exhibit was necessary to establish the state's theory that this duct tape was sufficient to be the murder weapon," said attorney Jeff Ashton.

The defense had argued vigorously against allowing the video into court, saying it presented just one of many possible scenarios and would serve only to inflame sentiments among the jurors.

But Orange County Chief Judge Belvin Perry agreed to allow the video into evidence. Determining the role of duct tape in the girl's death was "highly relevant," he said.

Judge Perry also denied a mistrial motion made by the defense, related to the video, at the close of Friday's proceedings.

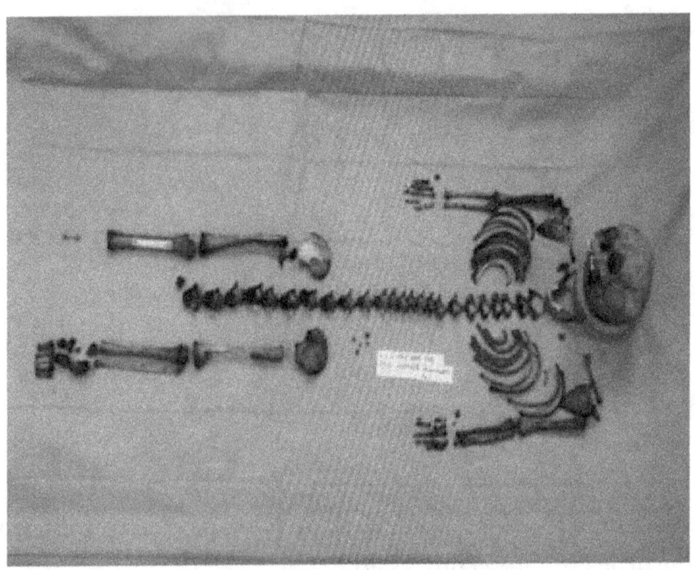

Caylee's Skeletal Remains from Autopsy Photo the right foot bones are missing.

Earlier Friday, the chief medical examiner in the case said the way in which prosecutors say Caylee's body was discarded left no doubt that the girl was intentionally killed.

Dr. Jan Garavaglia testified that Casey's failure to report her daughter missing for more than a month was just one of three red flags that strongly indicate foul play.

The others were the discovery of the girl's remains amidst black garbage bags in a wooded field - "tossed in a bag to rot" was her testimony and the presence of duct tape on the girl's skull.

"There is no child that should have duct tape on its face when it dies," Garavaglia testified. "There is no reason to put duct tape on the face after it dies."

The duct tape and its position on Caylee's skull have been points of discussion in the trial for two days.

Early Friday, a forensic anthropologist who examined the skull, John Schultz of the University of Central Florida, said under questioning from defense attorney J. Cheney Mason that the tape was not covering the nose hole on Caylee's skull when he examined it.

Schultz said that one image, which showed Caylee's vertebrae—the bones that made up her spine suggest that she was left at the site where the remains were discovered before her body decomposed.

He explained that in children, in order to allow room for growth, individual vertebrae are not yet fused together. Because Caylee's were found in one location, it suggested they had been held together by soft tissue when they were placed there, he testified.

Schultz testified that Caylee's body could have been in the woods for about six months, about the length of time that had passed between the times her family last saw her in June 2008 and the discovery of her remains in December 2008. The bones showed no evidence of any injuries or trauma prior to her death, he said.

By Saturday, testimony reached discussion of bugs and larvae found in Casey's trunk, where the prosecution alleges Caylee's body was kept in garbage bags for days after her mother knocked her out with chloroform and taped her nose and mouth.

While forensic entomologist Neal Haskell credited the bugs to decomposition, the defense argued and Haskell admitted the bugs could be attributed to a trash bag found in the trunk.

The prosecution also called Arpad Vass, a senior research scientist at Tennessee's Oak Ridge National Laboratory, who testified Monday about his examination of items from the trunk.

Vass said he was "shocked" by the high level of chloroform in the trunk carpet sample and had an immediate reaction when he opened the can containing the sample.

"I essentially jumped back a foot or two," Vass said, before confirming to Assistant State Attorney Jeff Ashton that he believed the smell was human decomposition. "The odor was extremely overwhelming. I was shocked that that little bitty can could have that much odor associated with it."

During a combative cross-examination, defense lawyer Baez attempted to cast doubt on Vass' testimony, accusing him of having a financial interest in the case and questioning his testing methods. Vass acknowledged that he has a pending patent on a device designed to detect clandestine graves. But he rejected the suggestion that his testimony in the high-profile trial could potentially inspire interest in the device and its applications.

Tuesday and Wednesday brought key testimony of the four-legged variety. Deputy Jason Forgey of the Orange County Sheriff's Office, and Sergeant Kristin Brewer of the Osceola County Sheriff's Office, detailed the efforts of cadaver dogs Gerus and Bones, who searched critical areas in search of human remains.

Gerus detected human decomposition in both Casey's car and in the Anthony's back yard, Forgey testified.

Within three to four minutes of being given a command to search in the yard, "I saw there was an area of interest he kept going back to and sniffing pretty hard," Osceola County, Florida, sheriff's Sgt. Kristin Brewer said of her dog, Bones. The dog made a second lap around the backyard and then gave his final alert, sitting down, she said.

The alert was within six to eight feet of that made the same day, July 17th, 2008, by Gerus, Brewer said, although she did not find that out until afterward.

She said she and Bones returned to the Anthony home the following day, but several crime scene units were working there and "a lot of dirt, mulch, pavers ... changed the landscape quite a bit."

Bones did not alert to any locations in the yard on the second search, she said. Gerus also did not alert the second day, Gerus' handler, Orange County sheriff's Deputy Jason Forgey, testified Tuesday.

Gerus also alerted to the smell of human remains in the trunk of Casey's car, Forgey testified Tuesday. When the dog passed around Casey's white Pontiac Sunfire on July 17th, 2008, "he started indicating in the rear of the vehicle," Forgey said. "I could tell he was working something."

After the trunk was opened, Gerus put his front paws inside and then lay down, signaling that he had detected the scent of remains.

Forgey explained the conflicting results in the Anthony backyard by saying that he believed Gerus alerted to a scent on the surface of the land. Once technicians disturbed the surface, he said, the scent was diminished "where the dog wouldn't find it. It was gone at that point."

On cross-examination, however, Forgey said he does not know the real reason behind the conflicting alerts. Still, he said, "in every single time (Gerus has) had an alert besides this case, he's had a find," that is, he found remains.

Brewer offered a similar explanation on Wednesday. "Whatever he was alerting to could have been moved or destroyed or dissipated because of all the work that had been done," she said, "or they may just not have dug enough to find what was below the surface."

During cross examination, Forgey and Brewer agreed that the dogs are not infallible when it comes to identifying remains and, "like humans," are imperfect.

A bag of trash found in the trunk, which had been sitting there for weeks during a Florida summer, has been suggested as a possible source of the odor. But Forgey told Burdick his dog does not alert on trash, and has been trained around garbage.

Forgey also told Baez that he's smelled human decomposition on numerous occasions and "I smelled it clear as day" in Anthony's car.

Also Tuesday, FBI forensic chemist Michael Rickenbach testified he analyzed pieces of Casey's trunk liner, carpet and parts of the spare tire cover, among other items.

On those, he said, chloroform "residue" was found, but it was at low levels. But he did not want to offer specific levels, saying it would not be appropriate because he conducted qualitative testing, confirming chloroform's presence, rather than quantitative testing, which would detect its level.

Under questioning from prosecutor Jeff Ashton, Rickenbach said the samples were sent to him in a cardboard box, not a sealed container, which could have allowed some of the chloroform to evaporate, lowering the levels present. Having the car trunk open for a time might also lower the levels, he said.

Though Wednesday and Thursday's testimony on computer forensics was less graphic compared to what was to come, it represented some of the prosecution's most critical evidence so far.

Through the testimony of three computer experts, the prosecution worked to establish premeditation, a factor essential to convicting Casey of first-degree capital murder.

The jury heard more evidence about searches conducted on the Anthony family computer on March 17th and 21st of 2008 included "chloroform," "how to make chloroform," "household weapons" and "neck-breaking," according to testimony.

A computer examiner testified Wednesday that someone conducted keyword searches on "chloroform" using a desktop computer located in the home Casey shared with her parents. The searches were found in a portion of the computer's hard drive that indicated they had been deleted, Detective Sandra Osborne of the Orange County Sheriff's Office testified.

However, she told jurors, deleted material remains on a computer's hard drive and can be retrieved until it is overwritten by new data. It had not been overwritten on the Anthonys' computer, she said, and "a complete Internet history" was obtained.

The searches using the keyword "chloroform" were conducted in March, three months before Caylee disappeared, according to testimony.

It appears the computer user first searched for "chloraform" on Google and received results for "chloroform," said John Bradley, owner of the software development company that created the software used to retrieve the data. One of the search results was from Wikipedia.org, which was accessed, he testified.

It also appeared searches were conducted using terms such as "inhalation," "self-defense," "meningeal artery," "ruptured spleen," "alcohol" and "head injury," he said. The user either typed those terms in to search, Bradley said, or in some instances might have clicked on links on the Wikipedia site to go to a different page.

Searches were also conducted on "how to make chloroform," "neck breaking" and "making weapons out of household products," Bradley testified.

During his cross-examination, Baez attempted to show that the user apparently did not spend a great deal of time looking at the pages referencing chloroform. Only a few seconds elapsed in some cases before the next site was accessed, Bradley said.

Bradley agreed with Baez's assertion that the links do not tell jurors what was on the websites accessed, and that some could have been jokes or information on self-defense. He also agreed he could not say how closely the user was examining the websites or whether a user was looking at multiple browsers.

While there were two user-created profiles on the computer, Osborne told Baez she could not tell who performed the searches.

She also testified she found no reference to chloroform on a computer belonging to Ricardo Morales, Casey's former boyfriend. Shown a photo Morales earlier admitted posting on his MySpace page featuring a couple with the caption, "Win her over with chloroform," Osborne said either it had been deleted and overwritten or posted from another computer.

She said a keyword search would not necessarily have located the picture, since the keyword was embedded in pixels in the picture. Morales earlier testified he posted the photo as a joke.

Osborne said she also was asked to find any records on the computer relating to a Zenaida Fernandez-Gonzalez.

Osborne testified she found searches for Gonzalez on people search sites, Google and high school class reunion sites, along with the social networking site MySpace. All of those searches were conducted on July 16th, 2008—the day after Caylee was reported missing to authorities, she testified.

But Osborne said she found no searches for Gonzalez before that date, another blow to Casey's claims to authorities that she had been frantically searching for Gonzalez and her daughter during the month before police were notified Caylee was missing.

Week 4 is expected to bring the close of the prosecution's case and possibly the start of the defense.

Week 4

As the prosecution rested in the Casey Anthony murder trial and the defense took the helm this week, emotions ran high, both inside and outside the courtroom.

People eager to snag one of the 50 tickets allotted each day to spectators grabbed headlines on Friday with a pre-dawn scuffle. Police were called when a violent brawl erupted after some hopeful spectators cut in line.

And on Thursday, three years to the day that, according to testimony, Caylee was last seen alive, a group of trial followers released balloons in Caylee's honor. When interviewed by the media, one of the participants, David Wood, cried as he lamented over how, as he put it, anyone could hurt a child.

Inside the courtroom, the usually calm Jeff Ashton, assistant state attorney, became less so as the focus shifted to the defense.

On Thursday, the day the defense began to present its case, Ashton objected when defense attorney Jose Baez asked Heather Seubert, a DNA analyst and serologist for the FBI, whether she conducted a DNA paternity test on Casey's brother to determine if he was Caylee's father.

Ashton said Baez's question falsely implied police had requested the test. While Judge Belvin Perry Jr. allowed the question after instructing Baez to ask it in a different manner and Seubert answered that DNA samples excluded Lee as a possible father. Perry admonished both attorneys for raising their voices.

"I don't have a hearing problem," Perry told the attorneys. "And the amplification of questions, objections, I don't need them."

Tempers ran especially high on Friday, when Ashton objected to Baez's questioning of entomology expert Tim Huntington. The defense attorney had asked the witness to testify about alleged decomposition stains, a subject of importance because the prosecution asserts that a stain in the trunk of Casey's car came from human decomposition. Ashton argued this was outside the witness's area of expertise.

Following Ashton's objections, Judge Perry dismissed the jury to allow a discussion of the matter. Ashton shook his head in frustration and accused Baez of texting when he noticed the defense attorney checking his phone. Perry allowed testimony on the stain, but did not let the lawyers' exchange go unchallenged.

"I'm not going to say this ever again. ... I do not want to hear editorial comments," Perry said in reference to Ashton's mention of texting. "Let's stick to the facts. I care less what Mr. Baez may be doing or not doing. ... I do not care if Mr. Baez is standing on his head, standing on one leg."

This outlash directed at Ashton was unusual for the judge, as Baez had more often taken the brunt of Perry's frustrations. But Perry's harsh words fell on Baez yet again on Saturday, when the judge threatened to file contempt proceedings at the end of the trial because Baez failed to tell prosecutors about a witness's planned testimony.

"Mr. Baez, to be quite frank, both sides have engaged in what I call game play," Perry said. "But this is not a game."

Saturday's threats followed Baez's questioning of witness William Rodriguez, a forensic anthropologist. After the prosecution objected to the testimony, the jury was temporarily excused.

With the jury out, Rodriguez told Perry he planned to testify that no conclusions can be drawn from duct tape found near Caylee's remains because of decomposition and possible movement of the bones by animals.

Rodriguez also planned to criticize the prosecution's earlier use of a video that superimposed Caylee's living face with a picture of her skull and the outline of a piece of duct tape. Rodriguez's testimony would be used to rebut the prosecution's theory that duct tape found on Caylee's remains was essentially a murder weapon.

Rodriguez's opinions, however, were not shared with prosecutors or contained in the report the defense filed with the court. This violated Perry's rule that expert testimony must be shared with both sides.

"It appears to me that this was quite intentional," Perry said to Baez as Casey and the rest of the defense team sat stone-faced. "This was not some inadvertent slip."

Perry ordered Rodriguez off the stand, but said Rodriguez would be allowed to testify Monday after the prosecution has a chance to interview him. Excluding his testimony would be "totally unfair to Ms. Anthony," Perry said.

Saturday's testimony also included Dr. Werner Spitz, another forensic anthropologist. Spitz said he believes the tape found on Caylee's skull was placed there long after the body had decomposed. He believes the tape could have been an effort to keep the jaw bone attached so the body could be moved.

Spitz also criticized the Orange County medical examiner, Dr. Jan Garavaglia, for not opening Caylee's skull when he examined the remains. Failing to do so, he said, resulted in a "shoddy autopsy."

"Based on this examination, the cause of death remains unknown for those who did the first examination and for me to some extent as well," Spitz said.

Spitz closed out three days of forensic testimony from the defense, which worked to rebut the prosecution's key evidence. This evidence includes a shovel that Casey allegedly borrowed from her neighbor, and carpet samples, hair and bugs found in Casey's trunk.

DNA expert Seubert testified Thursday no DNA was found on the trunk materials, but during cross-examination added that does not rule out the possible presence of decompositional fluids. She also testified that no blood was found on the trunk materials, but that the lack of blood does not eliminate the possibility of a crime.

Friday's testimony came solely from entomologist Huntington. In addition to his discussion of stains formed by decomposing bodies, he eventually told jurors that he didn't believe the stain found in Casey's trunk came from human decomposition. He also discussed the bugs found in Casey's car.

Jurors previously heard from prosecution witnesses who testified that the discovery of one leg of a blow fly, a kind of fly commonly found around decomposing bodies, as well as more numerous examples of a different kind of fly, suggested that a body had been in the trunk for no more than three to five days.

Huntington testified Friday that one blow fly leg was not significant.

"If we assume that there is a body in a car trunk, you would expect to find hundreds, if not thousands of these adult blow flies," Huntington testified.

After introducing 59 witnesses and submitting 323 pieces of evidence, the prosecution rested their case Wednesday June 15th. This was immediately followed by a motion for acquittal by the defense, presented dramatically by defense attorney Cheney Mason.

Mason, who typically takes a back seat in court proceedings, presented the motion outside the presence of the jury. Giving what could be a preview of closing arguments, he said there was not enough evidence to support the prosecution's allegations of murder, and that the possibility of a drowning had not been successfully rebutted.

"In this case, there is not any evidence of anything other than a caring and loving mother-child relationship," Mason said as he raised his hands in the air. "There is no confession. There is nothing but circumstances that the state is trying to expand into some proof."

Assistant state attorney Linda Drane-Burdick handled the rebuttal in her standard, matter-of-fact style, re-emphasizing the prosecution's key arguments and asserting that premeditation had been established.

"When Ms. Anthony decided to place duct tape on the child's face, not one application, not two but three, sufficient time had passed for her to understand the nature and quality of that act and that premeditation has been established as a result," Drane-Burdick said.

After taking 45 minutes to consult case law, Judge Perry denied the defenses motion for acquittal.

Week 5

The defense continued its efforts to cast doubt on evidence presented by the prosecution. Cindy testified that she, not Casey, searched for "chloroform" on the Anthony family computer in March of 2008.

Earlier in the trial, computer experts testifying for the prosecution said someone in the Anthony residence made searches for "chloroform," "how to make chloroform," "neck breaking" and "shovel," among other terms. Prosecutors alleged the searches proved premeditation and that records showed Casey was the only one who could have made the searches.

Cindy said she began by searching "chlorophyll," because she feared her dogs were getting sick from eating plants in the yard.

"Both the dogs would eat the bamboo leaves in the back so I started looking up sources from the back yard that could potentially cause her to be more sleepy," Cindy said. "I started looking up chloroform - I mean chlorophyll and then that prompted me to look up chloroform."

Prosecutor Linda Drane-Burdick questioned Cindy on her work records, which indicate she was at work during the searches.

"It could have been an error if my supervisor filled out my time card in my absence if it came on a day that our time cards were turned in," Cindy explained.

Cindy conceded she does not remember specifically searching for "how to make chloroform," "shovel" or "neck breaking," though she remembers seeing a pop-up, which included the words "neck-breaking." Cindy also said this testimony does not differ from her 2009 deposition.

"I remember looking up chlorophyll back in March of last year, and I am not sure if I looked up chloroform as well," she said in the deposition. "I looked up alcohol and several other things like that—like ethyl alcohol and peroxide, too."

On Friday, Cindy also testified that she came home to find her pool ladder was up on July 16th, 2008, the day the defense alleges Caylee drowned. Cindy tearfully recounted how she would swim frequently with her granddaughter and that the 2-year-old required minimal assistance to get in the pool.

"My hands are on her but not firmly, just like a light touch," Cindy said as she tearfully referred to a picture of her helping Caylee into the pool. "Even at that point she could climb into the pool by herself."

Cindy acknowledged during cross examination that she initially said the incident with the ladder could have been on June 17th or subsequent dates.

Mark Lippman, attorney representing Casey's parents, told reporters at a press conference this week that his clients just want to know the truth.

"They have no idea what happened," Lippman said Thursday. "They just want both the state (prosecutors) and the defense to do their jobs."

The press conference was held after *CNN* reported that Lippman told him that Casey's parents don't think their daughter is innocent, but they also don't want her to receive the death penalty.

Also on Friday, Lee, Casey's brother, provided tearful testimony for the defense. He said when he first noticed Casey's pregnancy; he confronted her and Cindy but was brushed off.

Lee cried on the stand as he acknowledged that he "regrettably" did not go to visit Casey in the hospital when Caylee was born.

"I was very angry at my mom, and I was also angry at my sister," Lee said as he began to break down. "I was just angry...that they didn't want to include me and didn't find it important enough to tell me especially after I'd already asked."

During cross examination, prosecutor Jeff Ashton questioned Lee's emotional testimony, noting he was not emotional during his 2009 deposition, which covered the same topics. Ashton also noted Lee's unwillingness to meet with prosecutors before testifying.

Ashton asked him why he ultimately chose to contact defense attorney Jose Baez and meet with the defense instead.

"The last time I was in court," Lee said, referring to his June 1st testimony, "I was present during a discussion where information came out that I thought it was important for Jose specifically to be made aware of...I took it upon myself to do that."

Lee did not say what the information was but confirmed it has not been brought into the case thus far. Lee's testimony supports the defense's allegations that the Anthony family was dysfunctional and secretive, which Baez says drove Casey to lie about Caylee's death.

Lee and Cindy also testified this week that Casey's Pontiac Sunfire, which the family bought used, had numerous stains in the trunk when it was purchased. The prosecution alleges the stains indicate a body could have been in the trunk.

This week, jurors also heard testimony rebutting the state's key forensic evidence. On Monday, botanist Jane Bock testified that leaf debris found in and on Casey's Pontiac Sunfire was not consistent with the leaves at the place where the body was found.

She also testified to the defense's theory that the body had been moved, saying it could have been at the spot where it was found for as little as two weeks. She said during cross examination that it could have been there much longer.

Wednesday brought four scientific experts, including FBI forensic examiner Maureen Bottrell. She said she was unable to match soil from Casey's shoes with soil from the scene where the remains were recovered. She could not say whether soil could have been present on the shoes at an earlier time.

FBI forensic chemist Madeline Montgomery also testified Wednesday. She tested the hair mass found with Caylee's remains for depressants, including Xanax and Klonopin, sometimes referred to as a "date rape" drug. The results were negative for those drugs, but she was unable to test for chloroform.

Michael Sigman, a chemist who helped take air samples from the trunk of the defendant's car, testified Wednesday that he cannot conclusively say if decomposition had occurred inside Casey's trunk. This contradicts the prosecution's forensic expert, Dr. Arpad Vass, who testified that there was likely a decomposing body in the car.

Karen Lowe, a FBI hair and fiber analyst, testified Wednesday that the duct tape found with the remains was dissimilar to a piece of duct tape coming from the Anthony house.

Court came to an abrupt end on Saturday after the defense and prosecution argued about forensic witness Kenneth Furton. Furton was expected to testify about decompositional odors. Judge Belvin Perry called the attorneys into his chamber for a conference, and then announced a recess until Monday morning. However Perry indicated that the recess was unrelated to Furton.

Prior to Saturday's early recess, Perry anticipated the jury could have the case as early as next Friday evening with the defense resting on Wednesday. The judge has not offered an updated timeline.

Week 6

The defense wrapped up its case on Thursday, June 30th, after calling to the stand every member of the Anthony family this week except for Casey. She only made a cameo when she personally addressed the judge to answer one of the trial's biggest questions, whether she would testify. She declined the opportunity to testify in her defense.

In true finale form, this week's testimony was emotional, drama-filled and, thanks in part to a spectator who made an obscene gesture at prosecutor Jeff Ashton, not without a few surprises. Even the weather set the tone, storming so loudly on Friday that the thunder could be heard inside the courtroom.

After 33 days and more than 100 witnesses, the murder trial of Casey Anthony is inches from its end and only Sunday's closing statements remain before the jury deliberates.

Casey's father, George, was a key player in the defense's final testimony, taking the stand twice during the final week. On Tuesday, he denied an affair with Krystal Holloway, a one-time volunteer in the search to find Caylee and the woman who claims George told her Caylee's death was an accident.

George said his relationship with Holloway was platonic, and he only visited her apartment because she told him she had a brain tumor and needed someone to comfort her.

Holloway testified the following day, retelling a conversation she alleges she had with George.

"He said it was an accident that snowballed out of control," Holloway said. "But I was caught off guard with it and by the time I looked up he had tears in his eyes, and I didn't say anything after that."

Holloway stood by her version of the conversation even when Ashton, the prosecutor, confronted her with the differing statement she gave to police. She told police George said, "I really believe that it was an accident, and it just went wrong and she tried to cover it up."

On Wednesday, questioning of George turned combative when lead defense attorney Jose Baez suggested he faked his support for Casey in jailhouse conversations while pointing the finger at her behind her back.

George admitted he pulled Orange County detective Yuri Melich aside on July 15th, 2008; the first night law enforcement visited the Anthony home. He admitted he told Melich the car smelled like decomposition and that his daughter was lying.

"Casey was the last one that I saw with Caylee," he responded angrily to Baez. "One and one adds up to two, sir, in my mind, and no matter how you're trying to spin it I'm upset because my granddaughter is missing."

Wednesday also brought George's second denial of accusations that he molested his daughter as she was growing up and a full breakdown when he recalled the day Caylee's remains were found.

"I felt a deep hurt inside, tears, the whole gambit of such an emotional loss, seeing what my wife went through, what my son went through," he said through sobs.

The defense also suggested Wednesday that George attempted to take his own life in a hotel room in 2009 because he was overcome with guilt. He admitted he consumed a mixture of pills and alcohol because he "wanted to be with Caylee."

In rebuttal, the state introduced into evidence George's eight-page suicide note, full of praise for his wife, longing for Caylee and lots of outstanding questions.

"I sit here falling apart, because I should have done more," he wrote. "She was so close to home, why was she there? Who placed her there? Why is she gone? Why?"

Prosecutors argue these questions about her death prove George did not know how Caylee died, contradicting the defense's allegations that Caylee drowned and he helped cover it up.

In the note, George also seems to express uncertainty about Casey. He closes the letter by saying, "I Love you - Cynthia Marie...Caylee Here I come...Lee, I am sorry...Casey—"

In a move the defense hoped would highlight the Anthony family's dysfunction, the defense called Cindy, who during direct examination agreed she testified six months ago that she thought Caylee was still alive.

"There was still a part of me that believed Caylee was alive at that time," she said Wednesday.

Cindy also played a role in the defense's unexpected final line of questioning: the manner in which they buried their family pets over the past two decades. During testimony from George, Cindy and Lee, the defense suggested Caylee was disposed of in the same way the family buried their pets, wrapped in a blanket and placed in garbage bags secured with duct tape.

During cross examination, prosecutors pointed out that Casey was also familiar to the family's burial techniques. The defendant was in high school when their last pet died.

Highlights of the week also included testimony from Casey's former fiancé, which the jury will never hear. With the jury out of the room, Jesse Grund testified that Casey told him she was molested by her brother.

"She told me at one point in recent years that she woke up one night with Lee standing over her in bed asleep," Grund said outside the jury's presence. "And in another instance was groping her in the middle of the night."

Judge Belvin Perry ruled the testimony was hearsay, and it was not admitted.

Roy Kronk, the meter reader who discovered Caylee's body, also took the stand this week. Baez alleged in opening statements that Kronk is a "morally bankrupt person who took Caylee's body and hid it."

Kronk denied moving the body or touching it before December of 2008, saying he spotted what he thought was a skull in August of 2008. After several unsuccessful attempts to direct police to what he thought could be the remains, he left the matter alone until December when he returned to the same area.

"I still didn't think it [the skull] was real so I very gently took it [the meter stick] and put it into the right eye socket and I gently picked it up," Kronk said describing the moments before he called police. "I looked down and I realized what it was and I set it down as gently as I could."

The week came to a close Friday with the state's rebuttal. Witnesses included Cindy's former supervisor, who testified company records show Cindy was at work during the times she claims she was searching for "chlorophyll" on the family computer. Earlier, a computer forensics expert had testified that he found searches for "chloroform" among the computer's deleted files, but no searches for "chlorophyll."

Court will resume Sunday with closing arguments. The jury is expected to begin deliberations Sunday evening.

Closing Arguments

Just before closing arguments began, Perry prohibited defense attorneys from bringing up allegations that Casey was allegedly sexually abused by her father or brother.

The defense had sought to explain Casey's behavior during the month before Caylee's disappearance was reported to police by suggesting she had been schooled from an early age to hide her feelings after her father began abusing her when she was 8.

Baez said in his opening statements that Casey's brother, Lee, also abused her, but "it didn't go as far" as that with her father.

Perry said there are "no facts in evidence or reasonable inferences that can be drawn ... that either Mr. George Anthony or Mr. Lee Anthony molested or attempted to molest Ms. Anthony."

As Casey alternately cried, glared and shook her head, prosecutors told jurors in closing arguments on Sunday, July 3rd, that evidence in the case points to only one conclusion, that Casey murdered Caylee.

"When you have a child, that child becomes your life," prosecutor Jeff Ashton told the jury. "This case is about the clash between that responsibility, and the expectations that go with it and the life that Casey Anthony wanted to have."

Defense attorney Jose Baez, however, told jurors, "I probably think you have more questions than you have answers." And the central one, he said, remains how Caylee died.

In his closing, Baez attacked the state's case, saying it does not constitute the kind of evidence that jurors need to make a decision in such a serious matter. Prosecutors' allegations are based on "fantasy (computer) searches, fantasy forensics, phantom stickers, phantom stains (in the trunk) ... and no real, hard evidence," he said.

At one point as Baez spoke, Ashton could be seen smiling or chuckling behind his hand, prompting Baez to refer to him as "this laughing guy over here." Ashton objected and the judge called a sidebar conference, then a recess.

When court resumed, Perry chastised both sides, saying both Ashton and Baez had violated his order that neither side should make disparaging remarks about opposing counsel. Both attorneys apologized, and Perry said he would accept that for now but warned against a recurrence, saying if it happened again that attorney would be excluded from the courtroom.

Following Baez's remarks, defense attorney J. Cheney Mason talked to jurors about the law and their duty, cautioning them to not take Casey's refusal to take the stand in her own defense as evidence of her guilt.

In the prosecution's closing argument, Ashton outlined the state's case against Casey by several witnesses as the odor from human decomposition and the items found with Caylee's skeletal remains in December 2008.

He started with the fabrications, telling jurors Casey "maintains her lies until they absolutely cannot be maintained any more" and then replaces it with another lie. "Call it Casey 3.0, the new version," Ashton said.

Ashton attacked the defense's theory in the case that Caylee drowned on June 16th in the Anthonys' above-ground pool, and that Casey and her father, George, panicked upon finding Caylee's body and covered up her death.

The defense's arguments, Ashton told jurors, "require you to suspend your common sense," likening them to "a trip down a rabbit hole" into a world where loving grandfathers do nothing when they find their granddaughter dead; cover up an accident; and where "a man who buries his pets will take the granddaughter, who is the love of his life, and throw her in a swamp. This is the world the defense invites you to occupy."

But Baez said the drowning is "the only explanation that makes sense." He showed jurors a photograph of Caylee opening the home's sliding glass door by herself. There were, he said, no child safety locks in the home. Both of Casey's parents, George and Cindy, testified that Caylee could get out of the house easily, he said.

Although Cindy testified that Caylee could not put the ladder on the side of the pool and climb up, Baez alleged that Cindy may have been the one who left the ladder up the night before. She didn't admit to doing so in testimony, he said, but "how much guilt would she have knowing it was her that left the ladder up that day?"

Ashton detailed the numerous stories Casey told her parents and others after Caylee was last seen on June 16th, 2008, and the lies she told police after Cindy reported her missing 31 days later. He reminded the jury that during those 31 days, Casey's friends and acquaintances testified she was shopping, hitting nightclubs and staying with her boyfriend, but did not tell them Caylee was missing. If they asked her daughter's whereabouts, they said, she often said Caylee was with her nanny, Zenaida Gonzalez.

Ashton also went over items found with Caylee's remains, including a Winnie the Pooh blanket that matched the little girl's bedding at her grandparents' home, one of a set of laundry bags with the twin found at the Anthony home, and duct tape he said was a relatively rare brand.

"That bag is Caylee's coffin," Ashton said, holding up a photograph of the laundry bag, as Casey turned her head to the side, pressed her hand to her mouth and closed her eyes.

But Baez, the defense lawyer, told jurors his biggest fear is that they will base their verdict on emotions, not evidence.

"Caylee Anthony was a beautiful, sweet, innocent child who died too soon," he said as Casey began to cry. "And that is not disputed by anyone."

But, he said, prosecutors "gave you two weeks of testimony that was irrelevant," in an attempt to make the jury hate Casey and play on their emotions, something Baez called "improper."

"The strategy behind that is, if you hate her, if you think she's a lying, no-good slut, then you'll start to look at this evidence in a different light," Baez said. "I told you at the very beginning of this case that this was an accident that snowballed out of control ... What made it unique is not what happened, but who it happened to."

Defense attorney Jose Baez discusses a photo showing Caylee opening a sliding glass door during closing arguments on Sunday, July 3rd, 2011.

Baez blamed Casey's behavior on her dysfunctional family situation.

"Casey has issues," Baez said. "And these issues were there long before Caylee was ever born and long before June 16th, 2008."

He said he was "not proud of the way Casey behaved. I don't think anybody here can justify her actions, but they do not constitute murder."

"These people are different," Baez said of the Anthony family. "This girl is different. And this is why she behaved in this way."

He dismissed the state's alleged motive that Casey was tired of being a parent and wanted to be an independent 22-year-old as "nonsense."

"She had no motive," he said of his client. "Casey treated Caylee well. She loved that child." No witnesses, he reminded jurors, ever testified that Casey was anything other than a loving mother.

Baez continued the defense's efforts to focus suspicion on George, saying he lied repeatedly on the stand, even testifying against his daughter. George "doesn't have an ounce of paternal instinct," he said.

"George cares about George. Not about his wife, not about his daughter, not about his family, only about himself."

Ashton, however, said, "There is absolutely no possibility, reasonable or otherwise, that George had anything to do with disposing of this body. He is a doting grandfather who loved that child literally more than life itself," referring to George's suicide attempt in January 2009 after Caylee's skeletal remains were found.

Baez said the suicide attempt came because George was nervous at the authorities nosing around him.

He also tried to cast suspicion on Roy Kronk, the former Orange County meter reader who found Caylee's remains, alleging he knew where the remains were for months.

Testimony regarding the vile odor emanating from Casey's trunk, Baez said, "does not shed any light on how Caylee died, period." For all the witnesses that testified about the smell, other witnesses testified they noticed no smell in the car, he pointed out.

"We all know Casey acted inappropriately and made some mistakes and bad decisions," Baez said, noting Casey should have called the police and not attempted to "block this out." And if she committed a crime in doing so, he said, the state can charge her for it. But, he said, prosecutors have "overcharged" the case "... just because it's entertainment."

He said authorities focused on Casey from the beginning and "put square pegs in round holes," in an attempt to make the evidence fit their theory, rather than keep an open mind.

But the prosecution offered a very different story, trying to convince the jury that Casey killed her daughter because the conflict between the life she wanted and the life she had was "irreconcilable."

"The evidence in this case proves beyond any reasonable doubt that Casey Anthony decided on June 16th that something had to be sacrificed," Ashton said.

"We can only hope the chloroform was used before the tape was applied, so Caylee went peacefully without fear," he said. "But go she did, and she died because she could not breathe. She died because she had three pieces of duct tape over her nose and mouth. She died because her mother decided the life she wanted was more important."

Just after 6:30 p.m., before the prosecution could offer its rebuttal to the defense's closing presentation, Judge Perry dismissed the jury for the day.

"I want all of you bright-eyed and bushy-tailed," Perry told the jury. "It's been a long day, and it will be a long day tomorrow."

Because of the delay, the judge said he would instruct jurors on Monday, as a few jury instruction issues must still be sorted out.

Jurors are expected to start deliberations Monday even though it is the Independence Day holiday to decide if Casey is guilty of killing Caylee.

The Verdict

On the morning of July 4th, the jury began deliberating. They only deliberated for six hours this day. Then on the morning of July 5th, they pick up where they left off the day before.

At 8:30 a.m. Judge Perry called court to order. He called for the jury and immediately sent them out to deliberate. Jose Baez arrived too late for the brief proceedings. Cheney Mason spoke for the defense. Casey was very animated and spoke with the guards and Dorothy Sims.

At 1:25 p.m., even though the jury didn't ask to see any videos, they had no questions for Judge Perry. But they have a verdict. After ten hours of deliberations, the jury in Casey's trial came back with a verdict.

When the jury returned to the courtroom the verdict sheet was handed to the judge. He looked at each page one by one and when he finished he looked at each one a second time.

Many in the courtroom felt that they knew exactly what the judge was looking at. They felt in their hearts that Casey was found guilty for killing her daughter.

But the reason why the judge decided to reread each one of the verdict sheets was because he did not believe what he had just read; Casey was found not guilty on counts one through three regarding first-degree murder, aggravated manslaughter of a child, and aggravated child abuse, while finding her guilty on counts four through seven for providing false information to law enforcement:

Count Four: Casey said she was employed at Universal Studios during 2008, pursuant to the investigation of a missing person's report.

Count Five: Casey said she had left Caylee at an apartment complex with a babysitter causing law enforcement to pursue the missing babysitter.

Count Six: Casey said she informed two "employees" of Universal Studios, Jeff Hopkins and Juliet Lewis, at Universal, of the disappearance of Caylee.

Count Seven: Casey said she had received a phone call and spoke to Caylee on July 15th, 2008, causing law enforcement to expend further resources.

Clutching the hand of her defense attorney Jose Baez, Casey began to sob as the verdict was read. The rest of her defense team stood beside her, also clutching hands. She thanked Baez as she was swarmed by the defense team.

Following the trial, Casey's defense attorney Cheney Mason, blamed the media for the hatred directed toward Casey. He described it as a "media assassination" of her before and during the trial, saying, "I hope that this is a lesson to those of you who have indulged in media assassination for three years, bias, and prejudice, and incompetent talking heads saying what would be and how to be." Mason added: "I can tell you that my colleagues from coast to coast and border to border have condemned this whole process of lawyers getting on television and talking about cases that they don't know a damn thing about, and don't have the experience to back up their words or the law to do it. Now you have learned a lesson."

State's Attorney Lawson Lamar said, "We're disappointed in the verdict today because we know the facts and we've put in absolutely every piece of evidence that existed. This is a dry-bones case, very, very difficult to prove. The delay in recovering little Caylee's remains worked to our considerable disadvantage."

Jose Baez said, "While we're happy for Casey, there are no winners in this case. Caylee has passed on far, far too soon, and what my driving force has been for the last three years has been always to make sure that there has been justice for Caylee and Casey because Casey did not murder Caylee. It's that simple." He added, "And today our system of justice has not dishonored her memory by a false conviction."

Former Casey defense attorney Linda Kenney Baden shared Baez's sentiments. She believes the jury reached the right verdict. "We should embrace their verdict," she stated.

On July 6th, Assistant State Attorney Jeff Ashton gave an interview about the case on *The View*. Ashton said, "Obviously, it's not the outcome we wanted. But from the perspective of what we do, this was a fantastic case." He disagrees with those who state the prosecution overcharged the case, saying, "The facts that we had... this was first-degree murder. I think it all came down to the evidence. I think ultimately it came down to the cause of death." Ashton also explained that if the jury did not perceive first-degree murder when they saw the photograph of Caylee's skull with the duct tape, "then so be it". He said he accepts the jury's decision and that it has not taken away his faith in the justice system. "You can't believe in the rule of law and not accept that sometimes it doesn't go the way you think it should", stated Ashton, and explained that he understands why the case "struck such a nerve" with the public. "I think when people see someone that they believe has so gone away from [a mother's love for her child], it just outrages them." Ashton also made appearances on several other talk shows in the days following, and complimented Jose Baez on his cross-examinations and as having "the potential to be a great attorney".

Her sentencing for the four charges that she was found guilty of would take place on Thursday July 7th.

Cindy could face perjury charges for testimony she gave, one of the prosecutors in the murder trial said after the verdict was decided. Cindy testified that she was responsible for searches about chloroform on the family's home computer, but evidence indicated she was at work at the time.

Florida officials, meanwhile, are asking that Casey repay the state for the enormous cost of investigating the case.

In a motion filed the day after the verdict was released, the state called for a hearing so it can tally up costs and slap Casey with the bill.

"The efforts and costs of the investigation were extensive and not immediately available and accordingly, the State of Florida respectfully requests this Court to set a hearing within 60 days to determine total costs," the motion says.

The motion cites a Florida law that allows the state to fine defendants in criminal cases to recoup money spent.

Texas EquuSearch also wants its money back.

The company said it used 4,200 searchers and spent $112,000 looking for Caylee after the girl was reported missing in July 2008.

Tim Miller, the head of company, said that he now believes Caylee was never missing and he is contemplating a lawsuit.

"This is the money that really needed to go to families that need us," Miller told the media.

Later, Texas EquuSearch and Casey eventually settled out of court on October 18th, 2013. Texas EquuSearch was listed as a creditor to Casey in her bankruptcy case and was entitled to $75,000.

After the trial, one of jurors commented that the reason that the verdict was not guilty for murder was because the State could not tell them exactly how Caylee died. And because of that, they had only one option and that was to find Casey not guilty of murdering her daughter.

In the courtroom on the day of Casey's sentencing, Cindy, watched her daughter walk in and commented to her husband, "Oh my gosh, there she is, she looks so beautiful." Cindy commented to her husband that their daughter had let down her hair, after having kept it pulled back throughout the trial.

Cindy also commented that Lee had been strong throughout the experience.

A woman who was in the courtroom later said that Cindy seemed happy and was smiling and looking at Casey, but noted that Casey did not look back at her parents.

Outside the courtroom, a crowd of protesters holding signs attacked the jury's decision and the fact that Casey will be freed.

But some people were there to support Casey, including one man wearing a sign asking her to marry him.

On July 7th, Judge Belvin Perry sentenced Casey to four years in jail, one year for each of her four convictions of lying to police. But with credit for the approximately three years already served and good behavior, leaving her with six days left to serve. Denying a defense motion to reduce the four counts to a single conviction, Perry gave Anthony the maximum jail time he could by ruling that the four years be served consecutively.

He also fined her $1,000 for each count. Court papers show she is also ordered to pay court costs and fees totaling just over $600.

On July 15th, Casey's attorneys file an appeal to the convictions of providing false information to a law enforcement officer.

At first it was determined that Casey would be released on July 13th, but the corrections department's recalculation put that remainder at 10 days and making the release date for July 17th, not July 13th as originally planned.

Florida's Orange County Corrections said in a statement that the new date is a result of "a detailed recalculation of the projected release date," according the statement from Allen Moore, the department's public information officer. The statement gave no details on how the extra days were calculated. Court administrators say Casey was credited with 1,043 previous days in jail, plus good behavior while behind bars.

"I don't know how free she's going to be (but) she's going to be out of a cage," defense attorney Cheney Mason said soon after sentencing. "I doubt there's any place in this country that she could walk the streets freely."

Mason said that he fears for Casey's safety, and that measures are being taken to protect her. She will undoubtedly get counseling going forward, he said, adding that offers to help have poured in from across the country.

"I think she wants to get away from all this and try to find some way to start a life," said Mason.

Additionally, Casey will also have to deal with a defamation lawsuit from the real Zenaida Gonzalez.

Casey walked out of the front door of the Orange County Jail at 12:09 a.m. on July 17th, three years and one day after she was first arrested. She had her lawyer by her side and two Special Response Team officers with green vests.

Sheriff's deputies had two contingency plans laid out, but in the end opted to go with a public release.

According to the sheriff's department, the plans for Anthony's release were that she would be driven by jail guards to a secret location away from the grounds, but after that she would be on her own.

Her attorneys say she has received seven serious death threats, including one email photo with a bullet through her head, but the sheriff's department said the threats aren't credible and after her release she is on her own.

"We will not be providing any elaborate security or protection for Casey once she leaves," Orange County Sheriff Jerry Demings said.

"We have made every effort to not provide any special treatment for her," said Allen Moore, the spokesman for the Orange County

Corrections Department in a statement. "She has been treated like every other inmate in her custody class."

Casey had not received threats against her at the jail, but "this release had an unusual amount of security. So therefore, in that sense, it would not be a normal release," Moore said.

With $537.68 from her inmate account handed to her, Casey offered a quick thanks to a Special Response Team sergeant.

Her hair was pulled up in a tight bun and she had on a bright pink V-neck T-shirt, blue jeans and sneakers. She did not show any emotion.

Given the threats against her life by those furious at the not-guilty verdict, Casey's lawyers have not said where she will go next.

She then walked out of the jail building doors and into a dark-colored sport utility vehicle.

Casey leaving the jail with her attorney Jose Baez

Throngs of television camera crews and a crowd of about 1,000 people were at hand outside the jail to witness the release.

Most of those who waved placards in the jail parking lot were there to voice their opposition to Casey's release, but they did so peacefully.

People in the crowd lined up on both sides of the highway outside the jail chanted "Caylee, Caylee," and cars driving by honked their horns in response a sign saying "Honk for Caylee."

Police, some on horseback, kept a wary eye.

As Casey left, some demonstrators shouted and jeered. Some screamed, "Killer!"

Jose Baez and his team spent the past 10 days crafting an escape plan for Casey, a way to get her from the jail to the airport where a private plane would be waiting to whisk her away.

Jose Baez wrote about this night in his book Presumed Guilty, Casey Anthony: The Inside Story.

"There were too many crazies who were convinced she had killed Caylee while she danced the night away, and I feared for her safety," he wrote. "In addition to avoiding an army of media, we knew we were going to also duck the surveillance of a half dozen helicopters."

The plan was to get Casey into a car as quickly as possible before driving across the street to attorney Cheney Mason's building that had a multilevel garage. Once there, they planned to have one car block the garage's entrance while a small fleet of cars waited inside.

Casey and Baez would get into another car and all of the cars would leave the garage and head in different directions, leaving followers unsure of which vehicle Anthony was in.

"As soon as we walked out that door, I heard screams, the way teenagers screamed for Justin Bieber at one of his concerts," Baez wrote, describing the moment they exited the jail. "I'm certain they were yelling 'Baby killer' and the like, but after going from total silence to the sound of insanity, neither one of us could make out a single word they were saying."

They got in the car and headed for the garage where they quickly switched vehicles, which was not as smooth as Baez had hoped.

"I opened the door, grabbed Casey's hand, pulled her out, and I was so hopped up with adrenalin, I forgot she was there and slammed the car door on her leg before she could even get out of the car," he wrote.

'"Owwwwww," she yelped," Baez wrote. "'Oh, I'm so sorry,' I said. "I'm really sorry."

The vehicles took off from the garage and the plan worked, shedding all of their pursuers except for one helicopter.

A half-a-dozen helicopters over the airport prevented them from going there directly. They went to a lake, parked in a wooded area and waited until the helicopter trailing them gave up and left.

"We drove around, and I had no idea where we were, but Casey did," Baez wrote. "'You know about three blocks up on the left, do you know who lives there?' she asked. 'Zanny?' I blurted out. We cracked up laughing. 'Don't make me punch you,' she said."

With time to kill, the group went to an all-night Steak 'n Shake where Casey had her "first meal of freedom" a cheeseburger, fries and chocolate milkshake.

Casey and Baez eventually made it to the airport and took off for St. George Island, an island on the Florida panhandle near Panama City. The defense team had rented a house on a secluded beach.

Since it was the middle of the night, the small airport was closed and the plane had to land based on the flashing lights of a car waiting for them below.

"Meanwhile I said to myself, 'Oh my God. After all this, I'm going to die in a fucking plane crash with Casey Anthony. This is a blogger's dream come true,'" Baez joked.

That night, Casey climbed up the roof where a "wound up" Baez was sitting and "took photos of her first sunrise of freedom."

When the secret location was discovered by the press, Baez had Casey moved immediately.

"I had one of my investigators drive Casey to New York," he wrote. "While the entire national media was searching for her in Arizona and California, she was within walking distance of all of their offices."

Florida corrections officials, and Casey's lawyers, have offered few details. That's in part likely due to the intense emotions Casey's release has generated.

Orange County Sheriff Jerry Demings said that investigators are assessing threats to Casey's safety. While he said the department was not aware of any credible threats to her life, it's a concern that was clearly on his mind.

"Nobody has a right to take the law in their own hands," he said. "Casey Anthony had her day in court and the jury made a decision. I would hope people would step back and would not go out and commit another crime."

It's also a concern for her attorneys.

"Myself and other members of the team are concerned for her safety, very much so," one of her attorneys, Dorothy Sims said.

What Casey will do now is unclear.

"If I knew at this point, I'm sure you can appreciate that I wouldn't tell you," Sims said. "I don't believe that that has been resolved. My hope for her would be that she would be left alone and her privacy would be respected."

Defense attorney Mason, who once said he thought of Casey as a granddaughter, said he doesn't know what life holds in store for his client, but has hopes.

"She is only 25 years old. A decade from now, hopefully, she'll have some stability in her life and maybe a husband, and they can be somewhere in Montana and start over," he said.

With so much outrage over the verdict Judge Belvin Perry, Jr. rules juror names will remain secret until October 2011, citing public "outrage and distress" over the not guilty verdict. He also appeals to Florida legislators to bar the release of juror's names in some cases "in order to protect the safety and well-being of those citizens willing to serve."

Part Seven

The Aftermath

The story of Casey Anthony did not end in a courtroom in Orlando in July 2011. And even though the jury found her guilty of murdering little Caylee a report released one month later on August 11th, by Florida's Department of Children and Families.

The state agency found that Casey "is the caregiver responsible for the verified maltreatments of death, threatened harm and failure to protect" in her daughter's death.

A spokeswoman for the Department of Children and Families said the report was issued this week as a "professional courtesy" after the sheriff's office and prosecutors finished their work on the case.

She added that the state agency is mandated to conduct reviews when there are allegations that a child dies as a result of abuse, abandonment or neglect. The agency had no contact with the Anthonys prior to the girl's disappearance in the summer of 2008.

The Orange County Sheriff's Office will not take any further action as a result of the report, Capt. Angelo Nieves said after the report was released.

"This closes out the DCF case, and it does not create additional follow-up on our part," he said.

The report said: "The Department of Children and Families concludes that the actions or the lack of actions by the alleged perpetrator ultimately resulted or contributed in the death of the child." The report was signed by officials in the department on Wednesday, August 10th.

"The report does not address, or substitute for, judgments regarding the guilt or innocence of the caregiver in this case," the DCF spokeswoman said.

The state report found that Casey's "failure to act" in the 31 days between the time the girl was last seen and when police were alerted about the case "delayed and interfered with a law enforcement investigation and best efforts to safely recover the child."

The agency report noted there were "no indicators" that Caylee's death was caused by physical injury, and it was "not substantiated" that she died of asphyxiation which were both points of great contention during the trial.

In its recommendations section, the report said that "the maternal grandfather" in this case, George Anthony, "should have been interviewed for the missing person report."

Casey had been investigated by the agency, when state child welfare investigators determined on September 14th, 2008, that there were "verified findings" indicating that Anthony was responsible for "inadequate supervision and threatened harm" of her child, although it found "no indicators of physical injury."

Exactly a month later, a grand jury indicted Casey on murder and other charges, and the case was eventually reopened by the Department of Children and Families. No further detail was immediately offered as to why or exactly when the department chose to review the case, or why it came out this week.

The report released officially closes the department's investigation in the case.

Judge Perry made one more ruling regarding Casey. After the original judge, Judge Strickland, removed himself from the case, Judge Perry ruled on August 15th that she is to report for supervised probation in Orlando. This probation is for her check fraud conviction, unrelated to the murder trial.

Among other things, her probation forbids her to consume drugs or alcohol, associate with known criminals, or own a firearm, and she must report regularly to a probation officer. The only difference in her probation from the standard for this type of crime is that Perry's withholding her address for her protection. Since her acquittal in July, Casey was being called America's most-hated person, and throughout her probation the Department of Corrections will do their best to keep her safe from an angry public.

In early September Casey is once again in a court battle with The State Prosecutors office. This time her defense team is fighting a reimbursement motion filed by the prosecution.

The very public and drawn-out trial of Casey Anthony cost Florida a great deal of money, as did the investigation into Caylee's disappearance. While Casey was acquitted of the murder charges, the jury did convict her of lying to authorities on her daughter's disappearance, which arguably increased the cost of the search (especially since she admitted later to knowing Caylee was dead the whole time). Based on this, prosecutors are moving to have Casey cover these costs, which total over $500,000. Her lawyers are fighting the motion in court saying that billing Casey more than $516,000 for expenses incurred in trying and failing to prove her guilty of murder in the death of her daughter is little more than sour grapes.

Prosecutors say they have a right to demand repayment from Casey because she was convicted on four counts of lying to investigators in the disappearance of her daughter Caylee.

But defense attorney J. Cheney Mason said the bill is unfair after his client's acquittal on the most serious charge of murder.

"What about the justice for the defense that won?" Mason asked Orange County Judge Belvin Perry Jr. "We're now going to get whacked again ... pay for everything they did, their trips, their meals, their books, and their experts, none of which, none of which, had anything to do with the crimes of conviction," Mason said.

Prosecutor Linda Drane Burdick told Perry he should approve their request.

"The argument of the defense completely misses the point of my position as it relates to the costs of prosecution specifically," she said. "And that is that, but for Ms. Anthony's lying to law enforcement at the inception of this investigation, there would be no costs of investigation."

Perry did not rule on the request following the lengthy hearing, which Casey did not attend. He will research legal briefs due next week and research the law before issuing a ruling.

The Florida Department of Corrections said in a statement that Casey checked in with her probation officer as ordered under the terms of her sentence following her conviction on check fraud charges.

Casey told her probation officer that she is unemployed, has not earned any income over the past 30 days and has not enrolled in any educational or vocational classes. "No violations have been noted" of Casey probation the department said.

Casey's attorneys admitted she lied to authorities during the search for her daughter, saying she knew that she was dead.

In seeking reimbursement, prosecutors have cited a Florida law that allows the state to fine defendants in criminal cases to recoup money spent.

Prosecutors say the Orange County Sheriff's Office spent $293,123.77 on the case and the district attorney's office spent at least $140,390.60. The Florida Department of Law Enforcement spent $71,939.56 and the Metropolitan Bureau of Investigation spent $10,645.38, according to court documents.

But Mason said prosecutors are asking for reimbursement for items that have nothing to do with the crimes of which she was convicted. He said should Perry find that there is some merit to the state's motion, that he should limit expenses to only those costs related to police efforts to locate Caylee.

On September 15th, Judge Belvin Perry stated that under Florida law Casey can only be charged for costs that were "reasonably necessary" to prove the charges for which she was convicted. This limitation restricts her from being billed for any murder investigation or prosecution costs. A hearing determined that Casey cannot be charged with any costs after September 29th, 2008 since that marked the end of the missing person phase of the investigation.

Judge Perry gave Casey orders to pay the total of $97,676.98, which includes:

$61,505.12 to the Florida Department of Law Enforcement

10,283.90 to the Metropolitan Bureau of Investigation for electronic surveillance costs from July 22nd, 2008, through September 29th, 2008.

$25,837.96 to the Orange County Sheriff's Office

$50.00 to the Office of the State Attorney

Some of the expenses of the sheriff's department couldn't be broken down to determine what work was performed prior to September 29th, 2008. The judge told investigators to submit revised reports by the 18th, and the total costs could then be raised accordingly.

The State submitted its revised report and in doing so Casey's reimbursement bill more than doubled.

On Friday, September 24th, Judge Perry ordering that Casey must pay an additional $119,822.25 for expenses from the sheriff's office. This is on top of $25,837.96 that he previously said that department would receive. He ordered additional payments to other entities.

The new figure represents a significant increase from that detailed on September 15th. But the new reimbursement total of $217,449.23 is still less than half of the $516,000 that state and local offices had originally sought from Casey.

The governments had argued that if it were not for Casey's lies, investigators wouldn't have had to expend the time and money to find her daughter's body.

They unnecessarily searched for five months, eventually finding Caylee's skeletal remains in woods less than a mile from her grandparents' Orlando home.

Perry determined that Casey is liable for expenses incurred from in the two and a half months after July 15th, from when Caylee was reported missing to when the homicide probe opened.

But she was not ordered to pay back investigative costs as the state had requested incurred between September 30th and December 19th, 2008. The latter is the date when Caylee's remains were positively identified, eight days after they were found.

While it didn't agree fully with the initial ruling, the Orange County state attorney's office does not plan any more action to try to recoup money from Casey, spokesman Randy Means said.

"We're disappointed that our theory wasn't substantiated by the judge, but we will live with the results of the ruling," Means added. "We're pleased ... that some of the money will be returned to the taxpayers. Unfortunately, it wasn't anywhere close to what the state agencies thought they were due."

There was no reaction to the ruling from Casey's defense team to Perry's latest ruling.

Perry denied requests from the state attorney's office for reimbursement of its costs, beyond $50 "for the costs of prosecution of the three misdemeanor convictions."

On December 8th, Casey's lawyers return to court in her civil case.

Casey's attorneys have argued that she never identified this specific woman as the nanny named "Zenaida Gonzalez."

Attorneys for Casey and Zenaida Gonzalez, the woman who has filed a civil suit against her, return to court in early December to argue whether Casey should fully answer questions posed to her during her deposition in October.

In that hearing, Casey's lawyers invoked her Fifth Amendment right against self-incrimination 60 times. Attorneys for Gonzalez want the court to compel her to answer.

Gonzalez's defamation lawsuit alleges that Casey falsely accused her of kidnapping Caylee.

Gonzalez alleges that Casey defamed her and damaged her reputation when she claimed that a nanny named Zenaida Fernandez-Gonzalez had taken Caylee.

Authorities were never able to find the nanny. But they did find Gonzalez, who claimed she never met Casey or her daughter.

Casey's civil attorneys have argued that she never identified this specific woman as the "Zenaida Gonzalez" she was talking about.

Gonzalez's attorneys claim, according to questions asked of Casey in the October 8th deposition, that Gonzalez was questioned by the police in Caylee's disappearance, was kicked out of her apartment complex and lost her job and that she and her two daughters received death threats as a result of media attention in the case.

Casey herself said little in the deposition, but did acknowledge she was aware she was being sued by Gonzalez.

She also said she had not spoken to her brother, Lee, in the previous six months, and had not spoken to her parents since October 14th, 2008.

However, her attorney, Charles Greene, did not permit her to answer questions including whether she had ever met Gonzalez; whether a person named Zenaida was ever a nanny to Caylee; or whether defense attorney Jose Baez's assertion during Casey's criminal trial that Zenaida Gonzalez was one of Casey's "imaginary friends," was true.

She also was not allowed to answer questions about whether she considered herself a good mother to Caylee; the last day she saw the

2-year-old alive; and whether she drowned in the Anthonys' pool in June 2008, as the defense claimed during Casey's criminal trial.

Gonzalez was deposed for about 12 hours last month by Casey's attorneys.

Gonzalez's defamation case originally was filed in state court. It was moved to the federal bankruptcy court in Tampa after Casey filed for bankruptcy.

On June 11th, 2012, Casey's lawyers file motions for a new trial to have the convictions of counts of lying to police overturned. They claimed that she should have only been charged with one count of lying to the police as it was all involved in one criminal case.

The motion will be heard by the Florida appeals court.

Within days of filing the motion to have the convictions of counts of lying to police overturned, the world hears Casey say one more time, "I didn't kill my daughter."

Her message was the same but her "look" was different. Casey had died her hair blond.

Case broke her silence to CNN's Piers Morgan, saying she was rightly found not guilty.

"Obviously I didn't kill my daughter," Anthony said, Morgan reported on "Piers Morgan Tonight." The two spoke for roughly 10 minutes by phone.

"If anything, there's nothing in this world I've ever been more proud of, and there's no one I loved more than my daughter. She's my greatest accomplishment," she said.

"I'm ashamed in many ways of the person that I was," she told Morgan, reflecting on past interviews. "Even then, that wasn't who I am.

"I'm 26 now, and I've gone through hell," Casey said.

Casey told Morgan she didn't trust law enforcement, and that the public image of her is still wildly inaccurate.

"I've never been a party girl. I don't drink now. I've probably had a handful of beers since I've been on probation," she said.

"I'm not making gazillions of dollars at the hands of other people, or trying to sell myself to anyone willing to throw a couple of dollars at me," she said. "The caricature of me that is out there, it couldn't be further from the truth."

Then on November 20th, 2012 a television in Orlando reported that police never investigated Firefox browser information on Casey's computer the day of Caylee's death; they only looked at Internet Explorer evidence. The media learned about this information from Casey's attorney Jose Baez who mentioned it in his book on the case.

Some have wondered if the investigators searched the Firefox browser, if they would have found more information to prove a murder had actually occurred.

Then at the end of January, 2013 Casey received more good news when Florida's Fifth District Court of Appeals threw out two of the four charges against her for lying to police in regards to the disappearance and death of Caylee.

However, the courts struck two of these charges, arguing that they constituted double jeopardy. Double jeopardy insinuates being convicted twice for a single crime, and is not permitted under the law.

The lawyers for Casey argued that the four lies should be counted as a single offense. This was not accepted by the court, as there was a sufficient break in time between the two lies making them separate criminal acts. Casey has the right to appeal the remaining two convictions.

The same day as the ruling, Casey files for Chapter 7 bankruptcy protection. She claims to have almost $800,000 in liabilities, with just $1,000 in assets, including cash on hand and personal property.

On Monday, March 4th, 2013, Casey was forced out of hiding for the first time since leaving jail after her murder trial in 2011 to meet with the creditors in her bankruptcy case.

Casey pulled up in the back of a black SUV around 10:30 a.m. Monday. She was wearing a large-brimmed hat and black jacket in an attempt to cover her face. Only Cheney Mason and an unidentified driver were in the vehicle with her.

The driver was not allowed to use the courthouse's garage to drive under the building. Casey was made to walk in the front door, just like everyone else.

Mason had his arm around Casey, shielding her face from the cameras. Casey's hair was dark and about shoulder-length, a far cry from the short, blond hair she had in a video blog she recorded that leaked online more than a year earlier.

It was Casey's first public appearance since she walked out of the Orange County Jail in July 2011, less than two weeks after she was acquitted of murdering Caylee.

Mason is not representing Casey in her bankruptcy hearing. It appears he accompanied Casey to court to show his support and protect her from the media.

In the meeting room, Casey sat between her civil attorney, Charles Greene, and bankruptcy attorney David Schrader.

In court, Casey appeared calm and confident, saying she has no income, and lives off donations and help from others. Court papers listed her as unemployed, with no recent income.

"I don't pay rent. I don't pay utilities," Casey admitted. "So, I guess you could say I live for free, or off the kindness of the people I stay with."

When asked if she had any possible book or movie deals, Casey answers, "Not to my knowledge."

Casey said one of her biggest creditors was her former attorney, Jose Baez, saying she owes him $500,000. But she added she doesn't think he wants her money, and even said it was Baez who has given her cash and a computer.

When asked about photographs transferred to Baez, Casey said she sent "a few photos for him to sell to use to pay the defense." Casey said Baez sold those pictures to ABC News in 2008 for $200,000.

She rarely answered a question without consulting Greene first, something that infuriated attorney Scott Shuker, who is representing Zenaida Gonzalez in this bankruptcy case.

"I think it's improper for her attorney to answer her questions for her," said Shuker. "She is allowed to ask for clarification and advice from her attorney, but when her attorney jumps in before she says a word or even worse, on a couple of occasions interrupted her that's not proper."

Casey said she lives off of gift cards and cash given to her, estimated at less than $2,000. She added she has not been out of Florida for more than 30 days over the last five years.

She said she has no bank accounts and no car. If she needs to go somewhere, she said she takes the bus though as she walked out of the courthouse in Tampa and got into her attorney's black Mercedes Benz.

Creditors now have 120 days to file a lawsuit to stop Casey's bankruptcy.

Her list of creditors also includes Roy Kronk, the meter reader who found Caylee's remains in the woods, who is suing Casey for defamation after her defense team accused him of having something to do with killing Caylee.

Now all Casey had to deal with was the defamation lawsuit filed by Zenaida Gonzalez.

The defamation lawsuit would linger on for four years until a federal bankruptcy judge in Tampa Florida tossed out the defamation lawsuit against Casey on Friday, September, 18th, 2015.

U.S. Bankruptcy Judge Rodney May said that Casey's statements about the baby sitter were not intended to hurt Gonzalez and weren't malicious.

He also stated that Casey's description of the baby sitter actually did not match Gonzalez, May wrote.

"There is nothing in the statement or in the entire hour-long conversation on July 25th, 2008 to support Gonzalez's allegations that Anthony intended to portray her as a child kidnapper and potentially a child killer, or that Anthony intended to subject her to heightened police and media scrutiny," May wrote.

Five years after Casey was acquitted of murdering her daughter, a civil lawsuit connected to the case is still grinding through Central Florida bankruptcy court, with new developments.

The man who found Caylee's body in 2008 – Roy Kronk – filed a lawsuit against Casey in 2011, alleging that she, through her attorneys, falsely accused Kronk of killing Caylee.

In April 2016, transcripts of two 2015 affidavits of private investigator Dominic Casey were filed on the court docket in the matter of *Kronk v. Anthony* and picked up by news services in May 2016. In one affidavit, Casey stated that on July 26th, 2008, Baez admitted to him that Casey murdered Caylee "and dumped the body somewhere and, he needed all the help he could get to find the body before anyone else did".

He also claimed that Baez had a sexual relationship with Casey, and that "Casey told me she had to do what Jose said because she had no money for her defense."

Baez "vehemently" denied a sexual relationship.

"I unequivocally and categorically deny exchanging sex for my legal services with Ms. Anthony," said a statement from Baez's firm.

Dominic Casey has written two books with unsubstantiated claims about the case. Lawyers for Casey don't want him to provide testimony in the Kronk case, according to documents filed in the case.

Dominic Casey has been deposed by Kronk's attorneys and a transcript of that was filed on the court docket. Casey's lawyers have filed motions to strike Dominic Casey's deposition. They are also demanding to see records he claims to have.

Kronk's case was delayed when Casey filed for bankruptcy in 2013, but eventually it was moved over to the bankruptcy court, where Kronk is now arguing that her bankruptcy should not prevent him from recovering damages related to his claim of defamation.

In August Dominic Casey was sanctioned by a federal judge for skipping at least three dates to sit for a deposition under oath.

And the documents where he made the allegations have all been struck from the court record or sealed, according to the docket in the case.

Dominic Casey will have to pay for Casey's legal fees, for the time and effort involved in the three canceled depositions, December 30th, March 31st and May 9th according to the court record.

2017

Casey poses for a portrait next to a photo of Caylee

It has been almost 9 years since Casey first hit the front pages across America and around the world. And now in 2017 The Anthony's are back in the news once again.

In March, 2017 Judge Perry who presided over Casey's murder trial said, "The most logical thing that occurred, in my eyesight, based on everything I know about the case was that Casey did not intentionally kill her daughter," Perry told a Florida news station in an interview.

"I think upon the evidence, the most logical thing that happened was that she tried to knock her daughter out by use of chloroform leading to an accidental death."

"There was a possibility that she may have utilized that to keep the baby quiet ... and just used too much of it, and the baby died," Perry said.

Perry said he had no complaints with the jury that found Casey not guilty of first-degree murder, manslaughter and aggravated child abuse.

If jurors had reached the same conclusion as Perry, who retired from the bench in 2014, they could have found her guilty of second-degree murder or manslaughter.

"As I've expressed, the only person that really knows what happened was Casey," Perry said.

Casey breaks her silence in the first week of March claiming now, "I don't know what happened."

Casey knows that much of the world believes she killed her 2-year-old daughter, despite her acquittal. But nearly nine years later, she insists she doesn't know how the last hours of Caylee's life unfolded.

"Caylee would be 12 right now. And would be a total badass," she told the Associated Press in one of a series of exclusive interviews.

But discussing Caylee's last moments, the now 30-year-old Casey spoke in halting, sober tones: "I'm still not even certain as I stand here today about what happened," she said.

"Based off what was in the media I understand the reasons people feel about me. I understand why people have the opinions that they do."

This was the first time that Casey spoke to a news media outlet about her daughter's death or her years since the trial. Her responses were at turns revealing, bizarre and often contradictory, and they ultimately raised more questions than answers about the case that has captivated the nation.

She admits that she lied to police: about being employed at Universal Studios; about leaving Caylee with a baby sitter; about telling two people, both of them imaginary, that Caylee was missing; about receiving a phone call from Caylee the day before she was reported missing.

"Even if I would've told them everything that I told to the psychologist, I hate to say this but I firmly believe I would have been in the same place. Because cops believe other cops, cops tend to victimize the victims. I understand now ... I see why I was treated the way I was even had I been completely truthful."

"My dad was a cop," she added. "You can read into that what you want to."

At the trial, lead defense attorney Jose Baez suggested that the little girl's cause of death was drowning and that George helped to cover it up. Baez also accused him of sexually abusing his daughter, Casey. He has vehemently denied those accusations.

"Caylee would be 12 right now. And would be a total badass," Casey told the Associated Press. "I'd like to think she'd be listening to classic rock, playing sports" and putting up with no nonsense, she said.

Casey says that while she'd be "blessed" to become a mom again, it would probably be "dumb" for her to have another kid.

"If I am blessed enough to have another child — if I'd be dumb enough to bring another kid into this world knowing that there'd be a potential that some jackass, their little snot-nosed kid would then say something mean to my kid — I don't think I could live with that," she said.

"If I knew what actually happened, I'd be able to fill in those blanks. I've done enough research, I've done enough psychology seminars, I've been tested, I've gone to the psychological evaluations, talked about this to the point where I've been in a puddle and not able to talk about it for days afterwards," Casey said.

"She is still the central part of my life, the central part of my being, always will be."

Asked about the drowning defense, Casey hesitated: "Everyone has their theories, I don't know. As I stand here today, I can't tell you one way or another. The last time I saw my daughter, I believed she was alive and was going to be OK, and that's what was told to me. "

Casey lives in the South Florida home of Patrick McKenna, a private detective who was the lead investigator on her defense team.

She also works for him, doing online social media searches and other investigative work. McKenna was also the lead investigator for O.J. Simpson, when he was accused of killing his wife and acquitted; Casey said she's become fascinated with the case, and there are "a lot of parallels" to her own circumstances.

An Associated Press reporter met Casey as she protested against President Donald Trump at a Palm Beach rally.

It's unclear why Casey agreed to speak to the Associated Press She later texted the reporter, asking that the Associated Press not run the story.

Among other things, she cited the bankruptcy case in which she has been embroiled since 2013: "During the course of my bankruptcy, the rights to my story were purchased by a third party company for $25,000 to protect my interests. Without written authorization from the controlling members of this company, I am prohibited from speaking publicly about my case at any time."

In addition, she said she had violated a confidentiality agreement with her employer, and remains under subpoena and subject to deposition in her bankruptcy case.

Yet she had participated in five on-the-record interviews over a one-week period, many of them audiotaped.

She still dreads the supermarket checkout line for fear she'll see photos of her daughter on the cover of tabloid papers. Her bedroom walls are decorated with photos of Caylee and she weeps when she shows off her daughter's colorful, finger-painted artwork.

Occasionally she goes out with friends to area bars. But news that she is there spreads quickly; people whisper and snap photos, and she retreats to her newly purchased SUV so she can return home, alone.

Casey speaks defiantly of her pariah status.

"I don't give a shit about what anyone thinks about me, I never will," she said. "I'm OK with myself; I sleep pretty good at night."

On March 8th, the day after this interview was released to the public, Casey's father George's attorney released a statement.

In a statement from their attorney on Tuesday, Cindy and George said their daughter forced them to return to a tragic time in their lives from which they had tried to "move forward."

The statement also read: "George, who has continued to try and move forward from this tragedy and who was vindicated on multiple occasions, is once again forced to relive the hints, rumors, lies and allegations that are being made by Casey Anthony."

On October 27th, 2017 Cindy and George are warning their daughter that they'll sue if she decides to sell her story or stars in a reality television show, according to an interview to air on October 30th.

Cindy and George are scheduled to appear on Monday, October 30th, on "Crime Watch Daily," a nationally syndicated TV show hosted by reporter Chris Hansen. The Anthonys took the opportunity to send a stern warning to their daughter.

"Casey, be true to yourself, start being honest with yourself, and own everything," Cindy told Hansen. "Quit putting blame on everybody else."

Cindy said she thinks her daughter is "mentally ill" and suffers from seizures, leaving her unable to recall events when they occur.

But Casey's father whom she has accused of sexually abusing her and even covering up Caylee's death struck a much different tone in response to Hansen's questions, telling his daughter not to come near him.

"Stay away," George said. "Stay away from me. If she wants a relationship again with her mom, she's got a lot of explaining to do, but I don't want to hear it no more. I don't want to see her."

George said he recently saw Casey "in the flesh" at the couple's home, including one instance when she woke him up by tapping him on his head.

But both George and Cindy agreed that they'll head to court if their daughter decides to sell her story or star in a reality show, perhaps with O.J. Simpson. In Touch Weekly reported exclusively in April that Casey and Simpson were in talks to star in a reality show together.

"It will give viewers the inside story on the aftermath of living with the horrible crimes they were ultimately acquitted of," a source close to the matter said.

The Anthonys, meanwhile, also discuss defense attorneys' theory of how Caylee died. Casey may have had a seizure at the time of the girl's death, according to her mother. The couple also discuss George's suicide attempt.

In July 2017, Casey's lawyer Cheney Mason discussed the events surrounding the death of Caylee.

During an interview, Mason noted that Casey blacked out over the details of Caylee's death.

Asking Mason how it's possible that no one knows after all of these years what really happened to Caylee, Mason replied, "I believe that Casey's mind, in some dimension, I guess the common word would say 'snapped.' She didn't go crazy by any means but blackout completely a blackout of what went on and what happened."

Earlier in the interview, Mason detailed that he believed Casey retreated to what he referred to as "Casey World" during the time of her daughter Caylee's death and afterward.

"Casey, as we established with an expert witness at the end of the trial, grieved and comprehended differently than anyone else what happened. She went into what I call 'Casey World.' She shut it out," Mason explained.

He added, "She didn't know what she was doing or what she was saying. She knows she did not do this."

Mason was adamant that Casey was "close to, bonded to, and loved that child," noting that Caylee lacked for nothing and was never abused.

He added that Casey "snapped" when a testimony from a grief counselor was entered before the court.

"When that testimony came out, I was sitting next to her, and I don't remember whether I had my arm on her shoulder or was just holding her hand there while that testimony was going on, but she started shaking, and shivering, and she cried," he said. "All the time I've known her, and all the times I've seen her, I had never seen this. It was clear to me, my personal opinion, that it was the first time she consciously was actually aware that her daughter had died."

A Final Memorial to Caylee

The original cross at the memorial site

Distressing pictures have been released over the years showing Caylee's neglected memorial site that was meant to commemorate the little girl's life.

Amid the dirty, moldy toys and trinkets that were left years ago, there are also a few new items that suggest people continue to visit the site. The wooded area is located just around the corner from Casey's former home, is where Caylee's remains were found in 2008.

Over the years, people have come to the site to drop off toys, balloons, cards and other trinkets in remembrance of the young girl.

Years later, there was talk of building a memorial park in honor of Caylee, but the plans never came to be and the land has remained just a wooded area.

It appears to be abandoned, and a large tree has fallen just feet away from the memorial.

Over the years people have stolen the cross that adorned the site.

In August, 2016, a Sarasota Florida couple puts a new cross at Caylee's memorial site.

"We did it for that little girl, for people that still love that little girl and still miss that little girl," said Wally Goodnough.

Creating a lasting remembrance for Caylee has long been a passion project for Goodnough and his wife, Jeanine, who were involved in a troubled effort to create a permanent memorial on the site.

The new remembrance features a white, wooden cross adorned with Caylee's name, butterflies, flowers, angels and stuffed animals, surrounded by a short decorative fence.

"All those toys that people had left were just there being covered with leaves, covered with roots," Wally Goodnough said. "I pulled three trash bags of rotten stuffed animals out."

They returned to Sarasota, built the cross that night, then drove back to Orlando early the next day to create the memorial.

It's a trek they've made numerous times before.

Back in 2011, thcy and other volunteers made frequent visits to clean the site. When little-known charity Bring Kids Home announced plans to build a $200,000 memorial for Caylee, they were eager to help.

However, the Goodnoughs soon began to question whether the charity, which was soliciting donations, could keep its promises. Their concerns prompted them to leave the group.

The memorial plans eventually fizzled out.

Goodnough knows his latest remembrance for Caylee may not last forever; a previous wooden cross he erected at the site years ago was stolen twice, he said.

Still, "there has to be something there for that little girl, without a doubt," he said.

There are new toys left by visitors who continue to honor the little girl's tragically short life.

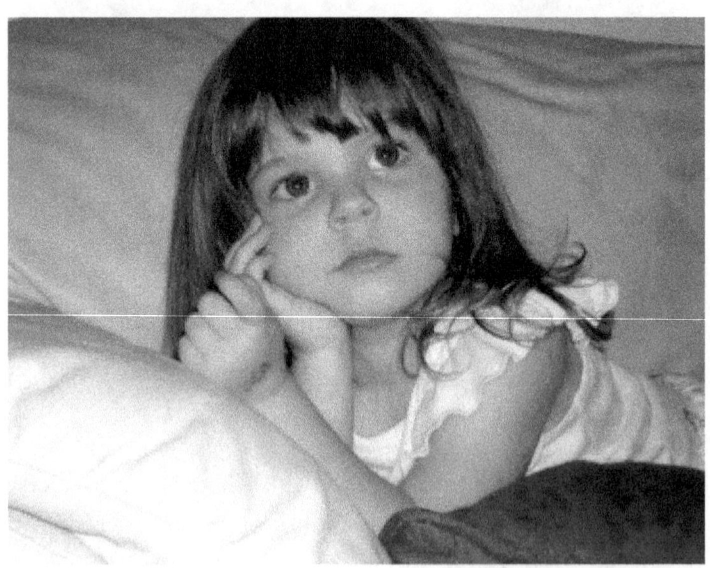

Closing

The one positive thing since the end of the trial, various movements have arisen for the creation of a new law, called "Caylee's Law", which would impose stricter requirements on parents to notify law enforcement of the death or disappearance of a child.

In response, Michelle Crowder of Oklahoma proposed 'Caylee's Law' on Change.org, a petition-hosting website, suggesting increasing the penalty to a fourth-degree felony for failing to report a missing child within twenty-four hours of their disappearance or one hour of their death. The petition quickly went viral and garnered over 1,300,000 signatures, pressuring lawmakers across the country to design such a law.

The backlash to the proposed law was almost as strong. Critics cited ineffective previous laws inspired by dead children and cautioned against making lasting legislature out of anger and fresh wounds.

Some experts have criticized the impracticality of the one hour and twenty four hour cut-offs, demonstrating the difficulty of determining time of death so precisely and offering complicating hypothetical situations. What happens if your child is at a sleepover and doesn't call home? Under this law, would you have to call your child at summer camp every day? What happens if your infant dies in his or her sleep? You might discover the death several hours later. Do we really want to punish a grieving parent in that situation with a felony? Although common sense should guide judicial rulings in these situations, there are many current examples of gross and insensible violations of justice.

Critics also fear that the law will make cautious parents falsely report absent children as missing, clogging up the police department's missing persons cases. The excess of false cases would obscure the real missing children cases and prevent them from being investigated in those first few crucial hours. Critics claim that the law will be unenforceable and ineffective in its goal of protecting children, merely entrapping innocent parents.

Despite these criticisms, several states have moved ahead with legislation. New Jersey Governor Chris Christie passed a 'Caylee's Law' in January 2012, making the failure to report a missing child age thirteen or younger after twenty-four hours a fourth-degree felony, punishable by up to eighteen months in prison and fines up to $10,000.

Governor Rick Scott of Florida signed House Bill 37 into law, another variant of 'Caylee's Law.' This law heightened to felony status the act of misleading a law enforcement official in a missing child case.

Louisiana's version of 'Caylee's Law', House Bill 600, passed, and declares that failure to report a missing child is punishable with up to 50 years in prison and $50,000.

Overall, thirty-two states filed some form of legislature in the past year to criminalize the failure to report a missing child.

But even with the new law the question as to why Casey was acquitted still weigh on people's minds.

Among the many differences between the opposing legal teams in the Casey Anthony murder trial, perhaps the key distinction is this: Where the prosecution sought to provide answers, the defense aimed to raise questions.

In his final opportunity to speak to the 12 jurors, who sat stone-faced, attentive and unreadable throughout the trial's intense six weeks, defense lawyer Jose Baez told them that the biggest question of all, how Casey's 2-year-old daughter Caylee died, remained unanswered.

"It can never be proven," he said.

In the end, the jury agreed. But still, we have to ask why?

Legal experts say the stunning not-guilty verdict is a result of several key factors, beginning with the lack of hard evidence tying Casey directly to the crime.

Prosecutors said Casey applied duct tape to Caylee's nose and mouth to kill her; Baez said the little girl drowned in the Anthony family swimming pool, an accident that was then covered up by Casey's father George.

The prosecution had a theory that Caylee was suffocated but it was only a theory. Nobody could say how Caylee died, when she died. We just don't know.

The bottom line is that the jurors did not completely believe the prosecution's theory and they chose to acquit. They were able to raise reasonable doubt in the jurors' minds.

What's more, Baez's repeated insistence that Caylee's death was "an accident that snowballed out of control" seemed to ring true with jurors, who were presented with extensive testimony regarding the Anthony family's dysfunctional dynamic.

Soon after the trial ended, the twelve jurors did not initially want to discuss the verdict with the media.Russell Huekler, an alternate juror who stepped forward the day of the verdict, said, "The prosecution didn't provide the evidence that was there for any of the charges from first-degree murder down to second-degree murder to the child abuse to even the manslaughter [charge]. It just wasn't there."

"It was such a horrific accident; they didn't know how to deal with it." He also said, "The family appeared to be very dysfunctional and instead of admitting ... there was an accident, they chose to hide it for whatever reason."

He also said he found the evidence regarding the smell in Casey's Pontiac Sunfire unconvincing, despite testimony from multiple witnesses including Casey's mother Cindy that the car reeked of death.

"You have to remember there were a number of law enforcement officers that responded to July 15th and none of them smelled the odor," Huekler said. "It was hard for me to accept that there had been a body in the car."

Juror number three,, a 32-year-old nursing student said, "I did not say she was innocent" and "I just said there was not enough evidence. If you cannot prove what the crime was, you cannot determine what the punishment should be."

She added, "I'm not saying that I believe the defense," but that "it's easier for me logically to get from point A to point B" via the defense argument, as opposed to the prosecution argument.

She said that she believed George was "dishonest." She said the jury "was sick to their stomachs to get the not-guilty verdict" and that the decision process overwhelmed them to the point where they did not want to talk to reporters afterwards.

Juror number two told the *St. Petersburg Times* that "everybody agreed if we were going fully on feelings and emotions, Casey was done". He stated that a lack of evidence was the reason for the not-guilty verdict: "I just swear to God ... I wish we had more evidence to put her away. I truly do ... But it wasn't there."

He also said that Casey was "not a good person in my opinion".

In an anonymous interview, the jury foreman stated, "When I had to sign off on the verdict, the sheet that was given to me there was just a feeling of disgust that came over me knowing that my signature and Casey Anthony's signature were going to be on the same sheet," but that "there was a suspicion of George Anthony" that played a part in the jury's deliberations.

The foreman stated his work experience enabled him to read people and that George, "had a very selective memory" which stayed with the jurors,emphasizing that the jury was frustrated by the motive, cause of death, and George.

"That a mother would want to do something like that to her child just because she wanted to go out and party," he said. "We felt that the motive that the state provided was, in our eyes, was just kind of weak."

Although the foreman objected to Casey's behavior in the wake of her daughter's death, he and the jury did not factor that behavior into their verdict because it was not illegal.

He said that they initially took a vote on the murder count, which was 10–2 (two voting guilty), but after more than ten hours of deliberation, they decided the only charges they felt were proven were the four counts of lying to law enforcement.

Despite public outcry over the verdict, this is the jury system. The whole point is that a jury of one's peers makes the decision, not the government. Casey had her trial, and the jury made its decision. And like it or not, we have to accept it.

CPSIA information can be obtained
at www.ICGtesting.com
Printed in the USA
BVHW030402080221
599613BV00011B/267